EDUCATIONAL ACCOUNTABILITY:

A Humanistic Perspective

I. David Welch
Fred Richards
Anne Cohen Richards

Library of Congress Card Catalog Number: 73-77970
International Standard Book Number: 0-88310-013-4

To Earl Kelley, an American Educator who spent his life humanizing education.

I. D. W.

To Diane Sorensen whose encouragement and support helped to make this book possible.

F. R.
A. C. R.

CONTENTS

III. Educational Accountability: A Humanistic Perspective

Introduction

THE DECADE OF ACCOUNTABILITY

Robert Zoellner cites an incident in a "Peanuts" cartoon which can serve as a paradigm for the controversial issue of accountability in education.[1] Little Lucy informs Charlie Brown she is a ballet dancer. When Charlie is skeptical, Lucy responds by performing three rudimentary dance-steps. Her repertoire exhausted, she turns to Charlie Brown and remarks, "That cost my Dad $11.50." The cartoon is, at one level, a gentle criticism of the occasionally over-indulgent American parent intent upon giving his little girl all the good things of life. On a deeper and more profound level, "it is a commentary on the American obsession with cost-accounting, with rendering every human activity . . . in terms of dollar expenditures."[2]

During the 60's, educators and educational institutions became the target and victim of increasing criticism. Holding schools responsible for all of society's ills and failures became a national fad. In addition, writes Gilbert Austin, many critics "believed that many of our severe and pressing educational problems could be solved almost exclusively by money. As that decade drew to a close, there was growing disillusionment with this concept. Although we had poured billions of dollars into the schools they did not seem to be producing a much better product than they had a decade earlier."[3]

The swelling cost of education and the seemingly small return on the public's investment in the schools triggered a call for accountability. Accountability came into vogue. While still in the process of being operationally defined, essentially "accountability means that public schools must prove that students at various levels meet some reasonable standard of achievement. The concept further implies that schools must show they use funds wisely — that expenditures justify educational outcomes."[4]

This is the Decade of Accountability. The Watergate inquiries, new guidelines for the use of human subjects in research, "Nader's Raiders," cost-accounting in the schools, environmentalist groups — these and more reflect the growing concern over the degree to which individuals and institutions should be held responsible for the consequences of their decisions and actions. That we need to be accountable is no longer in question. What continues to divide us, however, is the debate over what approaches to accountability should prevail.

Few oppose the idea that we must be able to show we are accomplishing something in our schools. It is possible, however, that the means we use to implement accountability may impede or destroy the very ends we seek. Like the young child enthusiastically placing his captured bird in a cage and later finding it dead, we may bind too tightly the educational process and destroy it. In order to prove that the educational system works, we, it appears, tend to measure what we already know how to measure easily and well. Consequently, grammar often becomes more important than communication, rhyming more important than poetry, the acquisition of information more important than the discovery of meaning.

Some educators have mindlessly embraced the present industrial model approach to educational accountability without first critically examining and, perhaps, redefining the priorities and purposes of education. They mimic the Kiki bird, now extinct but once notorious for its ability to fly backward. This backward mobility permitted the Kiki bird to become a recognized expert on where he had been. It also enabled him to avoid dealing with where he was going. Like some educators preoccupied with simply trying to do more efficiently what they have always done, the Kiki bird dealt with the present by staying in the past and refusing to confront the future. These educators, promoting the industrial model approach to accountability as a revolutionary breakthrough, "too often indulge in the pretense of change while flying into the past and the dangerous security it provides. Unlike the Kiki bird, however, they pass on their obsolescent knowledge and values, ill-preparing themselves and others for the future that daily arrives."[5]

Franklin Patterson, commenting on the impact of the technological revolution, calls for a process of education that will prepare persons to meet the challenge and shock of the future. Particularly critical, he warns, is the fact that we face a rapidly changing world "ill-armed in terms of our habits of mind and behavior."[6] An educational process, defining its accountability in terms of a limited application of a behavioral objectives approach, may well be educating for obsolescence and disaster. A more adequate educational process would emphasize also the "process of the continual discovery of personal meaning, the unmasking of distorted and ineffective perceptions of reality, and the disclosure of self in meaningful dialogue with others . . . . In a rapidly changing environment persons must be educated to re-educate daily their own perceptions of reality; they must be capable of perceiving and handling diverse, alternative points of view while continually evaluating their own perceptions."[7]

The debate over the issue of accountability is still with us. This book seeks to encourage and enlarge the discussion of educational accountability and to examine various approaches and their consequences from a humanistic perspective. Some of the articles take a concerned and critical look at the presently prevailing approaches to accountability. Others, written by humanistic educators, call for an approach extending and enriching, rather than limiting and dehumanizing, the concerns and goals of education in the schools.

REFERENCES

[1]Robert Zoellner, "Lucy's Dance Lessons and Accountability," **College Composition and Communication,** October, 1971, p. 229.
[1]*Ibid.*
[3]Gilbert R. Austin, "Educational Accountability — Hallmark of the 1970's," **The Science Teacher,** April, 1971, p. 26.
[4]Frank J. Sciara and Richard K. Jantz, Eds., **Accountability in American Education,** Boston: Allyn and Bacon, Inc., 1972, p. 3.
[5]Fred Richards and I. David Welch, "The Kiki Bird Versus Jonathan Livingston Seagull — A Choice of Educational Futures," **Egg,** University of Northern Colorado, Greeley, Colorado, May, 1973, p. 17.
[6]Franklin Patterson, "How Can Man Become Human," **Teachers College Record,** January, 1966, p. 252.
[7]Fred Richards and Anne Cohen Richards, **Homonovus: The New Man,** Boulder, Colorado: Shields Publishing, Inc., 1973, p. 115.

I

The Issue
of Educational
Accountability

Introduction

The successful launching of Sputnik by the Soviet Union in the 1950's brought pressure on educators to tighten up and compete more effectively with their Russian counterparts. While the Cold War has waned, criticism of our schools has intensified. The critics, often opposed to one another, have used the educational issue to promote their own points of view. Office-seeking politicians, protesting students, dissatisfied parents, enraged taxpayers, and increasingly vocal and influential minority groups continue to question the performance of educational institutions and remain powerful forces for criticism and change. The present issue in education receiving national attention is accountability.

Leaning very heavily on methods from engineering, industrial management and accounting, the accountability movement has been embraced by many as a radical and responsible effort to improve education. However, even those rushing to embrace educational accountability in its present form are having to confront several questions. If the schools are to be held accountable, to whom, it is asked, are they to be accountable? Also, for what exactly should the schools be held accountable? Equally important, where is the issue of accountability taking our schools? Finally, where does the push for educational accountability place us in relationship to what other countries are doing in their educational institutions?

Cold War Fallout in the Public Schools

PAUL P. MOK

A school system perpetually on the defensive is a school system that feels guilty. In order to expiate that guilt . . . we are in danger of investing greater energy toward seeking approval than in addressing ourselves to tasks which may not be currently fashionable and therefore low in approval value.

Those of us employed in public schools have become aware of a tightening up process that began in earnest . . . when the Soviet Union's space satellite dramatically alerted the nation to its educational shortcomings. Since that time school officials and parents alike have increasingly and more energetically concerned themselves with the staggering task of overhauling mediocre curricula and improving teaching methods, as well as with the search for talented teachers at all levels of the educational structure.

In this sense the intensity of heat generated by the Cold War with Russia has already had salutary effects on the American educational scene. But not all of the "fallout" that has filtered into the classroom has been so positive. The American school faces not only the threat posed by the Soviet Union and the fact that the Soviets have been pouring three times as much money into education in relation to gross national product, as the United States. A more subtle threat is posed by the effects of cold war competition. This is the tendency to compromise traditional ideologies that have characterized American education in the past under the pressure of national anxiety and the resulting desire to do anything which will help us keep pace with the Russians and prove to ourselves our educational adequacy.

Paul P. Mok, "Cold War Fallout in the Public Schools," **HGSEA Bulletin,** 6 (3), Fall, 1961. Reprinted by permission of the publisher and author.

Proof of the Pudding

The parents of our pupils, understandably influenced by the rash of alarmist school criticism, have been more vocal than ever in demanding tangible proof of the education pudding. How many times has a beleaguered school superintendent or principal stood up before a jury of parents at a PTA meeting and sought, with the aid of glossy graphs, charts, filmstrips and other audio-visual paraphernalia, to present the defense of his implicitly indicted school!

"Look at our pupils' test scores," he rails, "our sixth graders last year scored almost a year and a half above the national norms on a standardized examination in language usage! Look at the artist's sketch for the proposed new junior high school! Look at the new closed-circuit educational television schedule! Look, look, look!"

He sounds like the pitchman of old, but he is not selling a bottle of tonic guaranteed to cure backache, rheumatism, tired blood, and middle-age depression — instead he is trying, as never before in his life, to sell his school and its program to a critical public. The pressure we feel upon us to sell our programs, our services, our very selves as professional educators, demands a great toll on our energies and time and imagination — and even the rank and file classroom teacher has become an apprentice pitchman in the process.

A school system perpetually on the defensive is a school system that feels guilty. In order to expiate that guilt, be it rationally or irrationally determined, we are in danger of investing greater energy toward seeking approval than in addressing ourselves to tasks which may not be currently fashionable and therefore low in approval value.

For example, the ideology of recognizing and developing individual differences represents a traditional commitment in the American public school. Not so in the Soviet Union. There, human resources are viewed as national commodities to be developed along the lines of economic and strategic need, with individual choice playing a secondary role at best. If an individual pupil demonstrates tendencies that are not considered proper or valuable to his superiors in the educational structure, their development is not encouraged.

In the admittedly less efficient American system of public education, considerable attention has been given to the task of liberating and fortifying individual skill and talent along the lines of the pupil's naturally demonstrated interests. One is forced to wonder whether such idealism is currently being shunted into the back seat of the American education vehicle at the expense of the all powerful College Entrance Examination Board tests, the approved and fashionable extracurricular activities, and the high grade-point class standing.

Choice vs. Structure

Suppose that you, as a classroom teacher, designate a certain hour of the day as a "choice" time — a practice quite common in most elementary schools until the "fallout" of fear and anxiety become heavy in the classrom atmosphere. You feel that the time is justified because it may foster self-directed activities on the part of the youngsters. One seven-year-old boy spends the hour apparently scribbling on one sheet of paper after another until he has amassed a pile of forty-odd sheets on the floor. Each contains a mass of finely detailed but seemingly unrelated lines.

You watch the boy take his chair up to the bulletin board where he tacks up one sheet, then another, and another. The pieces fit together, each sheet a mosaic square. Spellbound, you watch as the forty-odd squares are transformed before your eyes into a mural. It is Saint George slaying the dragon. One square is the knight's gauntlet, another the hilt of his sword, another part of the blade, and so on.

You would like to get up before the throng of critical parents and defend the choice time. You know it is regarded as unnecessary, a valuable block of time in the school days which many pupils may be wasting to some degree. The parents are demanding more structured activities, an assurance that the schedule is as rigorous and demanding as possible. You would like to say that the youngster who did the mural did something in an original way — did something which you as his teacher could not have structured because you do not see things in the child's way. You would like to say that the boy's self-initiated project may have given him great satisfaction, may have excited the other children in the class, may be an important link in the development of a unique creative potential and original point of view which needs nurturing.

But many classroom teachers do not get up before the critical throng and make these statements. They recognize them as speculative. Intuitively they feel they are right, but they sense that anxious parents do not wish to hear intuitions and speculations. Instead, critics want evidence — tangible proof that what the child is doing today will help him meet society's competitive pressures, be they in the form of a 500-plus College Board score, admission into a first group college, or a class standing in the upper quartile.

If the public school has to prove — or feels it has to prove — the value of everything it is doing on the spot to a critical jury, it is going to move more and more in the direction of undertaking what can be proved readily. This is indeed unfortunate and frightening. Will the classroom teacher devote as much time to those activities which may not bear tangible results until the pupil is many years older? One teacher of my acquaintance, for example, used to allow her pupils approximately thirty minutes per day to write several paragraphs of their own choice about any topic or experience under the sun.

She felt the continued practice in self-expression would unleash the creative wellsprings and build self-confidence in verbal skills. She has not altered those convictions, but now she has cut the exercise to a weekly project. The pupils and their parents feel, she explains, that vocabulary lessons carry a higher premium these days. Although the daily writing assignment may have done more in the long run to build verbal skills, it was curtailed because short-range goals have come to carry greater weight in the minds of scores of taxpayers and school officials.

Mass, Chrome, and Marketing

A critical danger of adopting short-range educational goals as prime targets lies in the tendency to devote greater attention to pupils en masse than to pupils as individual entities. The pit is an easy one in which to fall, because all pupils share certain common learning needs. In the race for short-range proof of educational superiority, the teacher who dares to develop the idiosyncratic feels she may be lost come tenure time.

An equally pernicious aspect of anxiety fallout in the public school is the temptation to emphasize the chrome of education at the sacrifice of tuning up the machinery under the hood. Reacting to public pressure for new ideas, many administrators have become easy game for the salesmen of brave new teaching machines, evaluations on punch cards, and all manner of brightly packaged test kits. Many of these are so new they haven't been properly tested or validated. A teaching machine may be no better than the program fed into it, but to an anxiety-ridden school official or worried parent, it may appear to be the pot of gold at the rainbow's end.

Perhaps the most tragic symptom of anxiety on the school scene is the tendency of pupils to plan their education futures in the manner of junior account executives plotting a campaign for increased celery sales.

"How can I make myself more marketable to the Ivy League

colleges?" the pupil may wonder under the weight of increasing talk about college competition and overcrowding. "What gut courses are available? What activities will look best on my record? What ministers have the biggest prestige value on application recommendations? What tutors do the best coaching job for the College Board tests?"

No Pink Pills

There just isn't any pink pill that the public school can swallow to recover from the fallout effects. I have the uncomfortable intuition that we will be living with them for some time to come. However, as in combating any psychological malaise, the first step forward lies in confronting reality. For almost four years we have tended to assume that the disturbance was exclusively external in nature. My observations, gleaned from experience as a psychologist in the public schools during that period, suggest a contrary finding.

When we realized that the new Soviet education had made certain striking advances over our own, we first tried to modify our educational products while we scurried about flipping switches and searching for panaceas in the desperate hope of reasserting our superiority overnight. In some cases, as in Rickover's dramatic proposals, a willingness was expressed to scrap the traditional machinery itself.

Perhaps the reaffirmation of our democratic ideology will not come of its own accord. It would be wrong to assume that the education profession is apart rather than a part of the national population, that we school people are immune to our country's general anxieties. On the other hand, our professional image suggests the desirability of public leadership. Do we dare, in an era of power psychology, to reassert the values of individual discovery and development? Or will we postpone that task in favor of mass-producing a new generation of competitively designed and competitively operated, acquisitively oriented and security-starved cold war graduates?

Accountability: What, Who and Whither?

SCARVIA B. ANDERSON

Is it possible that the current fire of concern about education, which accountability has helped to fan, is at a sufficient height to lead to some receptivity to the idea of a drastic reformulation of education?

Accountability is already a powerful force in education for at least two reasons. First, it has managed in a relatively short time to accumulate the trappings of a discipline: parts of accountability have been delineated, the delineation of the parts has been reinforced by names for them, there are roles associated with the parts, and some techniques have been offered for carrying out the roles. Second, accountability is a large enough vessel to hold the concerns of many parties to the educational process; even if they are not all sympathetic, they are all involved.

Let us look first at the parts and then at some of the parties.

What?

Accountability has at least five major divisions or manifestations.

1. Performance contracting — establishing with a contractor a level of payment based on the level of student performance delivered. The contractor is usually a commercial company and frequently has educational curriculum products to offer. Standardized achievement tests provide the criteria of success. *Newsweek*

magazine predicted that 170 school districts would spend 50 million dollars on performance contracting [in 1971]. There are those who point out that performance contracting is associated more with training in the industrial sense than with education in the broad sense.

2. Turn-keying — the process whereby a program established under a performance contract is adopted by a school system and operated by its personnel. Some performance contracts specify the cost and effort required for turn-keying.

3. Auditing — the independent examination of an educational effort or performance contract to verify results, check on processes, personnel, and progress, and — frequently — make an independent report to an interested external agency. More auditors than performance contractors seem to come from nonprofit agencies. The demand for independent audit seems to be directly related to the distance between the program and the funding source.

4. Education vouchers — allowing education of children to be bought by parents in a "free market," through vouchers provided by school district officials or government agencies. This plan is associated primarily with James Coleman, economist Milton Friedman and the Harvard Center for the Study of Public Policy. It implies, in various of its proposed forms, regulations relating to selection of students, access to the schools for financial and program audit, standards of educational quality, and availability of evaluative data to potential purchaser-parents. The accountable party is the independently operated school.

5. Incentive pay — paying teachers on the basis of the performance of their pupils. This harks back to practices of earlier centuries, and so far it has met with little more popularity than any of the other merit-pay schemes advanced in recent years. Kenneth Clark of the Metropolitan Applied Research Center has made more headlines than headway in attempting to implement such an incentive pay plan in District of Columbia schools.

Coming to be more and more identified with "accountability" are another five activities or concepts. They come from other philosophical and operational sources with which they continue to be associated.

1. Behavioral objectives — statements of what the educational program is supposed to accomplish, the conditions under which it is to accomplish them, and the criteria whereby success in accomplishing them can be determined.

2. PPBS (Planning, Programming, Budgeting System) — a management tool first employed in national defense and designed to identify relationships between product outcomes and costs for various alternatives.

3. Needs assessment — a formal attempt to determine the

educational needs of a population or subpopulation.
4. Systems analysis — actually a conglomerate of techniques associated with operations research and computer simulation, recognizing always the interrelationships of a system's components.
5. PERT (Program Evaluation Review Techniques) and other network-based management tools — tools designed primarily to assist administrators in monitoring the effective operation of an ongoing system.

Who?

The parties to the accountability push — or debate — are more interesting than the techniques. They include teachers, administrators, minority groups, parents, psychometricians and, of course, external observers.
Teachers. Leon Lessinger has predicted that in education's accountable future the "teacher would become a manager, rather than a presenter of information." Fred Hechinger has explained in the *New York Times* the positive involvement of the United Federation of Teachers in implementing a plan to "establish procedures to hold the [New York City] schools and staffs accountable for their success in educating children" in terms of the lesser attractiveness of the alternatives: "Widespread difficulties in schools . . . can create outright community anger which tends to arouse often irrational demands that the schools be held responsible for overcoming all . . . social ills." He feels too that system-based attempts to upgrade performance are to be preferred by the union to performance-contracting with external agencies or the voucher system.
Robert Bhaerman, Director of Research, American Federation of Teachers, suggests in *Educational Technology* that accountability may be nothing more than "pie in the eye" of teachers. He reports on a resolution passed by representatives of the Federation in terms of such questions as these:
"Can 'the advocates' guarantee that performance contracting will not take the determination of education policy out of the hands of the public?
"Can they say, with a straight face, that performance contracting does not threaten to establish a new monopoly of education?
"How can they state that performance contracting would not subvert the collective bargaining process and reduce teacher input?"
"Is performance contracting not predicated on the false assumption that educational achievement can be improved in the vacuum

of a machine-oriented classroom, without changing the wider environment of the poverty-stricken child?"

W. A. Deterline in the same issue of *Educational Technology* questions the "justification for expecting [teachers] to do better, or for holding them accountable for doing so . . . unless someone else accepts accountability for teaching those teachers relevant skills beyond those they already possess, and unless the conditions that limit their effectiveness can be changed."

Educational administrators. Medill Blair, the Superintendent of Schools of Hartford, Conn., states unequivocally that state and local education governing bodies have no choice but "to take a leaf from business . . . and refuse to develop and promote new educational programs and techniques, refuse to commit public funds, and refuse to employ personnel, until we first establish clear goals . . . , until we develop ways to measure accomplishment of these goals, and until we set up logical techniques to employ in reaching them." L. L. Deck, Jr., the Assistant Superintendent in Nashville, Tenn., however, cautions that accountability for schools is different from accountability for other organizations. In general, school administrators seem more supportive of accountability than do spokesmen for other groups. Perhaps they agree with T. S. Barrows that it is primarily an administrative innovation and not an instructional one.

Black groups. Kenneth Clark, although supporting some activities associated with accountability, has "warned that the accountability proposals would be seriously undermined if they are to be used 'as a semantic cover for the old alibis' of why lower-class children cannot be expected to succeed." Representatives of other black groups are stating that accountability is what they have been talking about all along. But many add that they want it on their own terms — and under their own control.

Parents. This group, while increasingly vocal and active about the operation of schools if one judges by newspaper and television accounts, does not appear to have much specific representation on the panels currently arguing the case of accountability. But is it still safe to assume that — if their taxes are not raised and if their children do not have to travel too far to schools, are not underfoot at unscheduled times because of school closings, seem to be learning something and staying out of trouble, and eventually get into colleges or careers — parents will not care what the magic formula is called?

Psychometricians. Since test scores are viewed as the primary basis for determining whether educational objectives have been met and accountability established, it is only natural that those concerned with the properties of tests have had something to say about the matter. Mostly they have said that those letting and signing performance contracts are at best naive. R. E. Stake and J. L. Wardrop, for example, after reviewing the properties of gain scores, have concluded simply that "individual-student gain on a currently available standardized test should not be used as a criterion of successful instruction." R. T. Lennon has pointed to the frequent lack of congruity between the behavioral objectives of a particular instructional segment and the kind of nationally normed test that other stipulations of present performance contracts require. (Some have suggested substituting criterion-referenced tests.) Other issues raised by psychometricians include the validity problems associated with "teaching for the tests," comparability of alternate forms of tests, and the appropriate unit (individual, class, school, system) to which accountability procedures should be applied.

External observers. Fred Hechinger of the *New York Times* rejoices at least in the fact that the more sophisticated discussions of accountability recognize "that many factors contribute to a child's record" and the child alone cannot be held responsible for it. Sociologist Melvin Tumin in *Untangling the Tangled Web of Education* has written:

"It is sociologically axiomatic that when a number of parties are involved in any social enterprise, and when the enterprise fails, each party will lay maximum blame for the failure on the others, and will assume only minimum blame, if any, for itself. As a corollary, it follows that the *official* verdict of guilt for failure will be imposed on that party who is weakest or least able to fend off the imposition of the official stigma. . .

"There are numerous . . . evidences of the deep commitment of American education to blaming children for failing to learn as much as the 'standards' demand that they shall . . ."

"But all of this seems very much in the process of change . . . for nearly 20 years, starting just after World War II, the teachers of America, and *their* teachers, were attacked from all sides for the educational failures of children. Then, for a brief moment, until a temporarily successful counter-attack was launched, the families of children . . . were held to be essentially defective.

"Most recently, it is a combination of the educational establishment . . . and of the corollary lack of community control of the schools that has been made the major scapegoat . . .

"Whatever our supreme ignorance on many key educational questions may be, it seems quite clear . . . that family life, community organization, and the schools are all contributors to the educational outcomes of the children."

It would be cavalier to conclude this overview of accountability without even mentioning Texarkana, Ark., and Gary, Ind. So they will be mentioned — in the context of conclusions drawn from reviews of those performance contracts by another external observer, Minnie Perrin Berson. Mrs. Berson speaks regularly to thousands of teachers in the pages of *Childhood Education*, the journal of the Association for Childhood Education International. She asks: "Is it really fair to expect Gary's schools to be flourishing oases in the midst of the many unresolved urban problems that surround them? . . . can outside education-mechanics bring in magical learning solutions by converting a school into a skillshop?"

She continues: "Accountability is hardly achieved by simple test measures in which Mr. Lessinger so firmly believes. When children are continually given exercise sheets that resemble achievement test items, they can play the testing game with great savvy. So doing does not assure that they have mastered critical skills of reading comprehension and interpretation that differentiate mechanical mastery from fundamental learning growth.

"For the latter, more is involved than taking over a school, by-passing teachers, hiring aides for one-sixth of the salary, and giving them fancy titles for checking piece-work in the child-learning factory . . .

"Educational accountability worthy of its name requires that teachers, administration, and community be accountable to each other with honesty, compassion, and determination."*

And whither?

Educational accountability has become a catch-all for everyone's frustrations; many technical defects have been identified in applications of the tools associated with it. Nevertheless, it is enjoying a considerable vogue, and it is stimulating conversations between diverse groups concerned with American education. Where do we go from here? Many possibilities exist. Three — for different reasons — deserve special consideration:

The first is the most cynical. A few more performance contracts with the kind of bad press Dorsett received for Texarkana, the failure of capable organizations to devote their attention to refining present accountability tools and developing new ones, inadequate systems for disseminating information about appropriate

---

*Minnie Perrin Berson, **Childhood Education,** March, 1971, p. 342. Reprinted by permission of Minnie Perrin Berson and the Association for Childhood Education International, 3615 Wisconsin Avenue, N. W., Washington, D. C. Copyright © 1971 by the Association.

techniques and training educators to use them, a degree of cumbersomeness and expense associated with accountability ventures that makes administrators reluctant or unable to launch them, overemphasis on the engineering-financial aspects of accountability to the exclusion of the educational-personal ones, and predictions derived from the history of adoption of educational innovations — some or all of these could work to erase "educational accountability" from the vocabulary in a relatively short time, to be replaced perhaps by a new game for educators to play.

Second, assuming that accountability is sustained by positive events, developments, and climate, then in a few years we might see a great many educational systems and institutions with more precisely defined objectives, indices and measures compatible with those objectives, systems for collecting and analyzing data longitudinally, clear identification of who is accountable for what (with related schedules of reward and punishment), and management systems that facilitate operational planning and monitoring and that associate cost with effectiveness.

A rosy picture? It would certainly seem so. But let us pause for a moment to think about the fundamental emphasis of accountability.

The fundamental emphasis is on *output*. Many proponents of accountability would concern themselves with little else. They do not raise the basic issues of the nature of the population to be educated, the present requirements of our highly urban-technological society, and the needs of the individual for personal fulfillment. In other words, proceeding from the basic line of thinking about accountability, the most brilliantly executed and successful demonstrations of it stand little chance to do more than validate the present educational system — to show that schools are doing a good job of what they were supposed to be doing all along.

In *Education and the Cult of Efficiency*, R. E. Callahan talks about Bobbitt's approach to education: "The standards and specifications for steel rails were set by the railroads, not by the steel plant, and the specifications for educational products should be set by the community, not by educators. A school system . . . can no more find standards of performance within itself than a steel plant can find the proper height or weight per yard for steel rails from the activities within the plant."

This leads to a third consideration about where we go from here. Is it possible that the current fire of concern about education, which accountability has helped to fan, is at a sufficient height to lead to some receptivity to the idea of a drastic reformulation of education? Is it possible to invent a new system or series of systems —

that is conceptualized and operated in the context of the demands society makes upon individuals and the opportunities it offers them,

that takes into account the characteristics of various populations to be educated and is committed to the development of individuals rather than to teaching certain subjects.

that recognizes that development encompasses a broad range of skills and talents, ranging from self-understanding to interpersonal skills to advanced technological competencies, and including the abilities to restructure society,

that is dedicated to the propositions that development should continue throughout a person's lifetime and education should not be the responsibility of any single social institution, and

that is not constrained by structures and strictures from the earlier system, covered as it is by the band-aids of lowering and raising compulsory school age, social promotion, and the many other attempts to doctor creeping irrelevance?

Accountabilty leans very heavily on methods from engineering, industrial management, and accounting. Wouldn't engineers, managers, and accountants prefer to lend their talents, along with those of educators, legislators, behavioral scientists, and other representatives of our society, to the enterprise of developing new educational models appropriate to the waning years of this century, rather than to dissipate them in the thankless task of patching up or patinizing a system from another era?

Accountability: Bane or Boon?

WILLIAM R. BARBER

One of the most prevalent educational myths that has been hindering us for years is that learning is the result of teaching.

The past few years we educators have sat in innumerable meetings listening to the wind blow, and now and then latching on to pedagogical terms like "relevance" and "thrust". Now we have a new word that possesses relevance and is receiving lots of thrust — a new word that may help John Q. Citizen vote more dollars for the educational till. That word is Accountability.

Now, I, for fifteen years an elementary principal (and before that an elementary teacher) have always felt that I was accountable to someone for the quality of services rendered, although that someone who evaluated me and my services had to make some sort of value judgment about my work. Accountability, however, presupposes that someone is going to be able to make a fairly precise and objective analysis of how well my school is achieving the educational goals set (by someone) for my school and that I will be held accountable (penalties for default are not defined) for the results.

One of the most prevalent educational myths that has been hindering us for years is that learning is the result of teaching (by certified teachers, of course!). 'Taint so! *Some* learning does take place as the result of *some* teaching, but if teachers and principals would only regard themselves as learning facilitators, then possibly they wouldn't talk so much!

What we want to measure (and hold the principal and teachers accountable for) is *that part* of learning *that they have contributed*. This is going to be difficult enough for those skills that are quantifi-

William R. Barber, "Accountability: Bane or Boon?," **School and Community,** 14-15, April, 1971. Reprinted by permission.

able (e.g., math and reading), but I have long held that there are moral, ethical, and spiritual (heretical?) concepts that a teacher transmits through daily living with his pupils that are more precious and more important than multiplication tables. The school's business is not merely instruction, but the *life* of the child. Not all teaching that a teacher does is quantifiable or measureable, and *that* is exactly what makes a teacher a Teacher! I don't remember my second grade teacher (with much affection) because she taught me the consonant blends!

I'm not saying that Accountability has to be bad. The hard part comes in (1) determining *what* we want to measure, (2) *how* we're going to measure it, and (3) *what* we're going to do with the results. If we can identify school input and then the educational output, I'm certain we can subtract one from the other. We've been doing it for years and *have been held accountable for the results!* Accountability can be one of the finest things that has happened to our profession *if* we realize that at best the whole procedure is imperfect and full of holes. At least it will cause us to more precisely define our educational objectives and to keep our eye on them all the time.

Evaluation would be so simple if we could just pre-test, teach, post-test, and quantify, and apply the results. But children, teachers, and principals come in all varieties.

Consider the children as a case-in-point (since we nearly always attribute learning failure to them!). In some districts these children come from homes where learning, books, conversation, love, and understanding don't receive a high priority. These same children may go to antiquated schools with mediocre staffs and inadequate equipment. The rooms are crowded, attendance is poor, the teacher's time is taken up largely with keeping order, the principal is Chief Disciplinarian and Keeper-of-the-Keys, there is a general school atmosphere of frustration and depression, and the "expectancy level" of all inhabitants is quite low. Now, do we expect these children to show one year's gain during the school year, or, like Alice in Wonderland, do we have to run as hard as we can just to stay where we are? Please notice, we haven't even mentioned I. Q.!

We must derive some sort of statistical formula to measure the contribution that the school has made to its students in certain measurable areas. Now, Suburbia Acres School is in an affluent area, the principal boasts that 60 percent of his parents have college degrees, PTA meetings play to a packed house, the building is new, carpeted, air-conditioned, has a library of 10,000 volumes, the teachers are young, energetic and three-fourths have their Master's Degrees, and the pupils are regular in attendance and come in the front door just reeking of "Here I am, just burnin' to learn!" Now, the guy that's the principal of that school is going to have to have a handicap of 20 just for the front nine if he's going to play Accountability with me!

Obviously, then, we must have a statistical formula that will take into account *all* the important variables (here someone has to make a value judgment again) to arrive at a School Performance Index. Then, the principal of Suburbia Acres and I can play Accountability together, even if my teachers are lame, halt and blind, I have no library, the building is drafty, and the kids (when they do come to school) say "Well, here I am — let's see you teach me!"

Accountability? I think we're going to have a great time with this one, and, in the process, greatly benefit our students, our schools, our society, and our profession. I'm all ready to jockey for pole position — now, if I can just find where the pole is . . .

Whose Children Shall We Teach?

ROMEO ELDRIDGE PHILLIPS

*. . . the public schools by inheritance and default now must really
and completely "teach" all the children of all the public!*

The writer served on a panel with a political scientist and a
sociologist. The topic for the evening was given the ambiguous
title, "The Polarization in Our Society." Our assignment was to
ad lib as to our perceptions of this phenomenon.

The sociologist gave an analogy of the social stratification within
the American society and delivered an excellent dissertation on
acculturation and enculturation.

The political scientist, who has a degree in divinity, outlined
the whys and wherefores of the American political system and
how the church fits into it.

The writer supported the pontifications of the two speakers.
However, I stated that the public schools are the only places
where the sons and daughters of college professors, maids,
janitors, pimps, prostitutes, and preachers are found. In a typical
college town where there is only one senior high school, they
are found in the same building.

Teaching All the Children

It would appear plausible that the sons and daughters of
employers and employees meet on a continuum of sociality daily.
To look at this conglomerate of upper, middle, and lower income

Romeo Eldridge Phillips, "Whose Children Shall We Teach?," **Educational Leadership,** 27 (5): 471-474, February, 1970. Reprinted with permission of the Association for Supervision and Curriculum Development and Romeo Eldridge Phillips. Copyright © 1970 by the Association for Supervision and Curriculum Development.

youths, one realizes that the public school is truly an arena. The writer submitted then and submits now that the home and church have abdicated their individual responsibility to the young people of this nation. Therefore, the public schools by inheritance and default now must really and completely "teach" all the children of all the public! Let us cite some observations to support this hypothesis.

Many white Americans have contended that they did not leave the large cities to "get away" from black Americans, but because they desired a better quality of education for their children. On the other hand, many chose to live in a particular neighborhood because they, too, desired a better quality of education for their children. If a person's income permitted him, the movement became a living reality. One must remember, however, that an exodus from a given area does not render it a ghost town. To the contrary, living bodies remain — and in large numbers.

Let us follow the public school sojourn of a child whose parents have moved to a certain neighborhood in a typical college town. It is amazing how shortsighted we can be.

When one moves to a "certain" neighborhood, it is his intention to be with those of his kidney, that is, at his level within the bourgeoisie. It is reasonable to assume that the schools will be populated with these types of children. This assumption is one-third accurate: the middle-junior high school will have children from several neighborhoods; the senior high school will have children from all neighborhoods!

It appears that the runner ran in a circle. If one had wanted to expose a son or daughter to the "best" families, it would appear that this should be during the period of early pubescence when discriminate taste develops. During this period, it is not what Mom or Dad desires, it is what "I" want. We call this the period of adolescent rebellion. It is logical to conclude, then, that only the elementary school can supply the "quality education" sought by the mover-runner. Let us look into the high school where all three "types" are housed.

The teachings, mores, fears, prejudices, etc., of parents are placed on public display in the senior high school. It is in the senior high school that the 14-or-so years of neighborhood values training bear fruit. It is in the senior high school that the realities of heterogeneous living are tried. Truly, the senior high school is an educational arena. The public schools have been given the task either of curing all the social ills or of serving as a deterrent. For some 180-odd days each year the public schools face these problems head on.

Often potential teachers are heard repeating statements of

veteran teachers about certain schools in certain school districts. When reminded that they are seeking a certificate to teach in the *public* schools and not in certain types of public schools, expressions of ambivalence about teaching pour from their lips. The shock of being expected to teach *all* the children of *all* the public — including poor whites, blacks, American Indians, and Spanish speaking — creates a form of academic amitosis. One would guess that when they are reminded of this, the potential teachers may experience a form of ametropia. Sometimes it appears that such beginners no longer see public school teaching as before. Yet and still, a horrible disservice would be created if they were not made to acknowledge such a commitment as being realistic.

The writer has often been asked these questions: What types of teachers are in the public school? and, What sub-roles must we play, since the church and home no longer appear to really care?

Types of Teachers

There are five types of teachers currently drawing wages in the public schools. Each is easily recognized.

1. The Rebel — is against the entire system, but has no suggested plan of change.

2. The Retreatist — wants out of teaching, is constantly seeking other employment, and leaves, usually, with his or her leave bank empty.

3. The Ritualist — has retired on the job, and continues to repeat the same lessons year in and year out. This teacher can quote page, paragraph, and sentence of the text.

4. The Conformist — goes along with what is current without making an effort to contribute. In many cases this person and the ritualist are related.

5. The Innovator — sees the need for change and seeks to bring it about without antagonism. This effort ranges from his/her classroom to the district.

One who teaches must be conditioned to accept the following sub-roles:

1. . . . . a mediator of learning
2. . . . . a judge
3. . . . . a disciplinarian
4. . . . . a confidant
5. . . . . a parent substitute
6. . . . . a surrogate of middle-class values.

If, in fact, we have five types of teachers currently in the public schools and if teachers should subscribe to these six sub-roles, we must look at the teacher-preparing institutions.

Since the orbiting of Sputnik I, men with names such as Bestor, Rickover, Conant, Clark, Malcolm X, and McKissick have charged that the teacher education institutions are not doing their jobs. Of these various changes, the one heard most often is that potential teachers are being prepared to work with just one segment of our society — the middle!

The truth of the matter, they are saying, is that one does not really teach, per se, the middle segment. This highly motivated segment needs only guidance. Teaching must be at the extremes of the continuum. Because of this fact many veteran "teachers" obtain and seek assignments in such schools. Knowing this, potential teachers seek such non-available assignments. Teacher education institutions contribute to this dastardly deed by holding back two-thirds of the information needed — the fact that we have three types of communities within the public school arena. It is inexplicable why neophyte teachers must develop this awareness by empirical design.

Too many teacher education institutions have developed what the writers calls "slogan shibboleths." Many of these are really polite euphemisms, for they appear to be evasive in nature. One does not talk about "teaching the whole child" only to point out negatives, for example, "low IQ scores," a product of an illegitimate affair," and "too much freedom and money." Children may be dumb, but they are not stupid. They need not be told which type of teacher so-and-so is. They know that actions speak louder than words. For potential teachers not to be prepared to teach *all* the children of *all* the public is malfeasance. Potential teachers must be told what is expected of them and the professor is professionally obligated to "tell it like it is"!

Problem of Accountability

The problem on hand now is what must be done to teach students currently enrolled. The problem is compounded by the fact that many teachers are aware of these differences but choose not to adapt their presentations to fit the experiences of their charges. What can be done to rectify this situation?

Teachers unions appear not be concerned about making teachers accountable. If a teacher is accountable, it is a personal desire. Accountability in labor unions known to the writer revolves around wages. As a worker produces so is he paid. When he works up to expectations he is, naturally, praised; when he works under the basic standards he is moved. A teacher is protected by state law plus a master contract. However, unlike the members of labor unions, a teacher has no demands made on him to produce. He is not accountable and accepts all pay raises with no scruples of conscience. Knowing this to be true, citizens have resorted to extralegal means to gain teacher accountability.

In the suburbs, parents often check the content of their children's assignments. The same is true in "choice" neighborhoods in large cities and college communities. It is not unusual for Bobby's father, who is a professor of math at the local college, to challenge the teacher's math competency. Knowing the level of academic sophistication of his students' parents, the teacher usually shapes up or ships out.

The ghetto poor lack academic sophistication; they measure results. They know that they send their children to school for an education. The children may remain for some 13 inclusive years only to emerge lacking the ability to read. Parents are not stupid. They are now seeking methods of community control via the purse strings of school employees. They measure step-by-step what their children learn. If it is adjudicated that the learning did not take place, they want the teachers' wages affected, union master contract to the contrary notwithstanding.

When the ghetto poor rise up, it is unusual. A case in point is the Ocean Hill-Brownsville fiasco in New York in the fall of 1968. The public schools can expect more of the same as parents, ghetto poor parents, demand education of a quality comparable to that found outside their community. In the process the teacher education institutions will not come out unscathed. After all, it is they who trained the present cadre so inadequately. Pedagogics must expand to include the three socioeconomic levels. Teachers must be, so to speak, educational chameleons.

The business of teaching in this country is now, more than before, very serious business. Politicians no longer can afford to use the public schools as vehicles for reelection. Adequate funds are needed, and all three groups are united in this effort. Politicians react favorably to pressure. The ghetto poor know that a person without a marketable skill is a drain on society. They expect the public schools to provide the training. Our country has been made aware of the reality of the waste of brain power by not tapping the resources of the poor.

The Answer is Easy

Whose children shall we teach? It appears that the answer

is quite easy. We teach *all* the children of *all* the public, regardless of circumstances of birth, status of parents, and innate ability. If we do *not* believe in public education, we had better say so and commence to provide for those who will be eliminated. If we believe that the public *should* have the opportunity to be educated, then we had better act that way.

This means that the power structure, commencing with the teacher education institutions, must make the present and future cadre accountable. Ivan Pavlov used food with his dogs; perhaps money would be a viable control stimulus for humans, that is, pay would be determined by the quality of the work. No work — no pay! After all, we must stop the brain drain. If we can put men on the moon, surely we should be able to work with the known. Our greatest investments are our children. *All* of them must be taught!

Since the ghetto poor, like the members of the middle and upper class, desire and are now demanding results from their children's education, the public school arena has become a battleground. The "haves" have the resources to supplement via the tutoring route that which the public schools fail to accomplish. The "have-nots" do not have the resources, but they are demanding the same results within the same period of time. Since both sets of children are to compete in the same society, it is fair that both be given equal opportunities. The only "resource" available to the "have-nots" is the ability to destroy. We need not go into the psychological reasoning why this "resource" is used, for we know that it is used. We must concentrate our efforts so that the ghetto poor will feel that there is no need to use this "resource." Although they have nothing to lose, likewise they will not gain by using this "resource." It is better for the "have-nots" to gain a fair shake than for the "haves" to be reduced to the status of "have-nots."

The acculturation and enculturation outlined by the sociologist, as well as the role of the church and the politics of our society outlined by the political scientist, highlight the responsibility of the public schools. No matter how lucid the oratory about the need for a high quality of public education for every child, it boils down to what was said by the late Dr. Martin Luther King, Jr.: "Either we're going to live together as brothers and sisters or we're going to die together like fools." It appears that the only light in the lighthouse to guide our society is the public school. This light must not go out.

Educational Accountability Here and Abroad

HANNELORE WASS

On the whole, the indication is that other Western countries are responding to their industrial-technological revolution with a counter-revolution of humanistic education. America, on the other hand, seems to be well on the road toward industrializing her education and making it more technological.

America's schools today are more severely criticized than ever before. The charge is that they are not meeting the changing needs of society, are not educating a third of their population, and are causing too many youngsters to drop out physically and psychologically. Recently a powerful front of critics, backed by government and industry, have proposed their solution — accountability.

The principle of accountability has always been essential to education; new and revolutionary, however, is the recent redefinition of the concept. Critical aspects in the current view are: (a) improvement in education is imposed upon the schools; (b) measurable performance outcome is the sole criterion for improvement; (c) the economic model of cost efficiency provides the criterion for determining the degree of educational improvement, that is, learning is a commodity, and the question is how to get more for the tax dollar or, better, how to get the most for

Hannelore Wass, "Educational Accountability: Here and Abroad," **Educational Leadership,** 29 (7): 618-620, April, 1972. Reprinted with permission of the Association for Supervision and Curriculum Development and Hannelore Wass. Copyright © 1972 by the Association for Supervision and Curriculum Development.

the least; and (d) educational improvement is assessed by independent accomplishment audit agencies. Most ardent proponents of the new accountability promise nothing less than a "renaissance of American education."[1] They claim, in other words, that a rebirth or renewal of American education will be brought about by an economically motivated technique of coercing (inducing) educational change adopted from the industrial model.

This new approach to better education appears, at first glance, to make a good deal of sense. After all, our country is on the forefront in industrial and technological advancement; her size has made education a massive national enterprise involving millions of people in its operation; her present economic condition coupled with an antiquated tax structure call for a tighter squeeze; and an operational model that has proven successful in industry ought to work in education as well.

Add to this the fact that American psychology has, in the past half-century, developed an efficient technology of behavior modification. According to many hopefuls, its application to education will guarantee improvement provided the desired behaviors are predetermined and appropriate reinforcement schedules used. Add also the impressive number of tests produced by the testing movement over the years (1,219 according to the *Sixth Mental Measurements Yearbook*, edited by Oscar K. Buros, 1965), along with a sophisticated technology of testing. Learning for the test is not new in education. The current notion of accountability merely adds another dimension —*teaching* for the test; that is, the reward or punishment for learning goes to the teacher, or to the learning corporation that has entered into a performance contract with the school.

Production of Knowledge

Underlying the current concept of accountability is the belief that better education means increased academic production. This notion is not new either. When Sputnik went into orbit, America reacted fiercely with the demand that teachers teach more, sooner, faster, and with more rigor. This pressure has continued ever since. No doubt, the current wave of accountability demonstrates a total loss of confidence in the ability and willingness on the part of the teaching profession, but surely, it must also reflect a deep concern with the education of our young — a concern we share with other societies.

It may be worthwhile to take a look abroad to see whether other industrialized countries are facing a crisis in education as we are, and if so, how they are attempting to tackle the problem. The result of such a survey may come as a shock to many Americans. A recently published report of an international conference on the role of the teacher in educational change, held in Berlin, and attended by educational leaders from 31 nations (mostly European), may not be representative, but certainly is indicative of current educational thinking and developments in other industrialized coutries such as Germany, the USSR, Great Britain, France, and others. According to this report[2] and other recent publications,[3] [4] [5] [6] other countries share with us the recognition that educational change is desperately needed, that new scientific knowledge and insights must find their way into the schools, and must do so with less lag, and that modern technology and media offer useful means toward educational improvement.

The current American concept of accountability, however, is totally absent. The idea of coercing educational change, the focus on increased production and on the economic factor, and the notion of assessing effectiveness by agencies outside the field of education apparently have not occurred to other countries as a possible solution to their educational crisis. Rather, the trend is in the other direction:

1. The new American concept of accountability imposes, assesses, and reinforces educational change from the outside. This in turn reduces the role of the teacher from a professional to a skilled worker. European countries, on the other hand, hold firm in the belief that effective change must come from within the educational institution. They focus their attention upon the factors that might facilitate this process, such as broadening the teacher's competence, particularly his recognition of present societal needs, the school's role in society, and his own importance as an agent of change; involving him more actively in decision-making processes concerning matters that are essential rather than peripheral; and granting him more freedom to enable him to assume more responsibility.

2. The new American concept of accountability demands specification of more finely separated subject matter, and minutely detailed, hierarchically ordered specification of learning objectives, stressing ever more detailed skills. Other countries, on the other hand, have begun to stress interdisciplinary coupling, such as aesthetics with science (particularly in the USSR), and integration of traditional subject matter into more embracing, more meaningful, life- and problem-oriented entities, stressing broad relationships.

3. The new American concept of accountability requires that learning objectives (behavioral objectives) be predetermined and predefined for the learner by others. European countries unanimously have begun to emphasize self-propelled, self-directed "interest" learning by the pupil.

4. The new American concept of accountability implies that curriculum objectives and other important curricular decisions be determined by the "experts." European countries, on the other hand, are demanding shared decision-making involving teachers, scientists, parents, and pupils.

5. The new American concept of accountability defines the teacher's role as that of a learning engineer and subject matter specialist. Other countries have begun to stress such personality factors as sensitivity, positive self-concept, skills in interpersonal relations, autonomy, initiative, flexibility, openness to experience, and problem-solving attitude.

Thus it appears that production of knowledge is no longer the primary concern in other Western industrialized societies, and that a shift in emphasis is occurring from product to process, from curriculum content and methodology to the persons in the process, and from the strictly academic to the realms of personal development and interpersonal relationships. Most ironic is the fact, for instance, that America reacted to the Soviets' Sputnik with increased pressure toward academic performance, while at the same time the Soviets have been shifting their emphasis to character education and personality development.[7] [8]

These developments become the more noteworthy when the educational histories in European countries are considered. European countries are far more tradition-bound than the United States. Their schools are given less to fads and fashion, they have been less vulnerable to public pressure, they respond more slowly to changing needs, and when they do, changes tend to be deliberative rather than hasty. There is no question that changes now proposed or already in progress, in countries such as Germany, the USSR, Great Britain, and France, are radical departures from long-established educational traditions.

On the whole, the indication is that other Western countries are responding to their industrial-technological revolution with a counterrevolution of humanistic education. America, on the other hand, seems to be well on the road toward industrializing her education and making it more technological. Current approaches to accountabillity will indeed more quickly accomplish such industrialization and application of technology. Yet perhaps we need to pause and ask ourselves if that is what we want.

REFERENCES

[1] Leon Lessinger and Dwight Allen. "Performance Proposals for Educational Funding: A New Approach to Federal Resource Allocation." **Phi Delta Kappan** 51 (3); 136-37; November 1969.

[2] Alexander Schuller, editor. **Lehrerrolle im Wandel.** Padagogisches Zentrum Veroffentlichungen Reihe C, Band 21, Verlag Julius Beltz, Weinheim, Berlin, Basel, 1971.

[3] Klaus Goehrke. "Dienst die Gesamtschule der Demokratisierung?" In: **Gesamtschul-Informationen, Padagogisches Zentrum, Berlin** 4 (1): 41-45; 1971.

[4] Der Senator fur Schulwesen Berlin. "Bericht uber den Schulentwicklungplan fur das Land Berlin." Drucksache Nr. 1417 des Abgeordnetenhauses von Berlin.

[5] "Nachrichten und Berichte — Inland-Ausland." In: **Gesamtschul-Informationen, Padagogisches Zentrum, Berlin** 4 (1): 3-35; 1971.

[6] **International Yearbook of Education.** Geneva: UNESCO International Bureau of Education, 1968-1970.

[7] Ingrid Monch and Gesine Buhlow. "Differenzierung in der sowjetischen Einheitsschule." In: **Gesamtschul-Informationen, Padagogisches Zentrum, Berlin** 4 (1): 36-40; 1971.

[8] Urie Bronfenbrenner. **Two Worlds of Childhood — U.S. and U.S.S.R.** New York: Russell Sage Foundation, 1970.

II

Prevailing Approaches To Accountability: Some Critical Comments and Concerns

Introduction

Both those opposing and supporting the present approach to educational accountability realize it is not going to leave the schools or teachers unchanged. A growing number of educators, disturbed with where the behavioral objectives/performance-based approach is taking us, are increasingly exposing the weaknesses and dangers of that approach. Examining the history of the industrial model in education, they have brought attention to its misuse and abuse. Any model adopted out of frustration and expediency, they warn, could have disastrous consequences for education in a democratic society.

Others are challenging the idea that everything learned in a classroom can be reduced to exact and precise measurement. They warn that limiting ourselves to easily measured educational goals motivates us to ignore and overlook other equally important aspects of the educational process. Pointing toward the onrushing future, they insist we may be running a real risk of teaching ourselves into obsolescence and possible extinction. They call for educators to respond to man's needs for meaning and personal worth, and to strive for an approach to education and accountability that confirms and satisfies these human needs.

Apollo, Dionysus and the Cult of Efficiency

FRED RICHARDS

I. DAVID WELCH

ANNE COHEN RICHARDS

The cult of efficiency, supporting and sanctifying the behavioral objectives approach to educational accountability, is a symptom of future shock, of the inability of schools and education to confront and cope with the future that daily arrives.

The cult of efficiency pervading American society is no more evident than in the increasing application of behavioral objectives to the educational process. Our tendency to describe education in terms of the metaphor of business and industry has led us to evaluate the schools' effectiveness by accountings of their efficient use of public funds. However, the majority of those advocating the use of behavioral objectives to assure this efficiency have disregarded or overlooked the human consequences. They have disregarded the insight of the ancient Greeks and those who insist that a lop-sided devotion to a limited notion of order and objectivity is inevitably disastrous. They have suffered from a severe case of "future shock" and are a symptom of our schools' failure to cope with the onrushing future and the radically changing nature of change.

Education and the Greeks

The Greeks were well aware that an emphasis upon certain aspects of human experience at the cost of denying or neglecting others was a prelude to disaster. The truly educated person, they believed, was one integrating in his life and learning qualities too often viewed as antagonistic. In fifth-century B. C. Athens, the greatness of the Greeks was their capacity to reconcile or blend two modes of experience often perceived as mutually exclusive: (1) control, objective clarity, and the orderly pursuit of desired goals; (2) intuition, imagination, and an intense or spontaneous involvement in the process of accomplishing these goals.[1]

Apollo and Dionysus

These complementary modes of experience were represented by Apollo and Dionysus, Apollo was the god of order and reason, logic and objectivity. He was the form-giving force in human experience, the ability of humankind to order and direct its activities toward chosen ends. Dionysus represented the suspension of order and spontaneous abandonment. He was the god of ecstacy, imagination and madness, the inspiration and insight of the artist seeking its expression in the Apollonian.

The Need for Balance

The Greek's capacity to blend or merge these two modes represents the preeminence of the Apollonian in Greek culture. However, the victory of the Apollonian was a precarious one and only sustained by maintaining a creative relationship with the Dionysian.[2] The educational process which focused on the Apollonian and ignored the Dionysian proved to be, in the long run, completely inadequate. Order, objectivity, and the pursuit of predetermined goals - the essence of the behavioral objectives approach - were only humanly relevant and effective when informed by a healthy respect for the Dionysian.

Education and the Worship of Apollo

Unfortunately, education in American culture is displaying a dangerous and imbalanced devotion to the Apollonian. Focusing on that which is most easily objectified and measured in the form of standardized testing, behavioral objectives, performance-based criteria, cost-accounting, and prepackaged curricula, education in America worships at the altar of Apollo while neglecting to pay homage to Dionysus. American education reflects an unhealthy one-sidedness which, in the individual, announces a psychological breakdown and, in the life of the Greek tragic hero, brings about his fall. Disregarding the spontaneous, the intuitive, the joyful, the creative, educators perform, like some skillful but misguided surgeon, a psychological lobotomy upon those students in their care.[3]

The Cult of Efficiency

Stephen K. Bailey, in "Combating the Efficiency Cultists," warns that "in some circumstances narrow canons of efficiency are the enemy of efficiency."[4] In the long run, narrow views of efficiency prove ineffective. Developing a better management system to streamline the educational process provides only a superficial accounting of education. When such superficiality defines and establishes educational priorities - as is often the case - the efficiency cultists destroy the very process they set out to save.

One shudders at educational programs spending millions to develop thousands of behavioral objectives by which to evaluate the performance of their staff and students. The larger the number of these precisely-stated and measured objectives, the "less narrow and limited" the program is assumed to be. With two thousand behavioral objectives, how can anyone accuse us of limited goals! And considering the millions invested, who would be foolish enough to suggest we abolish the system and start all over again? Having invested millions, we convince ourselves it has to work! Such conviction is found in the response of a department chairman when asked if he believed his departmental members were competently doing their job. "I don't know," he replied, "but I'm developing a list of over three hundred objectives. I'll know soon!"

The Discounting of Education

Efficiency in education is an important aspect of accountability. However, the efficiency cultists are like those teachers who, as Earl Kelley once remarked, cover the subject so well they end up burying it forever. The Apollonian preoccupation with efficiency and cost accounting obscures or discounts much of what is vital in education. How do we efficiently determine the dollar value of those experiences many of us found most significant in our education: the small seminar in which professor and students shared the personal meaning of ideas; teacher and students dialoguing for hours over pitchers of beer; the warm and personal conversation resolving a conflict with a professor for whom you had a great deal of respect; the letter received from a teacher three months after graduation? Where are these entered in the books? What legislative or administrative lists of objectives leave room for such entries and, thus, reinforce and encourage such activities? Bailey cites a verbal interchange in response to the cost accountants and budget specialists who look askance at such frivilous and fuzzy activity. When a rural member of a state legislature was dumbfounded upon hearing that university faculty members taught **only** nine hours a week, the President of the university responded, "Sir, you are famous for your stud bulls. Would you judge their value by the number of hours a week they work?"[5]

The "Screw You Effect"

Recent developments in experimental, psychological research illustrate the limitations of the efficiency cultists. Research on psychological research has shown that the subject in the experiment is not a stimulus-response machine but a person whose own goals, needs, and perceptions color and affect his performance in experimental situations. Some subjects might, for example, "psyche out" the researcher's goals and seek to subvert them. Joseph Masling aptly refers to such subversion as the "Screw You Effect."[6] Similarly, many teachers are ingenius in devising ways to subvert a system attempting to define teaching in terms of directions sent down from "on high." On the surface, many play the "numbers game" to satisfy the efficiency cultists, while realistically going about the task of "educating for what is real."

The Utopian State of Affairs

Some researchers, responding to the "Screw You Effect" and similar phenomena, attempt to set up experimental conditions that remove or limit the effect of such "intrusions." Milton Rosenberg, seeking "a utopian state of affairs" in the experimental setting, concludes that future research should be designed to reduce the possibility of such unwanted behavior on the part of the subjects. Striving for clean data and pure objectivity, the researcher must control the experimental situation to prevent the subjects from "contaminating" the results.[7]

When the educational process is evaluated in terms of precisely-stated and predetermined goals, will the most vital aspects of education becomes intrusions, unrewarded and eventually extinguished aspects of learning? Will feeling, meaning, beliefs, values, perceptions - that which makes us human - become minor considerations simply because they don't "add up" to educational efficiency? The cult of efficiency and the search for a utopian state of affairs is what Richard Sennett describes as an adolescent search for a pure, coherent picture of reality.[8] Such a purification ritual is a desire to insulate oneself against the innovative and the new, against the Dionysian with all its surprise, spontaneity, and suspence. By forcing upon experience - and the educational process - this process of purification, one excludes, or attempts to exclude, all that is unpredictable, unknown, unexpected and imprecise. It prevents the disruption of one's utopian view of things. It helps support and perpetuate the illusion - and the belief of the efficiency cultists - that the real significance and value of education resides in what is most easily measured and most readily reduced to behavioral obejctives.

Future Shock and the Cult of Efficiency

The cult of efficiency, supporting and sanctifying the behavioral objectives approach to educational accountability, is a symptom of future shock, of the inability of schools and education to confront and cope with the future that daily arrives. It demonstrates, to use a phrase by Frank E. Ratliff, "our own intransigence in times of change."[9] While Alvin Toffler and other futurists warn us that we are caught up in an historic process demanding radical changes in our preceptions and values, the schools shudder and seek security in cost accounting and performance-based criteria. The schools react like the overwhelmed victims of a disaster, rigid and numbed when confronting an environment suddenly transformed and filled with novelty and change. They desperately employ what Toffler describes as the maladaptive strategies of future shock victims trying to escape the realities of our age.[10]

Denial. The future shock victim unknowingly denies the reality of radical change by closing out new information. He is threatened, seeks maladaptive closure, and, finally confronted with change, is overwhelmed. *He's a sure convert to the cult of efficiency.*

Specialism. The future shock victim has a narrow view of reality, what perceptual psychologists call "tunnel vision." While not fearing and denying all new information and ideas, he finds security in withdrawing to a narrow and specific area of life. *He's a candidate for promotion in the cult of efficiency.*

Reversion. The future shock victim retreats to former perceptions and behaviors once successful but now irrelevant. He is a dogmatist, obsessively, desperately, and meticulously continuing to do what he once did appropriately and well. *He is a spokesman for the cult of efficiency, insisting that being effective is doing more efficiently what we have always done in the past.* **Super-Simplifier.** The future shock victim "seeks a single, neat equation that will explain all the complex novelties threatening to engulf him."[11] He is the faddist finding salvation in easy answers. *He is also the "true believer" in the cult of efficiency, leaping upon the bandwagon of behavioral objectives.*

The Kiki-Bird Mentality

These maladaptive strategies display what two of the authors have described elsewhere as the Kiki-bird mentality:[12]

> The Kiki bird, now extinct, was well-known for its ability to fly backwards. Such expertise, while often rewarded in academe, was of dubious value in the world of nature. This backward mobility enabled him to become an expert on where he had been. It also enabled him to avoid dealing with where he was going. Like too many educators he dealt with the present by staying in the past and refusing to confront the future.
>
> Perhaps the Kiki bird's demise can be attributed to future shock. Unable to fly like the soaring and forward-looking Jonathan Livingston Seagull, the Kiki bird miscalculated and met butt-on the wall of the future, believing it to be a simple repetition of the past. Unable to deal with change and the radical change of change, he was destroyed by it. Fortunately, the Kiki bird had not educated others to repeat his disastrous mistake. His obsolete knowledge and values were buried with him.
>
> It is becoming obsolete, perhaps, to comment on the obsolescence of educational institutions which journey toward the year 2001 ill-prepared to respond to the realities of the 1970's. Numerous well-informed critics in best selling books have documented the terminal cases of future shock racking educational instutituions. Perhaps students, particularly, need no such clinical reports to remind them that too many educators seemingly withdraw into a catatonic-like state when confronted by change. . . .
>
> . . Such an educational process produces students who are trained for jobs that don't exist, who have to unlearn what they have learned in order to survive "in the world", who are not in touch with themselves and, thus, out of touch with others.

The Cost of Accountability

The Kiki bird collided with the future. His backward-looking confrontation with radical change guaranteed his tragic end. He is beyond saving. The cult of efficiency, seeking to account for and, thus, perpetuate rigidly defined educational goals, may lead us unknowingly toward a similar fate. We may fail to ask the questions: What are we trying to save in education? What will we destroy as a result of our efforts? Will we save the worst and destroy the best? In many cases, those suffering from future shock and employing behavioral objectives may simply pursue more intensely the very educational goals that have prompted critics to describe our schools as sterile, inhuman places in which to learn. Such persons may help to deny, diminish, or destroy the very experiences that make education worth the personal investment: being encouraged to follow a hunch, finding new purposes and directions, having a fact become alive and brilliantly clear, discovering the personal and social meaning of information, seeing something in a fresh and new way. Can we seek to measure so well and perform so efficiently that the peak experience, the moment of enlightenment, the imaginative insight, the new-found freedom, and the love of knowledge become messy intrusions rather than sought-after and celebrated goals?

The Final Reckoning

For the Greeks, those who worshipped Apollo exclusive of Dionysus were in danger of being literally ripped apart. To refuse to worship Dionysus was to become a victim of his agents, the Bacchae, divine agents capable of tearing apart, limb from limb, those obsessed with looking at and living life from the point of view of the objective and logical observer. While such a notion of detachment and "objectivity" has been idolized and rewarded by the efficiency cultists, it is a questionable and irresponsible posture for those in education. In its extreme form, it displays an irrational fear of change, a withdrawal from human experience, and a refusal to deal with the future that daily arrives.

We, accepting the limited and lop-sided application of behavioral objectives to the educational process, continue to carve out a secure corner in the cult of efficiency. We continue to worship at the altar of Apollo. We continue to be, too, the possible victims of the modern Bacchae: a climate of psychological imbalance in the schools, the inability to discover and communicate the personal meaning of knowledge, the unhealthy absence of openness, spontaneity and community in our college classrooms, the increasing confusion and frustration of teachers and students alike. We fail to face the human consequences of our commitment to the cult of efficiency.

> Today, the school is again being called upon to help a nation in great need . . . When we hear the call for acountability and respond to our critics, we must ask them and ourselves what are going to be the costs of our responses. . . . We can only guess at the cost of accountability in the future . . . But one thing we know for sure: some part of us will be included in the reckoning.[13]

REFERENCES

[1]H. D. F. Kitto, *The Greeks,* Baltimore, Maryland: Penguin Books, 1951, p. 25.
[2]Friedrich Nietzsche, **The Birth of Tragedy and the Genealogy of Morals,** New York: Doubleday and Company, Inc., 1956.
[3]Eugene A. Brunelle, "Apollo and Dionysus," **The Journal of Creative Behavior,** Vol. 5, no. 1, Winter, 1971, p. 37.
[4]Stephen K. Bailey, "Combating the Efficiency Cultists," **Change,** June, 1973, p. 8.
[5]*Ibid.,* p. 9.
[6]Joseph Masling, "Role-Related Behavior of the Subject and Psychologists and its Effects Upon Psychological Data," **Nebraska Symposium on Motivation,** University of Nebraska Press, 1966, pp. 67-104.
[7]Milton Rosenberg, "The Conditions and Consequences of Evaluation Apprehension," Robert Rosenthal and Ralph L. Rosnow, Eds., **Artifact in Behavioral Research,** New York: Academic Press, 1969, p. 280-349.
[8]Richard Sennett, **The Uses of Disorder,** New York: Random House, Inc., 1970.
[9]Frank E. Ratliff, "Accountability: At What Cost," **English Journal,** April, 1971, p. 490.
[10]Alvin Toffler, **Future Shock,** New York: Random House, Inc., 1970, pp. 319-321.
[11]*Ibid.,* p. 321.
[12]Fred Richards and I. David Welch, "The Kiki Bird Versus Jonathan Livingston Seagull - A Choice of Educational Futures," **Egg,** University of Northern Colorado, Greeley, Colorado, Vol. 1, no. 3, May, 1973, p. 17.
[13]Ratliff, *op. cit.*

Teaching for Profit:
The Deficit of Accountability

STAN ELAM

Are teachers who do not know history doomed, like politicians, to repeat it?

Revolutions begin when the time is ripe. The guaranteed-performance contracting revolution in education began a year ago in Texarkana, where everything fell in place: a special need; some federal money; a school administration willing to experiment; a teaching force unaware or unafraid of the threat; a state department without rigid regulations; and Loyd Dorsett's teaching machines, 13 years and $2 million in development.

But now school performance contracting with private industry is in trouble, because there was cheating in Texarkana.

Graham Greene wrote in 1935, "There's always money to be picked up in a revolution." Dorsett, or one of his employees, was a bit too eager to pick up his share.

Briefly, this is the story, as it broke in the public press in early July:

In late May a junior high student was taking his Iowa basic skills post-tests in one of the Texarkana rapid learning centers remarked that he was tired of answering those same old questions. (Post-tests are given to determine how much money Dorsett will get under terms of his contract.)

Martin Filogamo overheard him, and Filogamo is the school's dropout prevention project director. He is not paid by Dorsett. The cat was out of the bag.

From "The Chameleon's Dish" by Stan Elam, a column in **Phi Delta Kappan**, 71-72, September, 1970. Reprinted by permission.

Dorsett produces much of the software used in his teaching machines. A programmer in his organization had fed reading, math, and vocabulary exercises from the Iowa tests into the software used in Texarkana's rapid learning centers. Oh, there were differences — three choices instead of four in multiple-choice sections, for example. But Dean C. Andrews, the internal evaluator, said that 30 to 60% of the questions on 15 of 16 achievement tests may have been tainted. Dorsett said it was more like 6.5%.

Oddly enough, youngsters in the Texarkana rapid learning centers apparently made only small additional gains after Dorsett's "teaching to the test." But they had already done well enough to guarantee the contractor a profit. Dorsett's representatives had indeed snatched defeat from the jaws of victory.

At this writing, federal payments to Dorsett have ceased and a negotiated settlement is in prospect. The Office of Economic Opportunity has thrown out Dorsett's bids on other performance contracts. A USOE statement says, "We expect that as the accountability principle is applied more extensively in projects that we will learn earlier of problems such as these. Because of the flexibility provided by an outside performance contract, the USOE will be able to salvage aspects of projects with a minimum interruption of the program and student learning."

Has the performance-contracting accountability concept been dealt a death blow? By no means, At the July conference of the Education Commission of the States, where the Texarkana scandal broke just as panels were discussing accountability and performance contracting, it was revealed that about 150 school systems were negotiating with private firms to run experiments in upgrading student skills, with payments tied to "actual results." The USOE is dismayed but undeterred. It has made a grant of $281,000 to help finance a second year of the dropout prevention project in Texarkana (sans Dorsett, or course). A USOE spokesman says: "[The Texarkana situation] is merely indicative that problems will occur as new approaches and new methods are introduced into educational practice. Such problems do not invalidate either the concept of accountability or the specific method of performance contracting to achieve it."

Nevertheless, this observer would call attention to the little-known and unprepossessing history of performance contracting in Canada. Charles E. Phillips, for many years a distinguished educational historian at the Ontario College of Education, University of Toronto, wrote that history in succinct form in *The Development of Education in Canada* (W. J. Gage, Ltd., 1957).

In Ontario, from 1876 to 1882, Phillips says, a system of "payment by results" made financial aid from the province to high schools largely dependent on the number of students who passed an intermediate examination after a year or two of attendance. The system had already been demonstrated in England. "The effect was, of course," Phillips notes, "to narrow all school effort to the cramming of content most likely to be tested in the subjects prescribed for examination. The system also caused teachers to concentrate on the average and slightly below-average pupils, with whom their efforts would pay dividends through a larger percentage of passes, and to neglect other students — the bright because they would pass anyway, the dull because they were hopeless or at best a poor risk in terms of expenditure of time. But payments by results undoubtedly did lash both teacher and pupils to work harder at drill and review in order to avoid failure."

During the period when provincial support depended upon examination results, some schools made "amazing improvements." And unsuccessful headmasters and teachers were dismissed right and left. Then came the inevitable scandal. Says Phillips:

No doubt some of the teachers dismissed were lazy or inefficient. But nearly all were shrewd enough to take advantage of every new means that was offered to get results. Teachers' professional journals were filled with sample examination papers, model answers, and advertisements of little books containing notes on various subjects, the memorization of which would ensure success on the examinations. History teaching became the application of a system of mnemonics and the teaching of literature little more. Perth Collegiate Institute offered $10 to every pupil successful on the intermediate examination.

The Canada Educational Monthly stated editorially in 1881: "As matters now stand the high school master who does not deliberately coach his pupils for their examinations, study the pecularities of the examiners, get up old examination papers, and train for the examinations and the examinations alone, may be an honest man, but he is a Quixotic fool so far as his temporal interests are concerned."

Lists of questions likely to be asked on examinations were openly published and advance copies of actual examination papers were offered for sale confidentially by at least one enterprising individual. He was reported to have done an extensive business in examination papers for Second Class teachers' certificates, the equivalent of the intermediate examination, before being brought to trial in 1881.

Experience with payment by results in Ontario proved that it is possible to raise standards quickly if the criterion is defined as mastery of prescribed content. *But there was a storm of protest against the sacrifice of all other educational values for the attainment of this end.* In 1883 payment by results was abandoned in the province. (Emphasis added.)

Even some states of the U. S. have tried performance contracting in the distant past. In 1819, for example, the state of Georgia began paying schools on the basis of their product, according to Leon Lessinger. The experiment ended quickly.

The capitalist countries are by no means alone in unhappy experiences with payment by performance. Even Soviet school authorities, according to *The New York Times,* soon faced a professional disease known as "percentomania" when, more recently, they tried to hold teachers too narrowly accountable. Percentomania is jargon for cheating by teachers. Concluded the *Times* in a biting editorial (July 25): " . . . it would be a devastating commentary on American values if crass materialism of profit or less were to be the only hope for a brighter future of learning in the United States."

Are teachers who do not know history doomed, like politicians, to repeat it?

Education In A Gray Flannel Suit

HOWARD OZMON

*Naturally this has led an unreconstructed social critic like myself
. . . to ponder the application of the business approach to all
phases of education . . .*

In the last few months we have seen a not-too-surprising attempt
to apply the managerial ethos of business to the educational enterprise. We now talk about accountability which merges the word
"accounting" (certainly a highly business-like term) with "ability"
as if to suggest that ability (even teaching ability) can be accounted
for like money, i.e., in terms of dollars and cents. The most recent
suggestion along this line is the voucher plan (voucher certainly
being an equally relevant business term) whereby parents can
purchase education in the free-enterprise market, shopping around
(so to speak). That they might want to buy at the Klan School
for Retarded Cross Burners or the Old Time Bible School seems
not to trouble the business establishmentarians so long as schools
remain "accountable."

Naturally this has led an unreconstructed social critic like myself
(while checking my Spiro watch for the next radical-liberal meeting)
to ponder the application of the business approach to all phases
of education including kindergarden. Thus, at the John Pierpont
Morgan kindergarten, we might have a situation like this:

Howard Ozmon, "Education in a Gray Flannel Suit," **The Educational Forum,**
539-540, May 1971. Reprinted by permission of Kappa Delta Pi, an Honor
Society in Education and owner of the copyright.

CHARLIE: Hi, George.

GEORGE: Hi, Charlie.

CHARLIE: Sure is quiet.

GEORGE: Yeah, a bunch of kids got fired yesterday.

CHARLIE: What happened?

GEORGE: The market for hand paintings just fell right out.

CHARLIE: Gosh, I'm glad I'm on beads.

GEORGE: What's the rate of production in your shop?

CHARLIE: You have to string twenty-five a minute to keep up. I'm doing blue beads this week. What about you?

GEORGE: I'm still on paper flowers. We might get a bonus this Christmas. That's the rumor.

CHARLIE: I hope to get a raise soon myself. That's what they told my mother.

GEORGE: That's great. We should both get longer vacations this year too — with our seniority.

CHARLIE: I hope so.

GEORGE: Well . . . there goes the whistle. It's back to the old assembly line.

CHARLIE: I suppose you're coming tonight — to the meeting.

GEORGE: What meeting?

CHARLIE: You know — the union . . . !

Every Kid a Hustler

GARY SARETSKY

It is likely that, someday soon, a group of students may approach a teacher and say, "We understand that if we do well on the test tomorrow you're going to get a lot more bread than if we don't do well. Me and the brothers wonder what you intend to do for us if we do well tomorrow?"

For performance contracting to make "every kid a winner,"[1] must it allow some opportunity for every kid to become a hustler? Teachers and firms who have performance contracted may have placed new power into the hands of students, unwittingly making themselves accountable to the students.

Under most performance contracts, the measure of success — for the teacher or contractor — is the performance of students on tests. Contractors are rewarded for good student performance and sometimes penalized for poor student performance.

Students have the option of performing at a lower level on the tests than they are capable; that is, students have the potential to influence the financial rewards or penalties of the contractors. Therefore, students could have power over the contractor and force him to meet and satisfy the needs and desires of students.

The majority of students involved in performance contracting are the poor, blacks, Puerto Ricans, Chicanos, Appalachian whites, and American Indians. The schools have evidenced their inability to provide many of these students with even basic academic skills, which provide access to the usual rewards of schooling. Perhaps in reaction, many of these students have substituted hassling and hustling as sources of rewards.

Hassling, or making life difficult for teachers and schools — assaults upon and intimidation of teachers, school demonstrations,

Gary Saretsky, "Every Kid a Hustler," **Phi Delta Kappan,** 595-596, June, 1971. Reprinted by permission.

and school boycotts — has become a rewarding activity in which students can demonstrate their alienation from and discontent with the schools.

Performance contracts could serve as new ways to hassle the teacher, new methods for retribution.

Hustling, on the other hand, is the inner-city version of cost-effective private enterprise. Hustling is simply maximizing perceived payoffs from energy expended within the enterprise. That is; playing the numbers; dealing in drugs; theft; extortion; betting on handball games, basketball games, pool — these are means by which the hustler receives the greatest dollar-per-man-hour return. Where else can an inner-city resident get $25 for five minutes work? (Four kids can completely strip a car in less than four minutes for that payoff.)

Aside from material rewards, hustling provides the intrinsic reward of beating the system. This is a powerful reward for those who otherwise feel helpless in the face of the system. In fact, it may be far more powerful than a monetary reward. By making a teachers's salary or payment to a contracting firm contingent upon student performance, performance contracting has made those responsible for instruction vulnerable to being hustled.

The most obvious way that students can hustle the contractor is through extortion, threatening to perform poorly on the posttest unless the teacher meets certain demands. A more sophisticated and more profitable approach would be an offer, by a group of students, to perform poorly on the pretest. The students could then perform better on the posttest, regardless of the quality or effect of the teacher's instruction. Payment to the contractor (and his student coconspiritors) usually increases proportionately to student progress. If students realize that better performance will yield more financial rewards, hustling may actually serve to motivate students to learn how to perform well on the posttest.

Is it likely that, someday soon, a group of students may approach a teacher and say, "We understand that if we do well on the test tomorrow you're going to get a lot more bread than if we don't do well. Me and the brothers wonder what you intend to do for us if we do well tomorrow?" Is it just as likely that members of the Black Panthers, the Young Lords, or the SDS will soom approach a major commercial performance contractor and use similar leverage to get contributions for their free breakfast program or their free health clinic? Would a performance contractor who also has contracts with the Department of Defense be forced to choose among his clients because of student influence on the company's income? Certainly far more elaborate scenarios, concerning personnel selection, retention, and curriculum determination, could emerge from the possible dilemmas caused by the simplistic performance measures used in most current performance contracts.

Among the questions raised by the proposition that students can hustle performance contractors are: Why hasn't it happened yet? (or has it?) What changes in the student's self-image and his academic performance might result from his new power? Should the schools and the contractor attempt to close or utilize this loophole existing in many performance contracts?

Most students presently involved in performance contracting experiments are in elementary and intermediate schools and are not into hustling. Many of them aren't aware that others (teachers and commercial firms) are receiving money on the basis of their (the students') performance on a test.

Texarkana established the precedent for performance contractors to "pay off" students in the form of merchandise, green stamps, etc. Even those students "determined" the nature of some of the rewards, which the Dorsett company had not anticipated. The practice of providing rewards in the form of merchandise and money has been continued in most performance contracts. In essence, then, some of the potential hustlers have already been paid off. The more activist, underground-newspaper genre of public school student who might become a hustler has not been involved in performance contracting ventures; nor have the outside organizations which have organized and radicalized the high schools latched onto the potential inherent in performance contracts.

Hustling the contractor may increase the student's tendency to perceive his school experiences as dependent upon his own actions. Studies indicate that a person who has a strong belief that he can control his own destiny is likely to "be more alert to those aspects of the environment which provide useful information for his future behavior" and "place greater value on skill or achievement reinforcements and be generally more concerned with his ability. . . ."[2]

Industrial studies indicate that workers who participate in management decisions evidence greater productivity and satisfaction with their work.[3]

Wouldn't it be interesting to find that the inner-city student, when given this hustling leverage, increased his reading achievement?

If contracting teachers and firms have a responsibility that goes beyond facilitating student performance on some measure of cognitive achievement, they must be accountable for enriching the child's learning experiences and making them intrinsically more rewarding than hustling or hassling.

Until a better way is found, the loophole to which I referred may be the only means by which society, the immediate community, and the ultimate client, the child, can hold the performance contractor accountable for more than test scores.

REFERENCES

[1]L. Lessinger, **Every Kid a Winner: Accountability in Education.** New York: Simon and Schuster, 1970.
[2]J. L. Rotter, "Generalized Expectancies for Internal versus External Control of Reinforcement," **Psychological Monographs,** 80 (1, Whole No. 609), 1966.
[3]F. Herzberg, **The Motivation to Work.** New York: Wiley, 1959; and **Work and the Nature of Man.** Cleveland: World Publishers, 1966.

Commitment to Competency: The New Fetishism in Teacher Education

ROBERT J. NASH

In an overzealousness born out of frustration and defensiveness we are adopting a model which promises to bestow a magical kind of scientific-technological warrant on our professional endeavors.

More and more colleges of education are moving toward a competency model in teacher education. This commitment to competency is usually buttressed by the following assumptions:

1. Teaching can be reduced to a series of performance functions and can be analyzed according to types of teaching activities.

2. Because teaching consists exclusively of these various kinds of activities (e.g., explaining, guiding, demonstrating, testing and evaluating, skills imparting), the best teacher education program is one which develops training protocols that foster these skills.

3. The performance or competency curriculum is rooted in a set of very clear objectives. This competency curriculum provides knowledge and develops skills to reach those objectives. Also, it systematically measures its effectiveness by checking on how well its trainees are fulfilling the objectives.

4. Such a curriculum is not concerned with liberal education, specialized knowledge in an academic area, the values and attitudes of the trainee, or the dilemmas of the larger society within which the school is located. Its primary and exclusive function is to train learning strategists and communicators of skills. Its ultimate

Robert J. Nash, "Commitment to Competency: The New Fetishism in Teacher Education," **Phi Delta Kappan,** 240-243, December, 1970. Reprinted by permission.

goal is to produce the teacher who has mastery of specific professional competencies.

One recent spokesman for competency-based teacher education models has argued that teacher education ought to follow the pilot-training procedure. Like the pilot, the teacher trainee ought to pass through three phases: familiarization flights, supervised flights, and solo flights. And like the pilot program, progress through each of the phases ought to be governed solely by the trainee's performance and the concomitant demonstration that he can perform all of the skills which make up the goals of the program.[1]

According to the American Heritage Dictionary (1969), a fetishism is a belief characterized by an excessive attention or attachment to something. Often this belief impels the fetishist to bestow a kind of mystical or magical power on the thing he reveres. It is my conviction that, as teacher educators, we are racing slavishly to adopt a model for teacher education which is so out of touch with the contemporary zeitgeist that it has become but another unquestioned fetish in the arsenal of pedagogical ammunition. In an overzealousness born out of frustration and defensiveness we are adopting a model which promises to bestow a magical kind of scientific-technological warrant on our professional endeavors. What is happening, however, is that we are fetishizing techniques and trivializing the entire teacher preparation program. One of the consequences of a teacher education model which proposes the *reductio ad absurdum* of the student teacher's being trained as an airline pilot is the loss of many of our brightest, most idealistic students to the neoromanticists. Our students envy the romantic's willingness to question the mechanistic-positivistic assumptions which the competency model presupposes.

In recent years, the commitment to competency in teacher education has often been motivated for unassailably benevolent reasons. We have been deeply concerned about the deterioration of the educational process in low-income neighborhoods. We have realized, after much soul searching, that teachers must be more than self-sacrificing, dedicated sentimentalists. We have understood the necessity for producing the competent educational professional in the inner city who is capable of determining specific skill weaknesses in his students, and who, on the basis of his expert diagnosis, can then proceed to the implementation of a program of behavior modification — in order to increase student skill proficiency. Kenneth B. Clark, a psychologist-educator, has even proposed that teachers in the inner city be paid on the basis of their competencies in raising the reading, arithmetical, and writing skills of their students.[2]

Correspondingly, public school officials are becoming more convinced of the validity of the competency model and the requisite teacher accountability which such a model presupposes. Experiments in Ossining, New York, where a public school principal has "guaranteed" parents of an incoming kindergarten class that by the year's end 90% of their children will be reading at or above the national average, and in Gary, Indiana; Texarkana, Arkansas; and Camden, New Jersey; where public schools have contracted with private business and industry to teach the basic communicative and arithmetical skills to children, exemplify the move to competency in public education. Such programs also illustrate the basically humane motives of educators to deliver in the cities the kind of education which they have for years been promising.[3]

In spite of the above, it is my conviction that the failure of competency-based teacher education programs lies *not* in the humanity or integrity of those educators who have devised them, nor in the zeal with which they have been applied in the cities. Neither is the failure located in the predispositions of those teacher educators who desire more precise, operational training programs. Rather, the failure has occurred because we have made a fetish out of the competency model. We are in danger of reducing the entire teacher training program to such trivializing exercises as the preparation of general and specific instructional objectives. We are becoming excessively preoccupied with performance criteria, behavior modification, and a whole congeries of related competency concepts. We are in the process of gleefully devising an incomprehensible methodological nomenclature based on the precepts of operant conditioning. We are rapidly approaching the point where we are speaking a quasi-mystical language which bears little resemblance to the real world. Thus we hear of modules, entry and re-entry, tandem and chained schedules, differentiated staffing, mands, and tacts. Such mystagogy — the inevitable offspring of fetishistic thinking — would be laughable, if it were not for the legitimacy it is getting in many teacher education curricula.[4] Also, we are hawking the notion that what constitutes learning in any acceptable educational situation is only that which is observable, demonstrable, and objectively defined. Finally, we are conveying the belief that the most "professional" teacher is the one who concentrates solely on imparting a variety of skills to his pupils, while systematically detaching himself from the personhood of his students and from the bewildering social events which rage just beyond the walls of the school.

In retrospect, the ascendancy of such thinking has been predictable. For a least a century our culture has been guided by the values of post-Comtean positivism,[5] pragmatic immediatism, and opportunistic technologism. As positivists, we have insisted that demonstrably visible behavior which can be measured is the most acceptable basis of human learning. As pragmatists, we have maintained that the practical and the expedient in human learning take precedence over the claims of those who say that people can learn in ways that are *not* immediately reducible to utilitarian usefulness. And as technologists, we have devised educational technicways which allow us scientifically to utilize and to exploit our natural environment toward the satisfaction of our multiplying material needs. Small wonder that teacher educators, in the face of all the urgent social demands made on them, would rush with naive expectancy to a scientific model in order to validate and renew the teacher-training endeavor. As products of the larger culture's basic value system, we have embraced a model which promises immediate, demonstrable results. But what we have been asked to surrender is an epistemology which allows for the significance of non-cerebral, or non-intellective, learning. Also, we have been asked to ignore or underplay that dimension of human behavior which is activated by one's value perceptions. And, finally, we have been cautioned to suspend any substantive judgments about the morality of the system we are preparing students to face and to accommodate.

A result of such thinking is that our competency model has failed to inspire many education students. This generation of college students is questioning, at times with clarity and eloquence, the cultural life-style which is rooted in the values of positivism, pragmatism, and technologism. They recognize that solutions to the most pressing crises of our times will emerge only when we begin to challenge the melioristic-mechanistic axioms of progress and the good life which guide our thinking. Research studies by several social scientists have illustrated the extent to which contemporary college students are eschewing values rooted in practicality, achievement, scientific detachment, competitiveness, orderliness, and precision.[6] Instead, students are pursuing values related to self-expression, communitarianism, and a dedication to personalistic and humanitarian objectives. Also, as Theodore Roszak has so convincingly shown, a growing minority of our youth is forming a counter-culture in opposition to those technocrats who, in the name of science or expertise or competency, would reduce our human projects to the illusory busywork of the functionary-professional.[7]

When these students enter a teacher education program, they seek an alternative to the technocratic world view which has terminated in outcomes young people deplore: the narrowness of specialization, the depersonalizing meaninglessness of routinized tasks, and the suspicious interpersonal skepticism bred by a sterile competitiveness. They look to us for help in realizing their most ennobling aspirations. Pathetically, we give them more of what they have renounced. We insist that they temper their "idealism" with the stuff of realistic professionalism. Snidely, we demean their naivete, while undermining their goodwill. We suffocate them with the paraphernalia of systems theory, behavioral objectives, technological gimmickry, tests and measurements, performance criteria, behavior modification, and other related competency activities. Students implore us to assist them in their pursuit of personhood. We strive to turn them exclusively into competent functionaries by giving them a rigid, skills-centered curriculum which borders on the inconsequential and the nugatory. They ask for a program which balances the need for performative skills with the insights gained from concerted self-understanding and self-definition. We offer them our fetishes and insist on their allegiance.

Occasionally, the bizarre outcome of this is the image of the teacher trainee leaving his micro-classroom, or his simulation session, or his behavioral objective exercise, or his learning laboratory, with a copy of A. S. Neill's *Summerhill* under his arms. Rather than convincing this student of the validity of mastering specialized professional competencies in a laboratory setting, we have merely increased his demand for the neoromantics with their commandments of self-actualization, individualization, and autonomous choice. Men like Neill and Goodman, Kohl and Holt, speak to the subjective concerns of the idealistic and the alienated young teacher-to-be. Such authors share with E. E. Cummings the belief that the dimension of behavior which is most susceptible to quantification is of least importance. They stress that what is of central significance in preparing students to be helping professionals is not the technique or the function which they must perform, but rather how they live their lives and how they manage to subordinate the inordinate demands of a hungry technological social order to the realization of each of their students' finest human potentialities.

It is essential to note here that this is *not* an injunction to return to a pretechnological or prescientific age. Rather, it is my hope that we can begin to retrieve the young, gifted, and idealistic education student only when we understand his disillusionments with the social order. One of the purposes of teacher education ought to be to give young students the opportunity to question, to test, and to provide alternatives to the entrenched educational values of their day. Before we sell them on the validity of competency models, we have to respond to their ambivalent view of the school as an iatrogenic agent. We must face the fact that many of our brightest students come to see the school as a stigmatized symbol of their deepest sense of powerlessness, futility, and failure. They see the school also as the single greatest resistant force to significant social change. Paradoxically, they come into teacher education with a profound sense that education is where the final beachhead is going to be established against the insanity of the world bent on self-destruction. They demand a professional training which confronts the reality of values, attitudes, and social crises, as well as training which provides them with the basic skills they will need in the classroom.

The first step in revitalizing teacher education is to understand, as did John Dewey, that the primary responsibility of an educator is to begin with what troubles the student most deeply, and then proceed in such a way as to enable the student to gain rational insight into these concerns. C. Wright Mills always maintained that such an education must be carried one step further. Each professional educator has the additional responsibility of helping the student continually to translate his personal problems into public issues. That is, students must be given the training to understand that personal crises are inseparable from public or social crises, and that resolution comes only when the personal-social dialectic is clarified.[8] This is what Mills called the cultivation of "the sociological imagination," and it underscores the startling lack of this kind of imagination in teacher education.

I am proposing that the teacher education model balance its commitment to performative training with a sense of reformist zeal. In addition to becoming learning strategists, we might help students to become reform strategists. I am proposing that we ask four questions whenever we sit down to examine our curricula — four questions which will assess the degree to which we have fetishized the skills dimension of teacher training.

1. *To what extent is the curriculum confronting the education student with the realities of the school and the society in which he will be spending his professional and personal lifetime?* The older sentimentalist-progressivist model for teacher education has its modern analogue for irrelevance in the competency model which effectively insures that teachers never ask meaningful, disturbing questions about education, schools, and the social order. Until we sensitize students to the value dimension of human behavior, and to the resolute stubbornness of people and institutions to change; and until we help them to understand the complex interplay of personal, institutional, and social forces, we are only deluding students when we claim that competency training will enable them to face their professional careers realistically. Also, at least one contemporary critic of education has warned us that we must train teachers to be "futurologists." We must teach students not only to identify and to understand data, but to manipulate and to discard data. Likewise students must know when and how to discard old ideas and values, and how and when to replace them. Our students must be trained in learning how to learn. Such

training realistically prepares teachers for several possible futures.[9]

2. *To what extent are we including educational experiences which help students to get from the realities of the school to what they would like the school to be?* Currently there are very few courses in undergraduate colleges of education whch could aid the prospective teacher in moving from the "is" situation in the school to the "ought" desire for school reform. We offer no definitive work in tactical or strategic measures which a beginning teacher might employ in making his classroom a more "open" one, or in accomplishing substantial educational reform without alienating colleagues, supervisors, parents, or students. Current neoromantic notions of reform in education are doomed to failure, in part, because students are not being prepared to be change strategists. Similarly, competency-based models are failing because their notion of educational change is fixed on the micro-level of individual behavioral modification. Such micro-change strategies often miss the point because they ignore Mills' admonition that effective and enduring change occurs only when individualized behavioral modification is systematically related to the personal and social worlds.

3. *To what extent are we preparing the student to take his place in the classroom, the administrative office, or the counseling situation* as a critic *of the educational status quo, rather than* as a conformist in the name of "professionalism"? There ought to be opportunities for students in teacher education to examine those assumptions about education which educators themselves manage to conceal. Students should be given intense training in exposing the fallacious logic, spurious analogies, deceptive sloganeering, and superficial bandwagoneering which characterize the pronouncements of so many educational professionals.[10] So, too, students need extensive background work in being able to identify those forces in the school and community who will react most harshly and disproportionately to those criticisms. The most effective critic of education is one who has identified the problems, who is aware of the most resilient and sympathetic pockets of concern in the community, and who then proceeds toward a program of reform with a sense of resoluteness, reasonableness, and responsiveness to the feelings of those less commited to change than he. Students have to understand that they can be responsible critics of the educational status quo without having to resort to the self-defeating demagoguery of those who cry for change at any cost.[11]

4. Finally, we must ask, *To what extent are we as teacher educators becoming models for educational and social change?* Are we overly cautious about revealing our own deepest value

assumptions about education, or our most visionary dreams for educational and social reform? Have we become apoplectic apologists for a do-nothing professionalism? Or are we initiators of change in our committee work, our curriculum revision, our daily teaching, and in our frequent interpersonal relationships with colleagues and students? Do we raise issues over grading, arbitrary entrance and exit requirements, more pertinent course experiences for students, greater community involvement on the part of faculty and students, and a hundred other concerns which signify our personal interests in educational and social reform? Have we resisted the tendency among academicians to align with one or another school in psychology or philosophy? Or are we continuing to perpetuate the artificial divisiveness which is present in so many colleges of education in the name of behaviorism, or humanism? Such categorical enclaving precludes any consensual commitment among a faculty to educational reform, because faculty members begin to think in terms of positions consistent with their categories, rather than taking direct action on a number of specific issues which require ad hoc reform.

What can be said of teacher education at its worst is that it is bland, normatively obtuse, esthetically archaic, and intellectually insipid. At its best, teacher education can touch those hidden, unrealized potentialities in each of us so that we can create better lives for ourselves and others. It is my feeling that if we continue on an exclusive path toward performative competency in our curricula, we will be increasingly vulnerable to those who charge us with trivial, fetishistic thinking. We are capable of a great deal more.

REFERENCES

[1]Kevin A. Ryan, "A Plan for a New Type of Professional Training for a New Type of Teaching Staff," National Commission on Teacher Education, Occasional Paper No. 2, February, 1968.

[2]Fred M. Hechinger, "A Program to Upgrade Schools for the Deprived," **Sunday New York Times Week in Review,** July 26, 1970.

[3]See news items, **New York Times,** July 26, 1970, pp. 52, 56.

[4]For a stinging review of operant conditioning and its terminology see Alfred A. Baumeister, "More Ado about Operant Conditioning — or Nothing?," **Mental Retardation,** October, 1969, pp. 49-51.

[5]For a philosophical analysis of positivism and education see Michael B. McMahon, "Positivism and the Public Schools," **Phi Delta Kappan,** June, 1970, pp. 515-17.

[6]For a review of the recent research on college students and values see Nevitt Sanford, "The College Student of 1980," in **Campus 1980,** Alvin C. Eurich, ed. New York: Dell, 1968, pp. 176-99 (paper).

[7]Theordore Roszak, **The Making of a Counter Culture.** New York: Doubleday, 1969 (paper).

[8]C. Wright Mills, **The Sociological Imagination.** New York: Grove Press, 1969, pp. 186-88 (paper).

[9]Alvin Toffler, **Future Shock,** New York: Random House, 1970, pp. 353-78.

[10]A similar training is advocated for liberal arts students by a historian. See Howard Zinn, **The Politics of History.** Boston: Beacon Press, 1970, pp. 5-34.

[11]A hopeful example of responsible criticism is that made by a group of elementary principals in their journal, **The National Elementary Principal,** June, 1970. The entire issue was devoted to the theme: "Dehumanizing our society through education and with the active support of the public."

Ask Not What You Can Do
For the Machine . . .

DAVID A. THATCHER

*The preplanned educational system attempts to reduce the teacher's
role and the student's role to following directions, doing as one is
told.*

I watch a film showing the AIR-Westinghouse Learning Corporation system called PLAN (Program for Learning in Accordance
with Needs). Fifth-graders work in a self-pacing system, having
very limited choices as to what they study or how it's to be done.
I see the teachers patronizing students in the manner which shows
they're serving adult rather than student needs. Their words say
one thing but the meaning comes out as: "That's a good girl.
I knew this was the right choice for you" or "That's what you want
to do, isn't it?" I never hear the teach ask the crucial questions:
"What do you want to learn?" or "How do you see your situation?"

You can be sure if it's Westinghouse — but you better take
a careful look to see what you can be sure *of!* PLAN is another
system organized for the convenience of adults, neat little packages of activities designed to allay all adult worries about the
complexities of learning: "He passed the test; therefore I know
he learned it." I know no such thing. As a teacher I live with
mystery; there are always a great many more things I don't know
than things I do know. Project PLAN is organized so the student
and teachers serve the system — just as the tire molder serves
the machine.[1]

A leaflet tells me that "Individually Guided Education for all
children" provides for " . . . continuous progress for each child."

David A. Thatcher, "Ask Not What You Can Do for The Machine . . . ," **Phi
Delta Kappan,** 509-511, April, 1972. Reprinted by permission.

No way, man, no way. If it's happening that way it's because teachers are teaching to the test, preparing kids carefully to pass a test which usually covers some of the details, some of the trivia. Again, it's an organized effort to serve a system, like serving a machine.

The individual student starts with himself. He wants to know "Who am I? Who can I become?" As a teacher I afford him many opportunities to deal with these first questions. I encourage him to explore himself as an individual with his own integrity. As Carl Rogers learned from extensive work with client-centered therapy, each individual "knows" at some level of consciousness what he needs, what will help him to become. As a patient and perceptive living resource to him, I show my faith in his ideas and hopes and thus contribute to his becoming. But I still know only a little about him. Such living with ambiguity, such nondirective, nonthreatening aid can't be provided by the computers and the packages that are hawked as panaceas for our educational needs. The preplanned educational system attempts to reduce the teacher's role and the student's role to following directions, doing as one is told. So the hesitancy, the uncertainty on the part of the helper or the helped is to be regarded as unnecessary or unimportant. The system invites the teacher to take a tranquilizer and forget his doubts. After all, a distinguished team of experts designed this program — who am I to cast doubt on its efficacy? *I do.* I am learning to question the questions rather than blindly answer the questions.[2][3][4]

Do I Know What Is Best for Students?

There are a number of assumptions behind the systems and the packages. The people who develop them show no doubts that they know what is best for students. The Individually Prescribed Instruction (IPI) system breaks down the alleged skills of reading into component parts; a large number of worksheets present these parts in what appears to the expert developers as the optimum arrangement for the learner. By doing these worksheets at his own pace, the student will learn, they say.

This flies in the face of much we are learning about individuals, about the ways in which they perceive their world, about ways in which they interact with it. Torrance, for example, notes discontinuities in the development of creative interpretations of individual reality, while Gordon describes some dimensions of the reciprocal relationships of affect and cognition. Crutchfield reminds us of the complexities involved in problem solving. In a review of many studies of group influences on individual behavior, Thelen uncovers some of the psychological reality which teachers over-look at their peril. By contrast, the packages and systems are built on a primitive S-R model of human behavior: The adult or the system presents the tasks in a scientifically arranged sequence, the student responds.[5-10] For a real contrast, look at a humanistically oriented program, the language experience (LE) approach to reading. It welcomes the child to school as he is, rejoicing in the wealth he brings with him: language, ideas, experiences, readinesses, and feelings. It invites him to continue reaching out for more and more knowing relationships with the world, starting with what he already has. He draws pictures and the teacher writes down the words which he feels belong with the picture (if he feels any belong). Soon he writes down his own stories and may illustrate them. Pride of authorship and enjoyment in creative expression help the child gain confidence in himself and in others and his environment. Instead of the usual competitive situation, with winners and losers, everyone in the LE program is a winner. Vocabulary is individual, for different individuals seek different things. Yet there is much sharing as individuals ask others for help or go across the room to share an idea, a joke, or an enthusiasm. This program, in marked contrast to the IPI programs, takes into account many aspects of the individuality of each child. While IPI allows for self-pacing, which students like very much, LE allows the individual much freedom to create his own curriculum as well as freedom to work at his own pace.[11-14]

Canned Systems and Teacher Initiative

An unstated hope in most of the computer programs and the rigid packages is that teachers will use them with discretion and not to the exclusion of other methods and materials. The teacher manuals which accompany the SRA reading kits authored by Don Parker recommend usage for a period of weeks, then possibly for another period of weeks later in the year. They do not claim that the kits provide a total reading program. Yet some teachers use them as though they did. One of the insidious features of so many of these systems and packages is that they are convenient for the teacher and they subtly invite the teacher to let the machine take over — just as the regular teacher may take a break when the special music teacher comes in once a week. Or the teacher becomes involved in the paper work and record keeping which he sees as vital to the operation of the program: "I've got to write up all these results so we can turn them in on our Title III report." Then he has little time to observe which students need extra help or even some alternative to the system for a period of time. A particular girl may benefit from being allowed to put aside the Sullivan programmed reading for a few days and choose a book for herself. The teacher locked into the system seldom has time to talk with individuals in a private conference in which the student seeks confirmation of his importance as a personal seeker after selfhood.[15]

Too many teachers that I have observed in 20 years of teaching come to depend on a system or package. I've seen teachers who overused or misused such materials as Phonovisual, IPI, the many LAP's programs so prevalent today, the controlled reader, the SRA reading kits, and the Sullivan programmed reading. In this way, they tend a machine instead of teaching.[16]

'Don't Give Up — Now There's Di-gel!'

In many of these systems a substantial amount of time is spent in doing the exercises and the tests. For example, many of the LAP's, the IPI programs, and the Project PLAN programs require numerous activity sheets and tests. These tend to fill the student's time, to keep him busy, but limit his time for reflecting, guessing, imagining — and feeling like a person. The excessive busywork required of teachers in such programs discourages them and reduces their inclination to set aside time for personal communication with individual students.[17]

Can I Read the Future?

There is another reason why I cannot prescribe a curriculum for a class of 32 students or for one individual. I don't know what my futures will be, I cannot know what the possible futures of my students may be. It's true that accurate records on usage of long-distance phone lines and demand for aspirin tablets can give us some parameters of some futures. But, happily, many decisions made in many ways will influence other dimensions of those futures. My existential freedom gives me many opportunities to participate or not participate in given activities, or to participate in them on my own terms. By exercising my options I influence my own feelings and I influence other people, and so I influence not only my own futures but those of many others.

Since each person faces his own set of futures, his own opportunities, I want to give him the best preparation for meeting those futures, for exercising his options. To do so he needs flexibility, the opportunity to do lateral thinking as well as the straight-line thinking fostered in the packages. He needs encouragement to imagine, to suppose, to hypothesize, to try, to learn from failure, to tolerate ambiguity, to explore the possibilities he has if he is to emerge as a person. He also needs practice in these less structured activities; he, like me, learns by doing. I also play a part. By listening to him and by communicating with him about ideas and feelings he's ready to consider, I encourage his affective as well as his cognitive learning. I can help him learn how to learn.[18-20]

Students and Teachers Need Options

We express the hope that each student will feel okay as a person and thus will be willing to risk interaction with others. We may forget that the same psychological need exists for each teacher: to be thought of by others as an okay person able not only to take care of himself but also able to reach out to others in supportive ways. When I feel like somebody, as a person of worth, a likable and lovable person, then I am a person seen by students as one able to help them. Instructional programs and materials can help or hinder in this regard. Programs and materials which are designed to be "teacher-proof" can only hinder. If I am encouraged to use my professional judgment, to take risks in order to strive for a bigger payoff for the student, especially an affective payoff, then I am oriented toward human becoming and I will give my best to the many and varied encounters with students. After examining and experiencing a number of the mechanistically oriented materials, I must sadly say that they tend to discourage the teacher from displaying his best professional effort. Rather, they encourage passivity or lapsing into the routines, letting the system take over.[21]

Learning is an active process in which the individual enters into knowing relationships with the wider world. This requires that he commit himself to the continuation of search and the perpetuation of refining his understandings. I withdraw the security blanket of a "final" or "total" or "everlasting" answer to a problem. The programs and the systems with their one right answer to each problem or question deprive the student of the right to venture out and to grasp at his truth in his own way. They encourage a kind of passivity, a waiting, as though education were a preparation for life instead of life itself. If education as we practice it makes students feel it's only a preparation, then this may go a long way toward explaining the many apathetic adults there are.

No prescription for a humane way of life has much chance if millions continue in apathy.[22-24]

As a learner, I see interactions with what's "out there" which will validate my humanity, which will encourage me to continue my own unique search for meaning in life. I want to establish knowing relationships with wind, trees, and animals, to affirm a reciprocity with the natural world of which I am a part. I want to form human relationships in which I can explore myself. Hence I must declare my independence of the machines, the packages, the systems that would rob me and my students of these opportunities.

REFERENCES

[1]Phillip Sorensen, "Program for Learning in Accordance with Needs," **Phi Delta Kappan,** November, 1970, pp. 180-181.

[2]Carl Rogers, **On Becoming a Person.** Boston: Houghton Mifflin, 1961.

[3]Robert C. Burkhart and Hugh H. Neil, **Identity and Teacher Learning.** Scranton, Pa.: International Textbook, 1968.

[4]Hugh Prather, **Notes to Myself,** Lafayette, Calif.: Real People Press, 1970.

[5]E. Paul Torrance, "Comparative Studies of Creativity in Children," **Educational Leadership,** November, 1969, pp. 146-48.

[6]Ira J. Gordon, "Affect and Cognition: A Reciprocal Relationship," **Educational Leadership,** April, 1970, pp. 661-64.

[7]Wayne C. Frederick and Herbert J. Klausmeier, "Cognitive Styles: A Description," **Educational Leadership,** April, 1970, pp. 668-72.

[8]Elizabeth B. Higgins, "An Exploratory Investigation of the Valuing Processes of a Group of Fourth-Grade Pupils," **Educational Leadership,** April, 1970, pp. 706-12.

[9]Richard S. Crutchfield, "Nurturing the Cognitive Skills of Productive Thinking," in **Life Skills in School and Society.** Edited by Lewis J. Rubin, Washington, D.C.: Association for Supervision and Curriculum Development, NEA, 1969.

[10]Herbert A. Thelen, "Group Interactional Factors in Learning," in **Behavioral Science Frontiers in Education.** Edited by Eli M. Bower and William G. Hollister. New York: John Wiley & Sons, 1967.

[11]Dorris M. Lee and R. V. Allen, **Learning To Read Through Experience,** 2d ed. New York: Appleton-Century-Crofts, 1963.

[12]R. V. Allen and C. Allen, **An Introduction to a Language-Experience Program, Level I.** Language Experiences in Reading, Teachers Resource Book, Chicago: Encyclopaedia Brittanica Press, 1966.

[13]Russell G. Stauffer, **The Language-Experience Approach to the Teaching of Reading.** New York: Harper & Row, 1970.

[14]"They Can Do It," film available from Early Childhood Study, 55 Chapel St., Newton, Mass.

[15]Carl R. Rogers, **Freedom to Learn.** Columbus, Ohio: Merrill, 1969, pp. 221-37.

[16]Lewis Mumford, **The Pentagon of Power.** New York: Harcourt-Brace-Jovanovich, 1970.

[17]Clark Moustakas, **The Authentic Teacher.** Cambridge, Mass.: Doyle, 1966, pp. 37-58.
[18]Richard M. Jones, **Fantasy and Feeling in Education.** New York: N.Y. University Press, 1968, pp. 125-73.
[19]Philo T. Pritzkau, **On Education for the Authentic.** Scranton, Pa.: International Textbook, 1970, pp. 65-92, 133-45.
[20]Clark Moustakas, *op. cit.*
[21]Rollo May, **Love and Will.** New York: W. W. Norton & Co., 1969, pp. 28-33.
[22]Terry O'Banion and April O'Connell, **The Shared Journey.** Englewood Cliffs, N.J.: Prentice-Hall, 1970, pp. 140-70.
[23]R. D. Laing, **The Politics of Experience.** New York: Ballantine Books, 1968.
[24]Clark Moustakas, **Individuality and Encounter.** Cambridge, Mass.: Doyle, 1968.

Eichmannism and Accountability

FRED RICHARDS

If the demand is only for children who can be clearly characterized as confident, hard-working, appropriately dressed, sociable, ambitious, knowledgeable, and competent organizers and leaders, we will perform our duty and produce. But will we also be held accountable for the fact that these same characteristics were those listed in a dossier once filed with the SS and describing a promising young officer named Adolph Eichmann?

This decade may well be called the Decade of Accountability. A seemingly endless procession of journals, conferences, and legislative committees continues to leap into the growing national debate over the degree to which educators should be held accountable for the consequences of their actions and decisions. Stephen Barro writes that "the basic idea . . . is that school systems and schools, or more precisely, the professional educators who operate them, would be held responsible for educational outcomes — for what children learn."[1] Perhaps both institutions and educators may soon be judged, as John Dewey insisted they should, by the kind of humaness they foster, by their total effect upon man, and by the degree to which they facilitate the maximum growth of every member of society.[2] Thus, educators may soon be held accountable both for what children learn and for what they become as a discernible consequence of school experiences.

Our democratic society is an unfinished experiment. It is always at the crossroads of choosing to be either a humane or an inhumane society. The institution most clearly conveying the direction in which our society is moving may be the free public school system. This being the case, the state of our nation's schools

Fred Richards, "Eichmannism and Accountability," **New Voices in Education,** 2 (1), 6-8, Winter, 1972. Reprinted by permission of Tom Fauquet, Editor of **New Voices in Education,** University of Florida, Gainesville, Florida.

should disturb and alarm us. Dr. Charles Silberman, documenting the results of the 1970 Carnegie Study Report on Education, writes:

> It is not possible to spend any prolonged period visiting public school classrooms without being appalled by the mutilation visible everywhere — multilation of spontaneity, of joy in learning, of pleasure in creating, of sense of self . . . Because adults take the schools so much for granted, they fail to appreciate what grim, joyless places most American schools are, how oppressive and petty are the rules by which they are governed, how intellectually sterile and esthetically barren the atmosphere, what an appalling lack of civility obtains on the part of teachers and principals, what contempt they unconsciously display for students as students.[3]

Confronted and jolted into awareness and action by the civil rights movement and the student rebellions, we have, over the past two decades, set out to reform this same free public school system.[4] Believing the free public school system to be the basis of a democratic society, we may have chosen, however, to preserve the institution rather than save the children. We may have chosen to redecorate the system rather than rescue the children from dying "at an early age" in institutions often far less than humane.

Our programs of reform preserved the schools but made them perhaps no less obsolete. Despite our efforts, the educational base of our free and open society became no less repressive and undemocratic. As a result, we have been awakened to experience what Peter Schrag calls the "end of the impossible dream." Schrag writes that "if the school system fails, so does the promise of equality, so does the dream of the classless society. The school system has failed."[5] We are told the schools have failed and become, in the process of failing, the "killers of the dream." We who did our duty to preserve the institution, we who saw ourselves as the dutiful subordinates simply obeying the order of the day, find ourselves on trial. Despite our concern and commitment, we have been charged with "murder in the classroom." We are now being held accountable for decisions we feel we never made and for actions we felt duty-bound to perform. We are confused and threatened by this growing interest in accountability which now seeks to hold us responsible for the dehumanized products of our classrooms. Insisting we are responsible, Edward Sampson writes:

> How often do we hear people proclaim loudly, 'I had to do that!' and thereby seek to absolve themselves of all responsibility for their actions? And how often have we accepted their

nonresponsibility, granting them freedom from moral accountability? How often have we ourselves said to our students or friends, 'If only I were not a dean, if only I were not a professor; my *role* demands things of me and I must do them.'? This translates roughly in Eichmann's terms into 'I am not responsible; it is *my role* that has acted. I am just taking orders.' And what is worse, we believe it.[6]

Exterminating over six million Jews in Europe and escaping to Argentina after the fall of the Third Reich, Eichmann wrote in his memoirs: " 'It was really terrible but quite necessary. Anyhow the Fuhrer ordered it, and I did not have anything to do with the annihilation. I was not a killer but a man who executed orders.' "[7] Such "mindlessness", Silberman says, has become the climate of our schools.[8]

Perhaps the growing national interest in accountability means we have moved beyond such mindlessness. Perhaps it tells us we have heard the cries of our victims and, unlike Eichmann, have answered, "Yes, I am responsible and now commit myself to liberating my students to learn and grow." Perhaps not. Accountability may mean an insistence that educators merely do an efficient job of doing what they have done clumsily in the past. It may remain predominantly a concern with performance — not with facilitating humanness and fostering the full development of every member of society. Such a possibility moves James Cass to write in the *Saturday Review* (March 20, 1971): "If . . . the laudable effort to improve classroom practice . . . merely results in placing more intense and sophisticated pressures on the children to perform, the very principles will be denied in practice."[9] Accountability may mean the continual denial of the spontaneity, creativeness, and joy of the growing child. Indeed, we may still be in conflict over whether we want to save the children or simply preserve the institution while making it more efficient.

Accountability which concerns itself only with performance may become a search for a more efficient, precise, and cleaner way "to kill." It was Eichmann, the minister of death, who chose the use of a deadly acid as a preferred way of exterminating the Jews after he witnessed the crude, shooting death of a young child. Eichmann was noticeably disturbed and concerned with the deep psychological pain caused by such executions. The focus of his concern is clear in his statement to the commander of Auschwitz:

> We expect large quantities of people, and technically it will
> be very hard to finish them off by shooting them. The women's
> and children's shouts disturb the SS men in their actions and
> cause inconvenience.[10]

Barro writes that "what makes accountability an attractive idea" is that making educators responsible for educational outcomes will necessarily increase the quality of their performance.[11] This may guarantee that the public's financial investment in education will pay better dividends. Per dollar invested, students will produce and achieve more in areas given priority. The public will get what it pays for or someone else will be hired to do the job.

If the demand is only for children who can be clearly characterized as confident, hard-working, appropriately dressed, sociable, ambitious, knowledgeable, and competent organizers and leaders, we will perform our duty and produce. But will we also be held accountable for the fact that these same characteristics were those listed in a dossier once filed with the SS and describing a promising young officer named Adolph Eichmann?[12] Being told we are accountable, will we again simply execute the order of the day? Will we passively obey and again secure and hold, defend and preserve the institution and ourselves? Though accountable, will we continue to be in our classrooms the well-intentioned but, nevertheless, mindless "killers of the dream"?

These are crucial questions. The responsible answer is having the courage to stand and say, "When the door to my classroom closes, I, and I alone, am responsible for the human experience found, created, and shared there." The answer is in seeing the potential Eichmann within ourselves and others, that part of us willing to sit by pleasantly and passively while the impersonal values and repressive rules of our schools crush those we desired to set free. It's spotting the Eichmann within us willing to play the mindless subordinate, the little man who plays the victim and consequently victimizes others. It's seeing through the Eichmann who says, as teacher or professor, dean or chairman, "Don't take this personally, but it's what I have to do because they set it up that way. I'm just doing my job."

We must do more than simply do our job. We must do it humanely. Rather than defensively recoiling at the prospect of being compared to an Eichmann, we must choose to be responsible for the climates for learning and growth we create in our schools, our communities, and our nation. Accountability is here. We are now in the process of defining and implementing the concept. We must have a human definition. We must find and embrace the alternatives to a shortsighted definition that makes us do more efficiently what we have done in the past to create schools which stifle rather than free children both to learn and grow. We must not sit passively and follow the dictates of accountability wherever they lead. We must not simply follow the order of the day. Whatever direction the Decade of Accountability takes us, let us look for leadership from those who "ask why they are doing what they are doing" and who think seriously and deeply about the purposes and consequences of education.[13] Let us only support and abide by an approach to accountability that can "provide a more humane environment than is presently the case in many of our schools."[14]

REFERENCES

[1]Stephen M. Barro, "An Approach to Developing Accountability Measures for the Public Schools." **Phi Delta Kappan.** Vol. LII, No. 4, December, 1970, p. 196.

[2]John Dewey. **Reconstruction in Philosophy.** New York: The New American Library, 1950, p. 147.

[3]Charles E. Silberman. **Crisis in the Classroom.** New York: Random House, 1970, p. 10.

[4]James Cass, "The Crisis of Confidence — and Beyond." **Saturday Review.** Vol. LIII, No. 38, September 19, 1970, pp. 61-62.

[5]Peter Schrag, "End of the Impossible Dream." **Saturday Review.** Vol. LIII, No. 38, September 19, 1970, p. 68.

[6]Edward E. Sampson, "Evolution Versus Revolution in Psychological Character: Mechanicus or Man?" **Journal of NAWDC,** Summer, 1970, p. 154.

[7]Quentin Reynolds, Ephraim Katz, and Zwy Aldouby. **Minister of Death: The Adolph Eichmann Story.** New York: The Viking Press, 1960, p. 100.

[8]Silberman, *op. cit.,* p. 11.

[9]James Cass, "Accountable to Whom? For What?" **Saturday Review.** Vol. LIV, No. 12, March 20, 1971, p. 41.

[10]Reynolds, *op. cit.,* p. 140.

[11]Barro, *loc. cit.*

[12]Reynolds, *op. cit.,* p. 67.

[13]Silberman, *loc. cit.*

[14]Roland Callaway. "The Humanness of Behavioral Objectives." **Wisconsin Journal of Education.** Vol. 103, No. 6, February, 1971, pp. 10-13.

Competency-based Teaching and Trained Fleas

FREDERICK C. NEFF

Now, if you'll only get your eyes open, you'll see that the trained competency-based performers in our school and the trained fleas in the circus have more in common than you might suppose.

The Scene: *The office of Mr. Youngernaught, principal, Walden III Junior High School. Mr. Parent has come to discuss his son Harry's progress in school.*
The Year: 1984.

*   *   *

Mr. Youngernaught: Come in, Mr. Parent. Please sit down. What can I do for you?

Mr. Parent: Thank you. I've been wanting to talk with you for some time about the kind of education Harry is receiving here at Walden III. He is studying with several teachers who . . .

Mr. Y: Excuse me, but we don't use that kind of language here. We say that Harry's behavior is being subjected to operant conditioning at the hands of several trained competency-based performers.

Mr. P: I'm sorry. What I meant was that Harry is having problems with . . .

Mr. Y: Excuse me, but Harry doesn't "have problems." It is simply that Harry is so situated environmentally that he is called upon to respond simultaneously to two or more stimuli of fairly

Frederick C. Neff, "Competency-Based Teaching and Trained Fleas," **Phi Delta Kappan,** 480-482, April, 1972. Reprinted by permission.

equal intensity. In other words, Harry is confronted with conflicting contingencies of reinforcement.

Mr. P: Harry's having trouble with his math, dammit!

Mr. Y: Let's keep our voice down, Mr. Parent. Anyway, you'd better talk with Harry's mathematics performer, Ms. Dingbat, about that. Ms. Dingbat is now engaged in a trained competency-based mathematics performance in Room 104. You can talk with her in about half an hour.

Mr. P: It isn't that he can't do the work. Harry has a good mind.

Mr. Y: Excuse me, but Harry does not have a good mind. In fact, Harry has no mind at all. What you mean is that Harry is potentially capable of engaging in specific kinds of behavior designed to alleviate tensions in his environment.

Mr. P: Mr. Juggernaut, I wanted to ask you about . . .

Mr. Y: Youngernaught. The name is Youngernaught.

Mr. P: I wanted to ask you about Harry's gymnasium and swimming instructor. Harry tells me his swimming coach is a woman. Harry, well, he's getting to be a big boy now, and he tells me the boys swim without trunks, and I was wondering whether it might be better if a man were to . . .

Mr. Y: Mr. Parent, you do seem a bit old-fashioned. A directive from the State Department of Education has made one thing perfectly clear, and that is that no discrimination between the sexes will be tolerated in regard to either employment practices or the assignment of subjects. Ms. Ackerbath is thoroughly qualified in terms of the state department's performance-competency-based certification system. Besides, I'm sure her training in judo has adequately prepared her for any emergency that might arise with the boys.

Mr. P: But Ms. Acrobat is still a woman. I feel that Harry needs a masculine image to . . .

Mr. Y: Mr. Parent, we in education today no longer "feel." There are ample tests available. Moreover, the older distinctions between male and female behavior are no longer viable, being due to cultural conditioning. Your outlook strikes me as rather quaint. May I remind you that we are now living in the space age and that horse-and-buggy ways of doing things no longer apply. By the way, what sort of work are you engaged in?

Mr. P: I am head of the Aerospace Jet Propulsion Laboratory. Our work was largely responsible for the recent landing on Jupiter. My family and I moved here a few months ago, and I wanted to become acquainted with Harry's new school.

Mr. Y: Glad to have you here. Well, now that we've cleared everything up . . .

Mr. P: There is one other thing, Mr. Juggernaut, and perhaps it's the most important of all. Harry doesn't seem to be able to relate what he learns in school to anything like a system of values. He told me he once asked his science teacher about the purposes of science. The answer he got was that purposes and values were outside the province of science, and that they weren't very important, anyway. Even his literature teacher — I've forgotten her name . . .

Mr. Y: That would be Ms. Littermug.

Mr. P: Yes. Even Ms. Litterbug didn't seem to have any apparent purpose in what she was doing. She just seemed to be performing rituals. I want Harry to acquire a sense of values, to know the meaning of self-respect. I want him to achieve a measure of human dignity and human freedom.

Mr. Y: Mr. Parent, we are beyond freedom and dignity. Freedom is simply a hollow term denoting the absence of aversive stimuli. And dignity, well, there simply is no such thing as dignity, except as an inadequate explanation for certain kinds of conditioned behavior. When you say you want Harry to achieve freedom, what you mean is that you would like as many aversive stimuli as possible removed from his environment — that's freedom. And when you say you want Harry to achieve self-respect and dignity, you mean that you want his behavior to be positively reinforced in such a way that others will admire what he does — that's dignity.

Mr. P: But what about his teachers? They're human, aren't they?

Mr. Y: Correction — you mean his trained competency-based performers.

Mr. P: Do you mind if I loosen my collar? Well, whatever you call them, don't they have somewhere in their background of professional preparation some knowledge of educational objectives? A teacher can master ever so many techniques, store up a great deal of information, gain a lot of facts about child development, and be able to utilize all sorts of audio-visual aids — and still be a poor teacher. Why? Because he hasn't got straight on his objectives.

Mr. Y: In the first place, Mr. Parent, we no longer refer to teacher preparation. We speak of performance training. The persons you refer to as teachers are simply performers. And so they are not educated to teach — they are trained to perform. In fact, we are right in line with the state department's directive on this matter.

Mr. P: Could I have a glass of water?

Mr. Y: The water cooler is just behind you. Here. I'll read you what the state department has to say: "Institutional programs operating on a competency-performance-based certification system are required . . ." — *required,* mind you — "to substitute specific teacher-competency factors for generalized teacher-preparation objectives." There, now. What could be clearer than that?

Mr. P: What does it mean?

Mr. Y: It means that our trained competency-based performers — and I say this with a bit of pardonable pride — are products of training programs that have spared them the necessity for thinking about their objectives, thus releasing them from thought and freeing them to perform.

Mr. P: Could you open a window? I don't feel well.

Mr. Y: Our windows don't open. The state department doesn't think . . .

Mr. P: Mr. Juggernaut, I didn't come here to discuss the state department. What I am concerned about is the kind of education my boy is receiving.

Mr. Y: Youngernaught — spelled with a Y.

Mr. P: I see you have a copy of Charles Silberman's *Crisis in the Classroom* on your shelf. There's a passage I'd like to read to you if I can find it. I used to be a teacher myself. I've always remembered John Dewey's remark that "to act with an aim is all one with acting intelligently."

Mr. Y: We're beyond Dewey.

Mr. P: It seems to me that most of the people who think they're beyond Dewey are the ones who haven't yet gone through Dewey. The first piece of modern writing criticizing the schools was an article by Arthur Bestor in the *Scientific Monthly*. It was titled "Aimlessness in Education." What it criticized was the shallowness of teaching and education's lack of purpose. Now you have played right back into the hands of your critics. You've set education back 30 years. I am reminded of Robert Hutchins' observation, "If the object of education is the improvement of men, then any system of education that is without values is a contradiction in terms."

Mr. Y: We're beyond Hutchins.

Mr. P: Here. I've found the passage from Silberman: "The central task of teacher education, therefore, is to provide teachers with a sense of purpose, or, if you will, with a philosophy of education. This means developing teachers' ability and their desire to think seriously, deeply, and continuously about the purposes and consequences of what they do — about the ways in which their curriculum and teaching methods, classroom and school organization, testing and grading procedures, affect purpose and are affected by it." He then quotes Dewey on a related point: "To place the emphasis upon the securing of proficiency in teaching . . . *puts the attention . . . in the wrong place, and tends to fix it in the wrong direction."* Surely, now, you'll have to recognize Silberman as one of the most sane and fair-minded critics we've had.

Mr. Y: We're beyond Silberman.

Mr. P: Here is something I clipped out of last night's newspaper. It's something the Pope said, and I couldn't agree with it more. He says that "mere technology, without morality, can become an instrument of enslavement rather than of liberation." By the same token, might it not be said that mere performance, without objectives, can become for the teacher not an instrument of liberation but one of enslavement?

Mr. Y: We're beyond the Pope.

Mr. P: I don't think it is enough, Mr. Juggernaut, merely to say that you are "beyond." It is necessary to say what you are for, what your objectives are, in what direction you are headed. By the way, when did this directive from the state department become effective?

Mr. Y: About 10 or 12 years ago.

Mr. P: And why didn't those of you in education protest? Why didn't you strip away the jargon and take a long, hard look at what the directive really meant — while it was still a proposal and before it got enacted into legislation? Why didn't someone have the sense to point out that it meant behavior without thought, ritual without purpose, performance without aims, teachers without minds? You've become captives of a system that encourages you not to think — indeed, *requires* you not to think — about your objectives. I'm sorry to put it so bluntly, Mr. Juggernaut, but you've been brainwashed and you don't even know it. You aren't *beyond* freedom and dignity — you are simply *without* freedom and dignity. You're not even members of a profession any more.

Mr. Y: "Brainwashed" is a value term. I should prefer to say that we are products of institutional programs in competency-based performance training.

Mr. P: Jargon again. What you mean is that you've been led to believe you're paid to perform — and not to think. You've been converted from teachers into hired hands. Performance behavior is all right — so far as it goes. But when it gets cut off from the larger purposes it is designed to serve, it becomes hollow, empty, random, and blind. Nor is it enough merely to have a teaching objective — sound though it may be — without an educational objective. A teaching objective is procedural and specific — for example, to teach a youngster how to read, or how to compute, or to gain some facts about science, or to become acquainted with art, literature, and music. But an educational objective is long-range and general. It cuts across subject matter lines and has to do with relating what is learned to individual and social growth, with cultivating a life-style, with utilizing information in the gaining of cultural perspective, with progress in becoming a moral and humane person . . . . These institutional programs you speak of don't seem designed to turn out anything like master educators — they merely produce classroom mechanics . . . .

Mr. Y: I think it would be stated more technically than that.

Mr. P: I'm sure it could. But that's what it amounts to. Let's give it one more try, Mr. Juggernaut. Can you tell me in plain language just why my son's teachers are merely trained to perform and are not required to have given any serious study to the nature of their objectives?

Mr. Y: Let's make an analogy. Have you ever been to the circus?

Mr. P: Harry and I went last week.

Mr. Y: And what did Harry like best?

Mr. P: The animal acts.

Mr. Y: Precisely. They steal the show every time. And which of the animal acts interested Harry most?

Mr. P: The trained dogs, elephants, seals — but especially the trained fleas. Excuse me, but it seems awfully stuffy in here. Anyway, what has this to do with objectives?

Mr. Y: I'm coming to that. Try to stay awake, Mr. Parent. My point is that in order to perform with competence one does not need objectives — one need only behave. In fact, that is what is meant by "behavioral objectives." You said that Harry was especially taken with the performance of the fleas. Now, if you'll only get your eyes open, you'll see that the trained competency-based performers in our school and the trained fleas in the circus have more in common than you might suppose. Neither have been subjected to reflection. Both have been trained to perform.

Mr. P: Are you sure those windows won't open?

Mr. Y: Yes. Neither the fleas nor our faculty are judged on any other basis than their ability to perform. Both have been trained to perform, which is to say that both are trained performers! Really, the analogy strikes me as quite poetic.

Mr. P: And what about objectives?

Mr. Y: Mr. Parent — seriously, now — whoever heard of asking a trained flea what his objectives were?

Mr. P: I think I'm going to faint.

Mr. Y: Go right ahead. Make yourself at home. Oh, Ms. Robought. You'd better get the oxygen mask. I think Mr. Parent requires some attention. Meantime, if you need me, I'll be up in Room 312. Ms. Littermug is about to begin a trained competency-based performance of *Myra Breckinridge,* and I don't want to miss it.

Accountability: We Can Measure Just So Much

CALVIN GRIEDER

No argument that educators and school boards should not be held responsible will hold water. We seem to be extending the meaning of responsibility, however, by imposing a demand that the outcome of a given amount of human and financial resources be clearly demonstrable.

If accountability did not command a leading position among the concerns of school boards and administrators, I wouldn't have enough nerve to add my bit to the mountainous volume of exposition and exhortation that has been published about it. Yet much of what has been said seems oversimplified.

Accountability in education invites oversimplification, for if one digs into just what it can mean, he meets obstacles that cannot be readily overcome, if indeed they can ever be. I think this is the real reason why educators are cautious, and not because they are irresponsible or complacent about their stewardship.

Accountable or culpable?

The trend setters in education would not agree with me, however. To them, if you don't climb on the accountability bandwagon, you must be lazy, incompetent, prefidious or maybe all three.

It sometimes seems that they used the word, "accountability," in the same sense as culpability.

In some states teachers, administrators, and school boards are commanded by law to be "accountable."

They must submit evidence to the public — legislature, state board of education, community, parents — on the degree to which stated educational objectives are achieved. In short, the schools have to show what has been accomplished in return for funds and other resources committed for education, in terms of how well previously announced objectives are fulfilled.

No argument that educators and school boards should not be held *responsible* will hold water. We seem to be extending the meaning of responsibility, however, by imposing a demand that the outcome of a given amount of human and financial resources be clearly demonstrable.

This perverts the meaning of responsibility and creates a demand that human nature and the nature of education cannot possibly meet. Some outcomes, of course, can be and are being measured, including outcomes which are not of the most importance. But we're fooling ourselves or being fooled if we believe more than a small number can be shown to result from a specific allocation of resources.

Take grammar, for example. It encompasses skills amenable to fairly standardized evaluation, but who knows what specific input of resources results in the students' ability to understand subject and verb agreement?

To further complicate the problem, standards of acceptability undergo changes all the time. Look at the language arts where standards of pronunciation, grammar, and spelling change periodically. Teachers are now conjured, for instance, to recognize and accept black dialect, which departs in many respects from standard English (if there is such a thing).

When more complex or deferred outcomes in behavior and values are considered, one encounters insuperable obstacles.

Furthermore, the longtime effect of measurement and evaluation as called for by accountability enthusiasts is likely to be a trend toward standardization, a pattern of uniformity, as against individuality and diversity.

Pressure for success

Teachers will eventually learn to "teach for the tests" and other evaluative measures, as has happened in this country before (cf. the Regents' Examinations in New York State which used to be required of all college-bound high school seniors) and is common practice where passing exams is greatly emphasized . . . The kinds of exercises and behavior against which outcomes are measured are fraught with subjectivity, and the evaluation of responses is even more so. I don't think that a great push for accountability as it is being touted should be made. I do hope that ever more careful selection of prospective and licensed teachers can be made. Men and women are needed who have a broad general education, good command of their fields of study, deep knowledge of children and adolescents, and exceptional personal qualities suited to working with the young.

I would want these kinds of people to work under few restraints and compulsions except their own, and I certainly wouldn't want them to live and work under the threat that they were going to be "held accountable" in the threatening sense with which this term is frequently used today.

It's the Side Effects of Education That Count

T. ROBERT BASSETT

The conclusion can scarcely be avoided that, whatever else instruction accomplishes, its ultimate outcomes are indeterminable and unpredictable.

The Socratic bumper-sticker, "Knowledge Is Virtue" — today widely if less pithily paraphrased — makes of teaching a mission impossible. Mark these random quotes: "Education is the fundamental method of social progress and reform" (Dewey). "Because teachers are molding the minds of tomorrow's leaders, the hope for a better America rests upon their shoulders" (ex-teacher, ex-President Johnson). "On education, national survival itself depends" (take your pick). "In our schools, men may be educated for justice, liberty, and peace" (Truman). "Education is an investment in less crime" (President's Commission). "The teacher is the usher in of the true kingdom of God" (Dewey again).

Lots of luck.

But how come, when we've had so much education around for so long, we've also had the sleaziest war in our history, lies in high places, bigotry, brutality, and bribery unabated and not less crime but more. Our leaders are well educated. Where is their virtue? Did not their teachers teach them about George Washington and how presidents always tell the truth?

If it be protested that education needs more time to take effect, let's try a wide-angle glance back toward the Middle Ages. H. G. Wells suggests that in the medieval church's attempt to strengthen its grip on Europe by theological thought-control via

T. Robert Bassett, "It's the Side Effects of Education That Count," **Phi Delta Kappan,** 16-17, September, 1972. Reprinted by permission.

education, what happened was the precise opposite of what was intended. "Its conception of education," he wrote, "was not release, not an invitation to participate, but the subjugation of minds." Teaching by disputation, and hoping thereby to capture and contain man's intellect in webs of finespun argument, the church sought to defend the faith with reason and establish its doctrines with logic. But if subjugation was what it wanted, release was what it got. In trying to mold the minds of tomorrow's leaders, it succeeded only in setting those minds free and forfeiting its supremacy in Europe into the bargain.

There were, to be sure, other forces at work; but not least important, as a side effect of education, was the appearance of "common man, the unofficial outside independent man," as Wells puts it, "thinking for himself. Already in the thirteenth century there was a sense that a new arbitrator greater than pope or monarch had come into the world, that there were readers and a public opinion." Having been taught to employ reason in support of the church's teachings, men now employed reason to attack and undermine those teachings. Investing heavily in education, the church lost its political shirt.

It was in fact what Durant calls the medieval "dash into reason" that helped assure the triumph of humanism. Education nourished belief in human rights, civil law, experimental science, and freedom of thought — but not by teaching these things. It sowed the seeds of Renaissance, Reformation, and Revolution — unintentionally. With its spread came criticism, dissent, protest, rebellion — inadvertently. Maybe these phenomena constituted social progress and reform, but they were not exactly in the curricular game plan.

Whether one accepts this reading of history or not, the negative fact seems indisputable: In the long run, the church's behavioral objectives were not attained. The conclusion can scarcely be avoided that, whatever else instruction accomplishes, its ultimate outcomes are indeterminable and unpredictable.

Yet the belief persists that we could (if we played our cards right) control man's future through education. So we continue to insist that, if only the schools got on with it, they could make the next generation shape up and in the process rid society of prejudice, poverty, and pollution (not to mention VD, drug abuse, racism, and the oppression of women).

It would be nice, no doubt, if such reforms actually did get their start in classrooms. But they never do. National concern over the environment comes first, *then* environmental studies; the black movement, *then* black studies; women's lib, *then* women's studies. *After* we integrate society we can hope to integrate the schools. This is not because the schools fail in their duty but because it is simply not in their power to initiate planned social change. For the real teacher in the classroom is society itself, which can only be what it is, can only manifest its own nature, cannot transform itself through operant conditioning of its own behavior. Planned change must be forced upon it — by the direct action of a power wielder; it cannot be done through children, for they are themselves made in the image of the society educating them, partly in school, mainly outside. To hold teachers responsible for the shape of tomorrow's America is therefore both futile and unfair. It isn't that they don't want to bring about social progress and reform; it's that they can't. Education just doesn't pack that kind of clout.

What education does, as a social change agent (in the long run), is let loose forces that produce their own effects in and on society, and those effects can be neither prescribed, predetermined, predicted, nor prevented. They will be whatever future man, thinking for himself, decides they will be. For "thinking" implies nothing foreseeable about the conclusions it may lead to. Hence, when unthinking people genuflect piously toward the Ability To Think as the high aim of education, they seem unaware of its meaning (as it does mean) that two persons, pursuing equally valid lines of reasoning from the same starting point, may arrive at quite disparate end positions. To teach and encourage students to think for themselves is therefore to entertain the lively possibility that they may reject some of our cherished preconceptions in favor of their own variety of alien corn. We can't have it both ways: educate and at the same time keep the educand from having ideas of his own.

Here, Dewey (who gave considerable thought to thinking) comes up with the opposite word. "If we once start thinking, no one can guarantee what will be the outcome, except that many objects, ends, and institutions will surely be doomed. Every thinker puts some portion of an apparently stable world in peril, and no one can wholly predict what will emerge in its place."

Education releases. Liberates. (As we've always said.) But while liberating man intellectually, we have also tried (vainly) to program him behaviorally. The Southern States that made it a crime to teach blacks to read knew the truth. They knew that to keep people in hand you have to keep them in ignorance. Once let them learn to read and they'll turn and rend you.

We've got practically everybody reading now (not to say rending), and as education is self-escalating, the world is on an unstoppable education kick that will take us to who knows where. Universal education as a universal ideal has long since precipitated what Adlai Stevenson called the "revolution of rising expectations." There is nothing we can do about that now anymore — except pray that educated, thinking-for-himself man will in the future somehow take care of himself and the universe around him.

Carry it a step further. If the *social* fruits of education cannot be made to order, neither (given that education differs from training) can its effects on the individual. Not only do we lack evidence as to how the significant consequences of education are instructionally generated, but we are confronted with Everyman's testimony that he has retained from the classroom little of permanent value, his particular academic activities bearing almost no discernible causal relationship to any important aspects of his later life.

It does not follow, of course, that school attendance is necessarily without benefit to the individual; the point is that benefits are not likely to derive form the typical intensive-care treatment to which he is subjected in the classroom. Said Woodrow Wilson as president of Princeton early in the century, "College graduates will tell you without shame or regret, within 10 years of their graduation, that they remember practically nothing of what they learned in the classroom; and yet in the very same breath they will tell you that they would not have lost what they did get in college for anything in the world." (Happens to everyone, even today.) What they got was not so much learning, he said, but the spirit of learning.

Colleges have made too much of instruction, devoting themselves too exclusively to "well-conceived lectures and approved classroom method," Wilson added. "The mind does not live by instruction. Attendance on the exercises of the college is only a means of keeping the students together for four years" — to learn from each other, to pick up the habit of thinking for themselves, to have their minds quickened by the insights and incitements of campus life.

The end results of education (again as distinct from training) are thus indirect and diffused, not push-button-produced by instruction. It is not subject matter ingestion that creates the real educational product (which has been amply shown not to vary much with variations in the process). What counts is the fact that human beings are *in* school and *in* college, surrounded by an infectious ambience of words and ideas given off by other human beings. The broad impact, the total experience — these account for what in the end matters most.

So then, if we cannot through prescriptive education predetermine the future (either of the individual or of society) — if we cannot by teaching produce a manipulable citzenry — if it is not possible for education to solve on demand society's problems — if the people's behavior cannot be modified as lesson-planned — if education cannot guarantee national survival, liberty and justice for all, peace, virtue, and the kingdom of God — then we can afford to relax about these palpable misses and turn our sights on what education *can* do.

What it can do is help the individual make himself into the kind of person *he* wants to be. To help him we must first induce him to use the educational opportunities we are able to supply, which means (for starters) changing the school from being grim, joyless, and unrewarding to being appetizing, satisfying, and happy-making, a congenial place to live and work in, free of imposed goals and requirements, ready with a wide variety of learning situations to select from and complete freedom of choice in selecting them. We must grant him, with respect to his education, the basic human right of self-determination. We must treat him, not as a future citizen, but as a present human being; not as a means to social betterment, but as an end in himself. Besides embodying the democratic concept of the primacy of the individual person, this philosophy would almost certainly promote the solution of many school problems, which, as Emerson counseled, "solve themselves when we leave institutions and address individuals."

Dealing solely with the individual on his own terms, for the sake of *his* self-fulfillment, education would have a clear purpose and a built-in validity to justify itself. And if all we had to show for it was a society of self-fulfilled persons thinking for themselves (instead of behaviorized units of population), this might just possibly turn out to be our salvation.

Lucy's Dance Lessons
and Accountability

ROBERT ZOELLNER

*What the behaviorist does not claim – if he has a properly vivid
appreciation of the limitations of his model – is that lever-depressing
is all that the rat has learned.*

Some years back a *Peanuts* cartoon appeared which perhaps
can stand as a paradigm for the issue of behaviorism and accountability in the teaching of both composition and literature. Lucy, coming on strong as usual, informs Charlie Brown that she is a ballet
dancer. Charlie expresses his characteristic myopic skepticism.
Whereupon Lucy proves her point by *behaving,* by executing three
rudimentary dance-steps. First she extends her right foot, toes
pointed, head turned in the same direction. Second, she repeats
the same step in obverse, left foot extended, head turned to the
left. Finally she brings both feet together, looks straight ahead
in a fixity of beady-eyed concentration and, with ostrich-like
stiffness, executes a minute, almost imperceptible flexure of both
knees. In the last panel of the cartoon, her three-second dance-
repertory exhausted, Lucy turns to Charlie (who by this time is
glassy-eyed and freaked out) and remarks, "That cost my Dad
eleven dollars and fifty cents."
    On the most obvious level, the cartoon is a gentle putdown
on the affluent and doting American parent, usually suburban,
who is intent on giving his little monster all the "advantages."
On a deeper level, it is a commentary on the American obsession

Robert Zoellner, "Lucy's Dance Lessons and Accountability in English," **College
Composition and Communication,** 229-236, October, 1971. Copyright © 1971
by the National Council of Teachers in English. Reprinted by permission.

with cost-accounting, with rendering every human activity — intellectual, physical, religious, moral, even sexual — in terms of dollar expenditures and visible, here-and-now benefits obtained. One is reminded of George F. Babbitt's valiant efforts to reduce the cost per conversion at the Chatham Road Presbyterian Church: what works for the real-estate business ought to work for God. The point is that cost-accounting is inescapably a here-and-now operation. If Lucy's father should demand an accounting of Lucy's teacher, the only thing on which such an accounting could possibly be based is the *overt, visible behavior* of which Lucy is *now*, at this moment in time, capable. Since Lucy is a very little girl, that turns out to be three dance-steps. Eleven dollars and fifty cents divided by three gives Lucy's father what he is after: a cost-per-step of $3.83.

The assumption here, of course, is that Lucy's three childish steps — her three externalized, entirely mechanical bits of skeletomuscular activity — account entirely for what she has learned. But such an assumption represents simple-minded behaviorism and as a consequence simple-minded cost-accounting. The experimental rat placed in the stimulus-situation of the Skinner-box, for example, can easily be shaped by reinforcing food-pellet delivery to the point where he depresses a lever in order to get his pellet-reward. A counting mechanism can be attached to the lever to produce a learning-curve. What the behaviorist claims is that the rat has learned, by injection of reinforcement into the behavioral stream, to depress the lever. This is hardly arguable: the rat's observable behavior has been modified, and the learning-curve articulates that modification in statistical form. What the behaviorist does not claim — if he has a properly vivid appreciation of the limitations of his model — is that lever-depressing is all that the rat has learned. Conceivably the rat has learned dozens, perhaps hundreds of *other* responses, which are not useful in lever-depressing and therefore not emitted, or more probably simply not noticed because not incorporated in the parameters of the model. On a purely theoretical level, for example, the rat may have been twitching his tail to the left at the instant of reinforcement. He may also have been tightening one or another sphincter-muscle. Since both of these behaviors were simultaneous with lever-depressing, they would, theoretically, be simultaneously reinforced. But the Skinner-box is not set up to record them: *they are empirically invisible*. It follows that there is *no accounting* for the total learning of the rat. Even rat-learning, grossly simple though it is, is essentially *unaccountable*. If most psychologists, including Skinner, have not stressed this point, that is simply because psychologists are — as one would expect — intent upon deriving different meanings from the stimulus-response-reinforcement model than those that are of concern to a behavioral humanist. Behavioral scientists want to keep things tidy. Behavioral humanists want to keep them messy.

In any case, what goes in clubs for S. R. Rodent goes doubled in spades for Lucy. She is supremely unaccountable (just ask Charlie Brown) and so is the range of her learning. We would need a crystal ball or a ouija-board to develop parameters sufficient to account for the innumerable ways in which Lucy's $11.50 worth of ballet lessons have altered her behavior. But we can speculate a little. Surely, for example, there were other little girls in her dancing class; presumably she has learned responses appropriate to interchange with people who enjoy a community of shared special interests. Again, Lucy has certainly learned something about her own body as a vehicle for aesthetic expression. Since she is (as yet) short, stubby-legged, and dumpy, the behaviors of which she is capable fall somewhat short of the standards of the Ballet Russe de Monte Carlo, but they nevertheless represent an advance in aesthetic expressiveness. On a much more subtle level, Lucy has no doubt learned a good deal from her teacher, both as dancer and as person. Perhaps her teacher is beautiful as well as graceful; if so, Lucy must have an increased sense of the beauty of the human form (even her own), with a consequent increased capacity for behaviors springing from a sense of self-esteem. Finally, we know that Lucy is growing up in a world full of straight types: perhaps her father controls the Chevrolet franchise in Oshkosh, and her mother is a mover-and-shaker in the League of Women Voters. Hopefully, Lucy's dance teacher is a kook, perhaps the first adult kook that Lucy has ever encountered. If this is the case, Lucy may well have learned patterns of response to kook-stimuli which make her more open to life-styles and behaviors which differ from her own.

Now, none of these hypothetical behavioral alterations — social responsiveness, aesthetic expressiveness, increased self-esteem, behavioral tolerance — is really measurable. They are all therefore not accountable. Moreover, even if they could be codified as behavioral objectives, little would be gained. Lucy's organismic capacity for response is so immense and variegated that she might learn *none* of the things which I have suggested, and two dozen which I have *not* suggested. But even if this fact did not discourage us, and we persisted until we had developed and codified, say, 1500 behavioral objectives and accountability parameters for Lucy, most of them would be of minimal use for *another* little girl, because another little girl represents a different behavioral problem altogether. One of the central facts of Skin-nerian theory persistently, and I sometimes think deliberately, mis-understood by hostile humanists is the philosophical and methodological stress on organismic uniqueness. "Every human being," B. F. Skinner remarks in *The Technology of Teaching* (New York, 1968), "is the product of a genetic endowment and an environmental history which are peculiarly his own." The result, Skinner asserts, is "absolute uniqueness" for every human being (pp. 170-71). The point of all this is obvious: discrete-dance-steps-which-Lucy-can-perform, the only accountable con-sequence of her ballet experience, hardly scratch the surface of what she has learned. Organismic uniqueness makes Lucy intract-ably unaccountable.

Proponents of accountability in English, whether in composition or in literature, will argue, however, that this analysis of Lucy-as-ballerina misses the point. Accountability, they will retort, is not intended to cover all possible behavioral alterations in all possi-ble learning situations, but only a standardized few which can be applied to *all* students, forming a baseline behavioral repertory by which to measure the success or failure of a given English teacher's efforts. The argument has a certain validity: presumably the other little girls sharing a dance-lesson with Lucy have learned, more or less, the same steps as she, and of course, the lock-step formalisms of white ballet testify that differing, organismically unique human beings can indeed be brought to exhibit observable uniform behavioral patterns. Here, then, we reach the crux of the argument concerning accountability: uniformity of student behavior is the essential prerequisite to accountability for student behavior, in theme-writing or in anything else.

The problem, it turns out, is essentially one of *codification*. One must somehow come up with a *list* of behaviors, a *specifica-tion sheet* of some sort, a tabulative instrument accessible to department heads, principals, superintendents, school boards, and college deans, against which teacher success or failure may be measured. In some disciplines, or course, such codification pre-sents no particular problem. The student of mathematics can or cannot solve a quadratic equation at the end of the term; the shop student can or cannot use power-tools to build a bird-house in which birds will actually set up housekeeping for the summer. But things are not so simple in humane disciplines such as English. The humanities have as their province the totality of human activity, and in behavioral terms this means that the humanities must cope with the totality of response-possibility. Since human response is infinitely variable, specification-sheets encompassing it must verge on the infinite. The problem is illustrated by the list of behaviors which Lois Caffyn offers in *On Writing Behavioral*

Objectives for English (p. 72), a current NCTE best seller. "People with adult competencies in English," Miss Caffyn asserts, do the following things (I condense her list somewhat):

listen (eagerly, courteously)
attend (community meetings, clubs, concerts, lectures)
discuss (issues, beliefs, new knowledge)
explain (with clarity, patience)
share (experiences, humor)
habitually use (preferred language forms, appropriate degrees
of formality)
show (language courtesy, curiosity, emotional control)
demonstrate (thought through considered language rather than
through violence and profanity)
respond (to sensitivity, beauty, fine distinctions)

I suppose the most obvious thing to be said about this list is that it is suffocatingly middle-class, redolent of behavioral uniformitarianism and cultural coercion. I think immediately of Dylan Thomas, with whom I once spent twenty-four chaotically alcoholic hours in Chicago. (That, of course, is no distinction: everybody was doing it during the early fifties, and I simply helped pound another nail in the coffin.) Mr. Thomas, I can confidently assert, was not given to listening either "eagerly" or "courteously" (he seldom listened at all), had never explained anything with "patience" in his life, and commanded a much more effective way of reaching people than through "language courtesy" and "emotional control." Measured by the items in Miss Caffyn's Goody-Two-Shoes list, Dylan Thomas would have flunked flat. Yet he was the most humane and human man I ever met, and I think that his mastery of what Miss Caffyn calls "adult competencies" in English stands permanently beyond question.

One need not, however, resort to mad poets to illuminate the pernicious effects of codification of behaviors. Miss Caffyn's list simply does not apply to the students whom, as a Colorado teacher, I encounter in every class, superbly innocent young people fresh from high-country ranches and high-plains farms, for whom a different taciturnity and an economy of verbal expression stand at the core of a life-style which commands my profound respect. Neither does Miss Caffyn's list apply to the black student in my composition class, sporting Cuban shades and a funky Afro, who wrote me eight competent themes in the course of the quarter, but who sat in the back row for ten weeks in stony, expressionless silence, laying a quiet, unobtrusive, but totally effective mau-mau on the gesticulative white professor in the front of the room. He would have dropped dead before he would have listened "eagerly," he entertained a profound contempt for the Man's "preferred language forms," and he obviously did not feel that "language courtesy" would be of much use in winning the battles to which he was committed. I flatter myself that I am occasionally funny in class, but he never laughed, never cracked a smile — and it would have ruined my quarter if he had. He appeared at my office door after the last class and before I had assigned him a final grade, to inform me that the class had been, he thought, "all bullshit," but, as bullshit goes, "not bad, not bad at all." One settles for limited success in instances such as this: surely the ability to discriminante good bullshit from bad bullshit is an adult language-competency of considerable significance, but I do not find it in Miss Caffyn's list. The black student makes my point: one cannot codify human beings. It follows that neither can one codify their behaviors. Indeed, codification inevitably leads to stereotypical thinking: the only person that I know who really has achieved *all* of the behaviors in Miss Caffyn's list is Doris Day. I think it would be salutary for all of us who teach English to try to imagine what it would really be like to confront a class of twenty-five Doris Days at, say, eight o'clock, Monday, Wednesday, Friday.

Does all of this mean that there are no such things as behavioral objectives? Certainly not. A behavioral objective is one which springs from actual, here-and-now behavior of a given student or a given classroom full of students. The student behaves, or the class behaves (there is such a thing as group behavior), and *then* the teacher, at the moment, in the veritable transactional situation, comes up with a behavioral objective. This means that behavioral objectives which are devised ahead of time, and run off on the ditto-machine for distribution to the teaching staff, or (would you believe it?) stored in a behavioral-objective "bank," are not behavioral objectives at all, because they are not based on or derived from actual behavior. Rather, they are *educational* objectives. The distinction is of crucial importance. It involves the technical differences in behavioral theory between terminal objec- tives and intermediate objectives, between specification of final behavior and those *sub*-specifications which lead by successive approximations to the final behavior. We may, for example, decide that we wish the white rat in the Skinner-box to engage in lever- depressing behavior. This is a *terminal* objective, but it is *not* a behavioral objective because it is not based on the behavior of any actual rat. When, however, we place an actual animal, S.R. Rodent, in the Skinner-box, we have an on-going free-floating situation in which behavioral objectives can be developed. If S. R. Rodent tends to "freeze" in this strange situation, then our behavioral objective will be to reinforce movement, *any* movement, the moment it occurs. But perhaps S. R. Rodent is feeling "up" that day, is open to new stimuli, and is as a consequence very active, moving rapidly about the box in exploratory curiosity. If this is the case, then our behavioral objective is different, *because the rat's behavior is different.* Our behavioral objective in this case is movement *toward* the level or, if S. R. Rodent is really moving about, *touching* the lever. It all depends on what the rat actually *does.*

Like any English teacher, I have the general intention of fostering "appreciation of literature." But this is not a behavioral objective because it stands anterior to any encounter with any student. It is, instead, an educational objective. Behavioral objectives cannot be developed until I confront an actual student or class of students and *see what he does or they do.* Although class-behavior is no different, encounters with individual students illustrate this principle most clearly. For example, I recently taught Shakespeare to a large group of non-majors. During discussion of *King Lear,* I laid heavy stress — perhaps too heavy — on the fact that the "crazies" of the play say, in their cryptic way, most of the intelligent and true things. Part of the message of *Lear,* I suggested, is that reason is a kind of madness, and madness a kind of reason. That same day a male student — a science major — called the office to say he had to talk to me *right now.* When he arrived, he dropped unceremoniously into a chair and faced me squarely — and with as much hostility as I have ever seen in a student. "You *bastard,*" he said, "you don't know what you're doing to me." After considerable conversation, all of it hostile, it became clear what I was "doing" to him. He had, he told me, recently split from the drug scene on campus, and was busy "getting my head straight." He now equated drug use with unreason, and had simplistically assumed that in rejecting drugs he was now and forever safely back in the world of reason. Yet here was his English professor telling him that the reasonable world was in many respects mad. Edgar's assertion in the play (IV, vi) that Lear's rantings represent "Reason in madness!" had, he said, blown his mind, especially since he was at the same time reading *Catch-22* on his own. In a kind of terrible shock of recognition, he had made the connection (worth, it seems to me, an entire college education) between the psychotic contemporary world and the psychotic world of *King Lear.* At this point I was able to suggest that I stood at the end of a fairly long line of "bastards" who were "doing" something to him: Shakespeare, and Lear, and Gloucester, and Edgar, and Joseph Heller, and perhaps most of all, Yossarian. I hardly counted.

When, after an hour's conversation (and still full of hostility), he finally asked me if I knew of any other related readings which would further blow his mind, I was ready for the question. I had my behavioral objective, *based on observed, here-and-now behavior.* My science major was taking literature seriously for the first time in his life, for the excellent reason that his world-view was deeply threatened by *King Lear* and *Catch-22.* He was hostile and antagonistic because an *adversary relationship* with the literary artifact was the only way he could cope with what Shakespeare and Heller seemed to be saying. Hence my behavioral objective for this student was not "love of literature" or "appreciation of literature." For the time being it was, rather, to *maintain the adversary relationship* which the student himself, out of his own behavioral repertory, had established. No other relationship could be, for him, believable. So I sent him to Kafka (*The Trial* and *The Metamorphosis),* To Tom Wolfe (*The Electric Kool-Aid Acid-Test),* and to Ken Kesey (*One Flew Over the Cuckoo's Nest).* If I was going to be categorized as a mind-blower, I reflected, as good be hanged for a sheep as a lamb. The point of this anecdote should, I think, be obvious. There simply was no way for me to establish, *ahead of time,* a behavioral objective for this student. It would take a prescience far greater than mine to construct, *before the fact,* a behavioral objective stating: "Given the reading of *King Lear* and *Catch-22, the student* shall show his appreciation and love of literature by exhibiting fear, hostility, and aversive behavior." Perhaps those members of the profession busy codifying behavioral objectives for English have that prescience. Personally, I doubt it.

An equally compelling example of the difficulties of behavioral codification occurred a couple of years ago when I was teaching Faulkner's *The Bear* to thirty sophomores, twenty-nine whites and one lone black student — whom I shall call John — from out of state, a basketball player on an athletic scholarship, a sociology major, earnest and hard-working, but not exactly literary in his general orientation. In spite of my best efforts in class, John was badly put down by the other students' rather glib discussion of *The Bear* and most of the underlying symbolism. Most of them were well-versed in literary analysis, and he was not. After a few attempts at comment, almost always across the grain of the general discussion, John subsided into silence. Yet it was apparent that he was absolutely compelled by the story, and puzzled by the class's general approach to it. I therefore offered to spend a few hours with him in the office, where he wouldn't have to compete with the fast-talkers of the class.

It soon became apparent what the difficulty was. John did not want to discuss *The Bear* as a story-to-be-analyzed. Rather, he wanted to discuss the history of the McCaslin plantation, and of the black and white decendents of old Carothers McCaslin, as a series of events which had *actually happened.* His aesthetic premises were thus totally different from those of the rest of the class. They were engaged in *analytical behavior,* while my black student was engaged in a kind of *belief behavior.* During the last week of the Fall Quarter, John and I unraveled the compexities of Uncle Buck and Buddy's entries in the commissary ledger-books of Section IV, and John took the book with him when he went home for Christmas break. Shortly after the Winter Quarter began he appeared at my office door to report that he and his grandfather, who had had no schooling and who could read at only a functionally minimal level, had spent most of Christmas vacation together, going over Section IV of *The Bear* sentence by labyrinthine sentence, ledger-entry by cryptic ledger-entry. Faulkner's story had moved John's grandfather finally to relate, for the first time in John's hearing, his own family history which, it turned out, contained elements just as shocking as the most gothic features of the McCaslin chronicle.

John therefore returned to campus after Christmas even more inclined to treat *The Bear,* not as a story, but as *truth.* The persistence of this behavior, *John's behavior,* gave me finally a genuine behavioral objective: my job as teacher was to reinforce belief-behavior, and to treat *The Bear* in these terms. The result was a total shift in my teaching orientation. At one point, John and I were going over the passage where Ike McCaslin realizes that, despite all his woodcraft, he has failed to catch a glimpse of Old Ben because he has been relying on his own rationality, and thus withholding himself from the woods. So he hangs watch and compass on a bush, plunges into the green depths of the Big Bottom, and is soon hopelessly lost. It is at this point that Ike cuts the bear's trail and, following it, suddenly finds himself back in the clearing from which he started, the watch and compass gleaming on the bush where he left them, Old Ben glancing at him over his shoulder as he fades into the myriad and sundappled gloom on the opposite side of the clearing. When I suggested to John that Old Ben had *led* Ike back to the clearing, he turned to me in utter seriousness and asked, "Mr. Zoellner, do you really think a bear could be that smart?"

Thanks to my excellent Wisconsin training, my whole inclination was to say, "Look, John you *still* are not getting the drill. The bear is not a *real* bear, for heaven's sake, he's a *symbol.* You don't ask of a symbol, John, whether it's smart or dumb. There are no such things as *smart* symbols and *dumb* symbols." Fortunately, I did not say that. Because I had a clear-cut objective based on John's actual behavior, I took the question — which no student had ever asked me before about *The Bear* — seriously. I suddenly realize that I did indeed believe that wild animals could be as intelligent as Old Ben seemed to be in leading Ike back to his watch and compass. As a consequence I ended up doing what I had never done before, telling John about the ten-point mule-deer buck that I had once pursued through scrub-oak and aspen grove for a long Colorado winter's afternoon, only to find evidence in the snow upon back-tracking that the buck had made a huge, fast circle, and had been quietly following *me* for the last hour that I had been hunting *him,* keeping, as it were, a prudent eye on the bipedal idiot in the red hat. Once again, the point should be obvious: I cannot imagine a writer of behavioral objectives so prescient that, beforehand, he could assert: "Given the reading of William Faulkner's *The Bear,* the student shall treat it as *historical truth."* No one, not even English professors, commands that kind of crystal-ball brilliance.

In these examples I have stressed the development of behavioral objectives for individual students because the operation of the model is most clearly and dramatically seen in person-to-person office-confrontations. But the same principles apply to the classroom. Groups of students also behave, although seldom as clearly or incisively as individual students. As in the case of John and *The Bear,* there is no predicting what will happen in a classroom. One has to go there and see. Until one has done so, the construction of behavioral objectives is an exercise in futility. Classes are as unaccountable as individuals. I have also stressed objectives for literature-teaching rather than composition because the study of literature frequently leads to behaviors of a dramatic intensity not often encountered in composition classrooms. The processes are, nevertheless, the same. In the composition classroom, scribal behavior — or perhaps vocal-to-scribal behavior — must come *first,* and the development of behavioral objectives *second.* To attempt to construct and codify behavioral objectives for composition before the class engages in scribal behavior is to totally misunderstand the psychological model, and indeed to repudiate the whole meaning of the behavioral modification methodologies. It would, of course, be much simpler for all teachers of English — and for those who must evaluate English teacher performance — if behavioral objectives could be codified beforehand, dittoed up, filed in the principal's office, stored in banks, posted on walls. But teaching, as James Moffett has pointed out, is ineluctably a transactional activity, and any methodology which minimizes this fact is pernicious. Indeed, the failure of both teaching machines and most programmed-learning software to engage the interest of students beyond the Hawthorne period can be attributed to some Skinnerians, such as J. G. Holland, forgetting this central Skinnerian principle. Human beings cannot, in fact, enter into genuine transactional relationships with machines. All machines, and especially the binary computer, are simply too stupid to hold up their end of the relationship.

I must add, finally, that my rejection of predictive codification of behavioral objectives is consistent with what I have had to say before on matters behavioral. At the Cincinnati CCCC convention I was repeatedly, and not always in total amiability, accused of having shifted my ground on specificationism. Not at all. In "Talk-Write: A Behavioral Pedagogy for Composition" *(College English,* January, 1969), I suggested that the greatest weakness of current compositional pedagogy is "the almost total lack of intermediate or sub-specifications to bridge the often enormous gap between the student's actual scribal capacities and the invisible archetype at which we wish him to aim" (p. 301). The difficulty, I asserted, is "not the lack of an ultimate or terminal specification, but rather the fact that it *is* ultimate and, under the rubric of our present instrumental metaphor, intractably so" (pp. 283-84). Codified behavioral objectives, constructed ahead of time, are susceptible to precisely these objections: they are terminal and they are intractable, being totally unrelated to actual behaviors of actual students. They are, moreover, inescapably uniformitarian, coercive, and authoritarian. To correct these difficulties, I suggested techniques for the development of "intermediate specification of response" (p. 283) based on what the student vocally or scribally does. This procedure I called "autogenetic specification" (p. 301). By "autogenetic" I meant scribal specifications which have their genesis in the student himself, based on *his own behaviors,* either vocal or protoscribal. In these suggestions I was trying to persuade the profession to attend more to what a given student, or a class-room full of students, *does,* than to what he or they *ought* to do. I think we are still hung-up on that authoritarian *ought.* To burn the midnight oil writing codified objectives unrelated to the living and unique individual is, in my opinion, just another way to keep the behaving student, in all his terrible complexity, at comfortable arm's length. It is, in short, yet another pedagogical cop-out.

Humanism and Accountability

ARTHUR W. COMBS

We have to be concerned about the techniques we use in the search for accountability to make certain the side effects aren't so destructive that they eliminate the value of the thing we're trying to do in the first place.

Many of us humanists are concerned about the direction education is taking in the current efforts to achieve educational accountability. Concerned educators who identify with the humanist movement have a responsibility to speak critically and courageously about the humanistic aspects of accountability. Educators are great faddists. We are always in the hope we can find simplistic solutions, nice simple answers that are going to save us. For years we have searched for gimmicks which will make education what it ought to be. For example, we went through the testing movement, and then we thought T.V. was going to save us all. This was followed by the fad of teaching machines. I remember Earl Kelley saying, "Ten years from now there will be millions of dollars worth of teaching machines rotting away in the basement of schools all over the United States" — and it turns out his prophecy was true. Then we thought the new curriculum was going to do it: new math, new science, the new this and the new that. Of course, we have all learned a little something from these fads. Our efforts have not been entirely wasted.

Now we're engaged in a new fad, the movement for accountability. This present approach to accountability is an attempt to apply the industrial model to education. So now we're

Arthur W. Combs, "Humanism and Accountability." Adapted from an address at the Center for Humanistic Education Conference on Educational Accountability, Gainesville, Florida, October, 1972.

all up to our ears in PERTing and PPBS systems, computer controlled programming, systems analysis, behavioral objectives and performance criteria; techniques characteristic of industry in the last ten or fifteen years. It appears educators will have to ride this one through, just like we have lived through the others. We're going to have to let it run its course; but what a pity! It seems to me that this approach to educational accountability is leading us down some blind alleys. The question we need to ask is, what can we do about it? Do we merely have to go along for the ride? What stance can a humanist take with respect to this national debate over accountability?

It's not an easy thing to address ourselves to the issue of accountability, because whenever you set out to question a trend which is under way, everybody thinks you're being destructive. Of course, we do not desire to be destructive. In fact, I don't think anybody can be against accountability. Everyone ought to be accountable. What the humanist is constantly trying to make clear, however, is that accountability, as it is currently being practiced, is far too narrow a concept. And it is this narrowness that seriously injures the educational process. Unfortunately the humanist's concern is difficult to communicate when the accountability movement is sweeping the country. The concerned critic too often encounters the cry, "You're either for it or against!" Earl Kelley once said of dichotomies, "Whenever you can put an idea in an either/or category it's almost certain they're both wrong!"

The problem we face is not that current techniques are wrong. I wish they were. If they were wrong, we'd throw them out with no difficulty. The problem is that what we are currently trying to do is partly right. And because it's partly right, our partial success encourages us to keep on moving in the same direction. Donald Snygg once put it this way, "Sometimes you can sell more papers by shouting louder on the same corner. But sometimes you have to find another corner." Partly right solutions encourage us "to stay on the same corner." We think that if we could just do a little more and do it more effectively, if we could turn on a little more steam, if we could get more people back of it, if we could pour a little more money into it — surely it will provide the final answers. Such myths or illusions are almost impossible to dispel.

Unfortunately, communicating the goals and methods of the humanists is also not easy. To most people the humanist's position seems too vague, too imprecise. Humanists seem to others to be fuzzy-minded. "They're hard to pin down," some say. Others are heard saying, "You can't get them to give you a straight answer." Of course, it's difficult to live with unsolved problems and most people are continuously looking for simplistic answers. We need to remind ourselves that one of the characteristics of self-actualizing persons, according to Abe Maslow, is that they are able to tolerate ambiguity, able to live with unsolved problems. So if you find yourself being called fuzzy-minded, take a positive approach and see it as an indication of your self-actualization!

The humanist position always appears to be fuzzy-minded. Humanists talk about freedom and self direction and loving people — things that are important but imprecise. Besides, humanists, because of the kind of people they are, hate to organize. They want to be humanistic with each other instead of pushing each other around. So they will be just as happy to say, "Well it doesn't matter, the important thing is for you to do what you think is best." What happens then is that the organizers and managers just walk all over them.

Silberman, in his book *Crisis in the Classroom*, points out that a major sickness of American education is what he calls "mindlessness." Over and over we commit the same kind of errors because we have not looked at the basic issues with which we need to be concerned. I would like to suggest that if we are to forward the humanist movement with respect to the issue of accountability, it will be necessary to make clear to people what happens when you put any kind of technique to work in education. Whenever you introduce into the educational process any new thing, whether it be television, behavioral objectives, or a new technique or concern, there are always four criteria we have to consider.

The first of these criteria asks, are the objectives we're concerned with the truly desirable ones? Our failure to ask this one crucial question is a source of much sickness today in education. This is why a great many people are saying that education has become irrelevant, out of touch with people. It has also resulted in the alienation of young people and the opting out, copping out and dropping out that follows. In our society we can get along much better with a bad reader than a bigot. However, nobody is doing anything about bigotry. Everybody is attempting to do something about reading. Earl Kelley once said that he heard people talk so much about reading he had begun to think that the only reason for parents to have children was so they could have a good reader in the family! I'm not implying that reading isn't a good objective. What I'm trying to suggest is that when we wish to put any new technique into the educational process, we have to ask ourselves, "Are the objectives which we are attempting to achieve really the most desirable, the most important and significant ones?"

If objectives are limited, behavior is also limited. One of the things that many people have not understood about systems approaches is that a systems approach is a technique for making certain you reach the objectives you have in mind. That's all a system does. A system isn't right or wrong in itself. A system is simply a valuable way of addressing a problem and making sure that you arrive at the objectives you have set out for yourself. This is fine, except that if the objectives you are seeking are wrong ones then the systems approach will guarantee that your errors are collosal! What the humanists are trying to say at the present time is that some human objectives are far more important than some of the objectives currently being assessed in the accountability movement.

The second criterion is the question, "Is this the best way to achieve a particular objective?" We have to ask, "Does the technique we are using truly measure the objective we have in mind?" Behavioral objectives and performance criteria techniques are a fine way of achieving the simplest, most primitive aspects of the educational process. But education is much broader than this. We know statistically, for example, that people of higher intelligence have larger feet. The correlation between intelligence and size of feet is positive — low, but positive. We could decide to measure intelligence by measuring the size of people's feet, but obviously that would be leaving out a lot of other factors that contributed to the correlation while concentrating on things with comparatively little relevance. The argument of the humanist against the behavioral objectives movement is that it is measuring things we know how to measure and ignoring things we *ought* to measure. Humanists are concerned about the adequacy of the sample. Historically, in research and science the idea of the adequacy of the sample has always been a very important consideration. However, at the present time, as we go about measuring the outcomes of education, we behave as though the adequacy of the sample was a matter of no consequence. We continue to assess what we know how to test instead of finding ways to test things we ought to assess.

The third criterion to consider is the effect of techniques on the person who employs them. Whatever technique we use in accountability is going to have its inevitable effects on the teachers, the principals, the superintendents, the whole educational structure even down to the kinds of buildings we construct. Unfortunately, the question of what happens to the teacher is often ignored. Effects, however, are inevitable because whatever device we use to measure the outcomes of education necessarily concentrates the teacher's attention, focuses his behavior, and determines his goals — whether we like it or not. As a matter of fact these effects are exactly what the accountability experts want. From the humanist's point of view education is already concerned with much too narrowly-defined objectives. Take, for example, the teacher's plan book; the teacher makes a plan and thereafter becomes the victim of the plan. So many a good educational experience is lost because the teacher is locked into the preconceived system and is unable to break out of it. I think, for example, of watching a teacher with a group of children in a museum. The children were standing in front of a great big painting, looking at it pop-eyed, looking for all they were worth. And off to the side the teacher was saying, "If you kids don't hurry up, you aren't going to see anything!"

We've done a lot of research at the University of Florida over the last twelve years on the differences between good and poor helpers in various professions. One of the characteristics of good helpers, we find, is that their purposes are freeing rather than controlling. We have to ask ourselves then, "What is the effect of the techniques which we are asking people to use in accountability, upon these characteristics of the good helper?"

Finally, of course, the fourth criterion requires that we raise the question, "What is the effect of this particular technique or concept upon the student?" Here we have to be concerned, not only about the effect we have in mind but the side effects as well. In the medical profession, those working on a new drug carefully check out its side effects. Unfortunately, this is a lesson we haven't learned very well in education. We use a technique with no concern about the side effects whatever. We need to ask ourselves what a child is learning as a consequence of the techniques we employ and impose upon him. I remember some years ago my son came home from school talking about the grading system and he said, "Dad, how come you put up with this system of grading on the curve?" And I answered, "Well, what brought this on?" He responded, "Well, think about it for a minute. Grading on the curve makes it to my advantage to destroy my friends." And then he added, "That's a hell of a thing to teach young people." You know, that's true; a system which makes it to the advantage of the student to hurt his friends is indeed a very questionable device for education.

We have to be concerned with student self-concepts when deciding what to do about accountability. If in the process of teaching a child that two and two is four you also teach him that he personally is a failure, then we need to realize that teaching him that two and two is four may be less valuable than we have thought. We have to be concerned about the techniques we use in the search for accountability to make certain the side effects aren't so destructive that they eliminate the value of the thing we're trying to do in the first place.

I believe all of us in the humanist movement must also try to help people understand the basic inappropriateness of the industrial model applied to educational processes. This is a hard thing to do because all of us in this culture have grown up with respect for the industrial model; deciding what you want, establishing the goals, setting up the machinery, then testing whether you did it. The industrial model, we know, works beautifully with things. The difficulty is that it also creates the illusion of accuracy. It sounds so straightforward, so businesslike to say, "Determine your objectives, set up the machinery to accomplish them, then test to see if you accomplished them." It works fine in industry. It's also the technique we use in science, which all of us worship as a sacred cow. Unfortunately the model is not wholly appropriate for educational processes. The model is familiar to those who have lived on a farm and have had to bring the cows home from pasture. You start from the barn and go down the lane, opening the gates where you want the cows to go and closing the gates where you don't want them to go. Sometimes this is called the stockyard approach and it works fine for cattle. The only trouble is that people are always failing to cooperate. They escape through gates you've forgotten to close or they climb over the fences and scamper over the hillsides. We have a song, "Don't Fence Me In" which expresses the American spirit violated by this kind of approach to human beings. If you carry this conception to its ultimate conclusion, somebody's got to know where the people should go so the rest of us can set up the machinery to get them there. In the final analysis, this leads directly to a philosophy of dictatorship, a strange conception for us to be using in a society that espouses the democratic way of life.

There are other things which this approach to dealing with people does. It puts a terrible responsibility on the teacher, because the person who is supposed to be running the show cannot be wrong. He's *got* to be right. If anything goes wrong he is fully and completely responsible. This puts a terrible weight on the teacher, one almost impossible for a person to live with. It also creates a climate in which students view teachers with mistrust. One of the problems we have in education today is the deep feelings of dehumanization experienced by teachers and students everywhere. The bigger we make our schools, the more precise we seek to make our processes; the more we treat people as things, the more alienation we produce. To have a rich curriculum, we think we must have a large school. The trouble is people get lost in large schools. So then we have to set up a guidance department to find them again! Having created a group of specialists in human relations, teachers then don't feel responsible for dealing with human problems; "there's a specialist for that." Rather, teachers strive to produce those precise and measurable outcomes for which they are being held accountable — and the dangers of a very limited and narrow approach to accountability becomes disastrously evident!

I think we have to take a good look at what the industrial model did in industry. The application of precision management techniques gave the laboring man the feeling he wasn't important, that he was a victim of the machine. So what did he do? He got together with others who shared his dilemma and formed labor unions to combat the system. If you look around you in education today you can see that this is precisely what's happening with older students. Unfortunately, the little kids haven't got the power yet, so they have to live with it and endure.

It should be evident to us by now that the management techniques of industry constitute a different model than the one so urgently needed in education. In industry, the task is to produce a product. The task of the president is to see that that particular product is produced. And everybody else on down the entire management line has as his objective to see that his *boss's* objectives are realized. The worker has to make certain that the foreman's objectives are accomplished. The foreman makes sure that the supervisor's objectives are accomplished, and so on. But I would like to suggest that exactly the opposite model is required for education. What we need is a system in which everybody is trying to make certain that the objectives of the person *below* him are being accomplished. The principal ought to be helping the teachers to accomplish what they're trying to do. The teachers ought to be helping the kids to accomplish what is personally meaningful to them as students.

At present we are involved in much too narrow a view of the curriculum. The current movement toward behavioral objectives is almost exclusively preoccupied with the most simple and primitive aspects of curriculum. But the modern curriculum must go far beyond this. A curriculum which can be easily and simply measured is no longer adequate in our society as a consequence of the information explosion. We all know how tremendously the amount and rate of information has increased, so that never again will there be a time in American education when we can ever hope to have a curriculum required of everyone. The diversity of our society has become so great that we cannot predict what a person ought to be like even the day after tomorrow. At the present time in the United States we have 35,500 occupations from which a student may choose. This list represents a 33% increase in career possibilities in merely the last fifteen years. At present a child must be prepared for a lifetime in which he may change his occupation at least four or five times. As a consequence, any system which tries to define too precisely the nature of outcomes is almost certainly going to prepare persons for the wrong things. What we have to have as our objective is not people who know this or that but persons who can think, who can behave intelligently, who can respond to completely new situations creatively and effectively. Creativity and intelligence are not things which can be defined in advance with great precision.

We talk a lot about affective and cognitive education as though these were independent goals. People say, "Do you want to educate for intelligence or adjustment?" That's a lot of nonsense. It's as though we have to make a choice between smart psychotics or well-adjusted dopes! This is a ridiculous choice. It's also out of touch with reality. Psychologically, there isn't anything but cognition. Emotion is simply an artifact of behavior. Emotion has to do with the degree to which an idea, a concept, a cognition, has relevance to one's self. Let me give you an illustration. Let's think for a moment about the young woman who has a lover still in Vietnam. He's been there a long time. She gets a letter from him saying he'll finally be home in six months. Great news but not much to get too excited about. Time goes by and she receives a letter saying he'll be home in a month. Then, he's going to be home next week. He's on his way. He's back in the country. Time to go to the airport. Here comes his flight. There he is! Unless you are particularly hard-hearted, I suspect you share some of this young woman's emotion. The closer the event gets to self, the greater the emotion one feels. Emotion is simply the relevance of something to self. The snake on the other side of the glass at the zoo doesn't distress me at all. A snake the same distance away without the glass between us has a very different effect because it is more relevant. We need to understand that if we do not have affective education we aren't going to have any at all. If an idea is not important, if you don't have any feelings about it, then you can count on it not having any effect upon your behavior.

Rather than speaking of affective education, we need to speak of relevant or non-relevant education. Perhaps we need to stop talking entirely about affective education, because when we do people get uncomfortable and insist that "feelings have nothing to do with education" or "that's the kind of thing that should be dealt with in the home." So let's talk instead about relevant education. No one would fight much about making education more relevant. No parent is going to complain about education which will help people to feel better about themselves. But call it affective education and you're in trouble.

To deal with the humanistic aspects of accountability, we have to insist on the validity of human judgments for evaluation. We have sold ourselves a bill of goods in our insistence on being objective. Objectivity is fine when you have it. But judgment is what we use when we are unable to deal precisely and objectively with a particular event. If we throw out judgment in the evaluation of educational outcomes, we have thrown out a most important tool. Judgment is what education is all about; in fact, the goal of education is to improve human judgment. If teachers are not allowed to use judgment to determine what is happening then what we have done is rule out the very quality that makes them most effective in the long run. In our research at the University of Florida on good teachers, as well as good practitioners in other helping professions, we found that objectivity correlates negatively with effectiveness!

The heart of any profession is that, presumably, the professional person is able to make better judgments than the layman. Now, if we say to people in education that you may not, must not, use human judgment to make some kinds of evaluations, we've eliminated one of the most valuable tools of human experience. The teacher who gives up judgment has abrogated his responsibility. There are teachers who determine a child's grade by adding up scores on tests. They insist that their own judgment has nothing to do with evaluation. Not me. As a person of dignity and integrity who has spent forty years in the teaching profession, I refuse to abrogate judgment to any test that I have ever seen anywhere, anytime. My judgment is important. So is yours.

Many of the techniques we have to use in humanist measurement are presently crude and awkward. They don't have the nice, clean, clear-cut illusion of precision which you may feel you can get with a pencil and paper test. One of the things we need to do, however, is to understand that this is the way it has to be. The present humanist movement is a new effort to make education more relevant, and thus our techniques are bound to be fallible at this stage. We need to remind ourselves, however, that the first atomic pile under the squash court at the University of Chicago was also a very crude device. However, it helped make possible a whole new movement in the physical sciences. My good friend, the late Don Snygg, used to say when speaking of our struggles to find ways of accomplishing humane objectives, "You know, the Conestoga Wagon was a very crude means of transportation, but it made possible the opening of a continent." The humanist movement is only 20 to 30 years old and we have to expect that our techniques will frequently be less precise than we might like.

What we need is to get about the business of using what we can from the systems which have existed before us. We have to adapt the old systems wherever possible. But beyond that, we have to get busy developing new techniques for getting at the assessment of the human objectives of education. We need also to seek the funds to underwrite such efforts. Recently I said to a state department of education, "Look, you're spending millions of dollars on the behavioral objectives approach. How about giving us some funds to explore the humanistic objectives." In response, they told me they were already doing this. However, I've looked very hard on both the state and national levels and nowhere have I found any substantial efforts to deal with these concerns. We are pouring millions of dollars into the limited aspects of education amenable to behavioral objectives, performance-based criteria. I find this a frightening thing. It can only result in a distortion of the major thrust of education. It will encourage us to concentrate our attention on what we know already how to measure, while what we desperately need to assess is permitted to remain in limbo.

Finally, I think we need a new psychology for the humanist movement. Humanistic psychology does not deny the contributions of behavioristic psychology but goes beyond them. Let me use an analogy to illustrate how humanism doesn't deny or overlook the behavioral objectives approach to understanding human behavior. Think for a moment about the field of mathematics. As human beings reached the place where they needed to deal with things that could be seen and counted, they developed arithmetic as a way of dealing with countable facts. No sooner had they developed that system, however, when they began confronting new problems, that of how to deal with things which can't be counted directly, with unknown numbers which can only be dealt with by inference. So algebra was invented. But we know that algebra does not deny the validity of arithmetic; it goes beyond it in order to deal with things simple arithmetic cannot effectively handle. Then we had to deal with the problem of infinity and so we developed another system in mathematics called calculus.

The same thing is true in our understanding of human behavior. In our attempt to understanding behavior, we first developed behaviorism as a way of dealing with actions and behaviors which are easily observed and countable. Now we realize it is also crucial to deal with things going on inside the behaver, how he thinks, feels, and perceives himself and his world, and these can't simply be measured in behavioral terms. To deal with such important concerns and aspects of human behavior we now have the humanistic psychologies of Combs, Maslow, Rogers, and many others. These newer approaches to understanding human behavior do not deny the significance of behavioral approaches; they include them and go beyond to address themselves to human dimensions and problems not readily dealt with in behaviorism. They are especially relevant for confronting the great human problems currently in need of attention but often ignored by those jumping too quickly upon the bandwagon of behavioral objectives sweeping through the country.

So far, humanistic psychologies have only begun to influence and direct the focus of education. It is time they were used more often. It is time we humanists involved ourselves more in the process of providing and implementing a humanistic approach to accountability and other major concerns in education. We need to communicate clearly the fact that the humanistic psychologies can and do provide important insights and offer viable solutions to some of the most pressing human problems in our school system and, Lord knows, that system needs all the help it can get.

Rapunzel, Rapunzel, Let Down Your Golden Hair

MARTIN ENGEL

*The schools today function with a fallacious premise - the mythology of mechanomorphism. We not only **do not** believe the world to be animistic and alive, but our educational practice suggests that we do not even believe that people are animistic. Instead, we see them in the form of machines. It is the malaise of our technocracy.*

There is this magic show . . .
And some people live in the magic show . . .
And some people are the magic show . . .

And some people wonder what the magic show is all about . .
And some people wonder what magic is . . .
And some people never wonder at all.

From a film-short on a California sculptor

Of course we know what the magic show is. It is life, as flowing, mysterious, marvelous, felt experience. Learning is the growth part of that life and therefore is the natural, continuing, and constant process of individual creation and intuition in the mind and body of each human organism. It continues through each person's life span. That formal education should end for most people after twelve or sixteen years does not recognize this biological truth. We all learn through both the struggle of exploration and the wonder of discovery. Human beings are innately and intrinsically learning beings. As John Holt says: "Birds fly, fish swim, people learn!" We must greatly expand our narrow conception of learning, certainly far beyond the traditional limits of academic or manual skills. Learning is a process achieved by virtue of our total consciousness, interacting with our ever-changing perception of reality. Learning takes place as the human organism interacts with the reality he perceives and proceeds through the activities of probing, experimenting, trial-and-error, and self-determined repetition, as well as through dreaming and fantasizing. In other words, there is almost nothing that we do that is not a learning experience.

"Learn", "know", and "understand" are active verbs. Learning is the growth of knowing and understanding. It is a volitional, self-rewarding and self-purposive activity. The instinctive desire to learn can be strongly reinforced by the willing and active participation of the learner. One can learn consciously only what and if one wants to learn. Some believe that will has a significant bearing upon unconscious learning as well. The first priority of education, therefore, is to provide conditions in which the individual will *want* to learn, and is able to if he wants to.

No institution can ever help unwilling students to learn, because learning cannot be imposed from outside of the individual. Much of the learning that we attribute to the intervention of parents, teachers, and schools have taken place outside of, or despite these stimuli. When and if they have succeeded, these stimuli were *willingly* ingested within the learner's total experience. We should also understand that kids learn from parents and teachers very little of what is intentionally, consciously taught. What kids do in fact learn is modelled upon what we *are,* not what we preach; not what we *say,* but *how* we say it; not what we *ask* of children, but what we ourselves *do.* In other words, teachers and parents and schools, as well as peers, are themselves the hidden curriculum within which our children strain and test their own wings. To state this point another way, McLuhan's addage is singularly accurate in education: The Medium is the Message!

With young children especially, but most likely with all human beings, learning is not solely an activity of the "head", if indeed that is where we see the locus of the mind. Mind is an attribute of the entire person. It is contradictory, a short-circuiting, to expect a docile, self-controlled body to contain a dynamic, creative, and active mind in a youngster. Especially for young children, to sit still for any length of time in order to learn what we want them to learn, when we want them to learn it, is a counter-productive expectation. A short attention span is characteristic of young children, not a fault, and is the expression of an active mind. Young children learn through the immediate senses of touch and taste as much as through the distancing senses of sight and hearing. In fact, the process of growing up seems to involve the de-tuning of our oral and tactile receptors. For adults, learning is a more abstractive and distancing activity. For children it is one of immediacy. I am not sure that what we as adults have gained in that exchange is worth the price of what we have lost. One of the fallacies of our educative system is the insistence upon that exchange, and at an earlier and earlier age. Among young children, reality and the control over reality is naturally experienced through physical interaction with the world and this physical interaction is not merely a "head" process.

Learning proceeds primarily, as we have insisted, through doing. It is an active process, not passive. To be taught is passive. The point is that the body actively thinks as well as feels. "Head" activities, like verbalization, are primarily adult behaviors. People like Piaget, Montessori, and Rudolph Steiner have understood this and have urged the learner to manipulate, to play with, to physically feel with his body the sounds and letters and numbers with which we construct language. We cripple our children's capacities to learn by interpreting their activities as primitive or yet-learned adult behaviors. The fact is that their behaviors, in their physicality, are legitimate in themselves. The language of children — whereby they communicate and interact with the world — is body language. It is principally tactile and kinesthetic and non-verbal. Early childhood education has neglected this dimension because the *adult* goal of education is instrumental; that is, economic and social. Thus imposed upon children, it is a *means* to be endured in order to attain an adult *end*.

We are finally becoming fully aware of the fact that what we call "teaching" has really very little to do with learning. We usually confuse training and teaching. B. F. Skinner supposedly was overheard to say: "If you know what you are doing, its *training*. If you don't know what you are doing, its teaching!" Skinner is referring to measurable outcomes and therefore, by his criteria, golf pros and dog trainers are the best teachers. Training is in-struction; that is, structuring into someone. It is like computer programming. But it is not education. Words like "train", "course", "curriculum" and "instruction" all have an underlying relationship that points to externally controlled forces being applied to the mind of someone else. The verb "train" is closely related to the noun - a linear sequence of expectations with no choice of direction. A "course" is, of course, a pre-determined route, like the course of a ship. A "curriculum" was originally the ancient Roman race-track in their arenas. Yet, most of us can remember only one or two inspiring people in our lives who genuinely helped to shape our growth, helped us to learn, in a profound sense, and led us out of ourselves, if that is what "education" means. Kahlil Gibran tells us in *The Prophet* that no one can teach us anything unless it already lies half sleeping within us waiting to be born. Thus, the wise teacher is not one who beckons his students to enter *his* house of wisdom, but rather attempts to lead students to the threshold of their own experience. Even more explicit than Gibran's poetic insight, is Carl Rogers' *Freedom to Learn*. In it he writes:

> I have come to feel that the only learning which significantly influences behavior is self-discovered, self-appropriated learning. . . . Such self-discovered learning, truth that has been personally appropriated and assimilated in experience, cannot be directly communicated to another. . . . Hence I have come to feel that the outcomes of teaching are either unimportant or hurtful.[1]

Surely every child has the right to expect more from the school than simply the training of his mind, just as he has the right to expect much more from his home than the toilet-training of his body. Schools fail children insofar as they only in-struct and do not "lead out."

There are certain concepts which, while fairly well known to psychology, seem to have had almost no impact upon education and it is currently practiced. For example, a loved child can learn more and better than an unloved one. A loved child is healthier, physically and mentally, than an unloved one. A happy child learns more and better than an unhappy one. Learning and growth vary in direct (though approximate) proportion to the amount and quality of love and happiness, other conditions being equal. In order to implement or facilitate learning, the first function of schooling, though by no means the only function, must be to provide love; that is, a supportive environment for each child, and to reinforce happiness; that is, to reduce anxiety. This means success experiences in the child's own terms and when there is no success, there must be no penalty. It is unfortunate that these verifiable facts tend to be dismissed as folish romanticism. For it is demonstrable that punishment generates aggressive behavior and retards physical, emotional, and intellectual growth. Repression, authoritarianism, impersonal and de-humanized institutional relationships are anxiety-generating conditions which inhibit learning to a measurable degree. On the other hand, conditions of love, support, pleasure, sensory stimulation, warm companionship from adults and peers, confidence, respect, and the absence of fear stimulate all learning to a significantly measurable degree. Regretfully, most schools and their teachers persist in seeking to shape the small, visible portion of the iceberg, while ignoring or actively repressing the much larger, submerged portion which supports it.

We must make "the whole child" more than the platitude of conference speeches. Most educational practice dis-assembles the "whole child" and isolates the visible and measurable functions, addressing itself to these isolated and discrete skills exclusively. The schools today function with a fallacious premise — the mythology of mechanomorphism. We not only *do not* believe the world to be animistic and alive, but our educational practice suggests that we do not even believe that people are animistic. Instead, we see them in the form of machines. It is the malaise of our technocracy.

We deal with people as if they were mechanical. What works successfully in the auto factory, the production line, the industrial process — more precise and careful procedures, greater intensity of effort upon ever smaller isolated tasks, more efficient systems management, greater quality control, merit rewards for higher productivity, better designed assembly sequences — all the efficiency increases that serve to produce more cars and refrigerators, do not work to produce more or better literacy, problem-solving skills, decision-making ability, a higher ethical and moral purpose, more vital personal and social commitments, or any of the academic and non-academic desirable outcomes we seek to develop in our school systems. To pursue this industrial assembly-line process is what Dwight Allen has called the fallacy of the student as object. While we can indeed be "objective" about subjects, we simply cannot sustain this mind-set about human beings. What educators will not face up to is that the first priority of the school and school system is *not* to run efficiently. In terms of our avowed goals for education: "We cannot get there from here. We have to go somewhere else, first!"

Education is the disciplined facility for learning. Schools are only one of the means for providing educational services. And, as education cannot guarantee learning, nor control it, and in fact may inhibit it, so schools cannot guarantee education and may in fact inhibit that! Once we, as the educational community, can get our priorities straight, we may then and only then become genuinely helpful to others as they pursue learning. School systems, as bureaucracies, have become so self-serving and self-perpetuating that they are moving ever further from their stated purpose. Means and ends have become totally confused.

The human mind is infinitely more complex, mysterious, and "messy" than is indicated by the neat, linear, sequential, and modular image of learning. The American Dream is predicated upon images of cutting down vast forests, plowing sweeping plains, producing oceans of material goods, building ever more and ever better. But the human mind is not a forest to be cut, a field to be plowed, raw material to be molded or assembled, a building to be cast up toward the sky, or any other similar analogy. Yet, the data-oriented consumerism and competitive comparisons which characterize the national preoccupation with numbers and with print de-coding betrays our technocratic and positivistic values. In short, the schools must no longer be sustained by a mythology of *quantity* and *industry*.

The point of Toffler's *Future Shock* is that we can't memorize the future. The world we were educated to believe in and function in does not now exist, yet we are even at present perpetuating and compounding these past misguided efforts by preparing our young for the world as it is *presently* constituted. We cannot possibly know or anticipate what skills and knowledge are going to be essential for survival in the terra incognita of ten or twenty years hence. We must relinquish the notion that what kids today need is simply *more* of what we had. The learning of survival skills for the future must be generically, fundamentally different, stressing such basic attributes as creativity, sensitivity, flexibility, autonomy, the ability to improvise, independence, a tremendous capacity to accommodate rapid change, what Alan Watts calls the "Wisdom of Insecurity", and most important, a resilience and capacity for perpetual independent learning and thinking. Stressing the exclusivity of certain presently marketable skills, to the exclusion of the more fundamental ones such as concept formation or perceptual skills, is the worst possible way to help children prepare for their future. Perhaps the best way to help children is to recognize that learning is autotelic; that is, self-purposive and self-rewarding. John Stuart Mill put it very well when he said: "Men are men before they are lawyers or physicians or manufacturers; and if you make them capable and sensible men they will make themselves capable and sensible lawyers and physicians."

George Dennison has pointed out that most children who have difficulty with reading are not primarily reading problems. The written or printed word is an extension and application of speech. Reading is not difficult for those who have an adequate command of verbalization. The point is that aural and oral language cannot be by-passed. Nor can those opportunities which help a youngster to perceive and to think. Reading is best learned in the same spontaneous way that language is first learned. The reason that poor kids do not do well in reading is that they have been deprived of that verbally stimulating environment in which reading is looked upon as a desirable and pleasurable activity. Language usage must first be a norm as conversation before it can become a norm as reading and writing. If a conversation about Dick and Jane and their dog Spot is an uninteresting subject to a six year old, reading about them is surely even less desirable. Impressive reading gains can inevitably be found in verbally rich environments in which children are optimally free to speak with each other and in which adults take conversations with children seriously. Clearly, unless we teach children *to* read and *to love* to read, there is no point in teaching them *how* to read. The usual regimented way of unison reciting, one-at-a-time performing, constant correction and all those uninspiring, convergent techniques which stress rote, repetition and no whispering or wiggling in your chair are the worst possible way to learn to read, speak, write, or learn. It is ironic that though children prepare for reading best by freely talking, it is the *teacher* who does most of the talking in our classrooms!

It is nonsense to argue that the acquisition of reading skills will, in turn, generate self-respect and learning motivation, when the process of and technique for acquiring those skills is *itself* authoritarian, repressive, and extrinsically rewarded. We must get over the Puritan notion that in order for it to be good for us, it must somehow be distasteful, uncomfortable, and something we would avoid if we could. Teachers seem to look upon reading the way many parents see broccoli or spinach. As it happens, children really want to communicate freely. The schools, however, suppress so much communication that when reading and writing are taught, they are not taught as communication *which is what they are!* It's like trying to drive a car with the brakes locked. Reading is a sub-set of verbalization/language. Language is, in turn, a sub-set of communication, which includes the vast and fertile field of non-verbal human expression. All of which is a sub-set of thinking. Obviously, the schools have these priorities in an inverse order.

With the behaviorist educator's penchant for objectivity, testing and measurement have become crucial methods for attaining objective data about individual performance and levels of ability correlated against norms and numerical criteria. Almost all major decisions in the administration of school systems have come to be based upon this data. Unfortunately, we have not yet developed any means for conducting testing in a useful and reliable way. Testing tends to focus upon the most obvious and most superficial dimensions of an individual and ignores the more profound, dynamic and complex aspects of that individual caught in the throes of the rapidly fluctuating forces of growth and development. Because we are measuring people rather than, say, the average national rainfall, or, more to the point, conducting a laboratory-controlled experiment upon inert material, we can never be confident that our charts, graphs, and mathematical models do in fact accurately describe the ability of an individual. We will never screen out all such variables as Experimenter Bias, Hawthorne Effect,

Subject's perception of role, Halo Effect, Placebo Effect, and other biasing factors. What most testing can tell us is how well the tested individual can take that particular test at that particular time, and no more. Thus, tests can only measure test-taking ability. They tell us very little outside of the immediacy of that particular test. We have become so hard-data conditioned that we are no longer willing to rely upon our own powers of observation. We refuse to recognize progress with our own eyes and instead rely upon scores. Must *all* observations emulate the experimental-physics model, with hard mathematical data? Have we finally and *completely* confused measurement and evaluation and forgotten that the word *evaluation* contains the word value?

If we must measure children, let us at least measure them as people rather than as programmable learning components. Let us measure the child's "development quotient" which is the term a psychologist has given to the correlated synthesis of a variety of information. In other words, let us measure the *whole* child, not only his reading skills or his I.Q. Let us integrate his perceptual growth, his bodily functions, his social relationships, his memory and imitative skills, his manipulative and motor abilities, along with his intelligence. Schools have succumbed to the behaviorist addage that: "If you can't measure what you are teaching, then teach what you can measure." Thus we have rank-ordered certain limited and obvious skills above the more fundamental ones such as creativity and intuition, and thus we cheat the child.

What goes on in most early grades is a very poor excuse for Froebel's original concept of a kindergarten as a child's garden in which he may grow, and in that growth derive pleasure. What can grow in the right kind of learning environment is a great deal more than math and reading. The integration of thinking, feeling, inter-personal relationships, valuing, choosing, problem-solving, decision-making, accepting change, communicating (including read), non-verbal expression, creativity, and intuition: all these are basic skills. How many of them can we measure? How many of them can we actually teach? It is possible to be generously endowed with all of the skills just listed and still not be able to read, write, or do numbers. Conversely, it is possible to be able to read, write, and do numbers rather well but have very few of those basic skills listed above. Human growth can not be stimulated except by nurturing the entire child, his feelings, phantasy, dreams, play, and longings, as well as is capacity to manipulate symbols and decode print.

I don't think we ought to prepare children for schools as they are. Rather, we ought to be preparing schools as children are.

Schools, in their archaic and bureaucratic sclerosis, must relinquish their monopoly of learning as an institutionalized process so that learning as a life-time activity, pleasurable and autotelic, can be phased into all of our lives. I am sure that if we all put our imaginations to work, we could come up with lots of alternatives for helping children to learn and grow. There is nothing inherently sacred about the school system. Ivan Illich gives us our mandate "The 'age of schooling' began about two hundred years ago. Gradually the idea grew that schooling was a necessary means of becoming a useful member of society. It is the task of this generation to bury that myth." We should stop worrying about and investing in methods for patching-up and improving the existing schools and school system, and start asking basic questions about what kids need and how those needs may best be met. We must stop turning our children over to professionals and experts. We cannot be absolved of our responsibility to provide for our children's intellectual and emotional needs any more than for their nutritional needs. A list of the needs of the young child ought to be the objectives of a child-care center, nursery school, kindergarten, or elementary school:

1. His physical needs, his needs for exercise, large muscle activity, energy release, and his need for play.
2. His nutritional needs, especially for protein; his need for rest.
3. His needs for social interaction with his peers and with adults, that is cooperative rather than competitive; an early and continuing relation of trust with at least one adult; affection, support, and comfort; frequent attention from adults of sufficient duration.
4. His health and medical needs.
5. His need for small muscle development, manipulative skills, and coordination. ,
6. His need for sensory stimulation and opportunities for perceptual growth.
7. His need for affective development, his emotional needs; not only his *sense* development, but nonsense and fantasy growth.
8. His need for experiences that communicate knowledge of himself and respect for himself - as an individual and as a member of the family and community.
9. His need for early, frequent, and varied verbal activities.
10. His need for *familiar* places, things, and activities.
11. His need for order, regularity, and consistency in his surroundings, his schedule, and his treatment.
12. His need for varied, interesting, and challenging experiences.

13. His need for opportunities to explore his surroundings.
14. His need for opportunities for *mastery* and control of places, things, and people.
15. His need for *limits* that develop self-control and ability to cope with frustrations.

Do we not identify a good home for the child as one in which all of these needs are met?[2]

In asking for a termination of the "conspiracy against childhood", as Eda LeShan put it, I would like to stress a central theme found in all the arguments of the school reformers, regardless of their differences. This leitmotif was well stated by Dr. Don Davies of the US Office of Education: "A child's basic needs go beyond reading and math. They include the need for dignity and respect for another human being whom he can trust. A Teacher who cannot meet human needs is not likely to meet educational needs."

REFERENCES

[1]Carl Rogers, **Freedom To Learn,** Columbus, Ohio: Charles E. Merrill Publishing Company, 1969, p. 153.

[2]I am indebted to Dr. Earl Shaefer and Dr. Joe Lipson for many of these points.

III

Educational Accountability:
A Humanistic Perspective

Introduction

Concerned educators, opposed to the narrow focus and application of behavioral objectives, propose a more humanistic approach to educational accountability.

While in favor of accountability, some of these educators view the behavioral objectives mania as an unwanted intrusion into the classroom setting. Others seek to widen and extend the present use of behavioral objectives to focus on more humanistic aspects of education. Still others call for a national commitment to humanizing education and for the increasing use of present and newly developed instruments to encourage and evaluate such a commitment.

In many cases, these educators insist that the rising cry for accountability must be heard beyond educational institutions and demand a greater sense of accountability in the society as a whole. In every case, they have called for a re-assessment and a new understanding of the educational process in the modern world. They insist that educators committed to humanizing education must prove themselves accountable by embodying the humanism they propose.

Two Humanists: A Conversation with Arthur Combs and Sidney Jourard

F. MCLAUGHLIN

We keep looking for something, some gimmick that will make the difference, and I'm convinced that you're not going to change American education until you change the teachers. The change must occur in the hearts, understanding, thinking, beliefs, the values of the people who are running the business.

Arthur Combs and Sidney Jourard are two national leaders in the field of Humanistic Education. Both teach at the University of Florida (Gainesville) where they have been faculty members for more than ten years. Professor Combs has taught in the College of Education; he is past Director of the Center for Humanistic Education. Professor Jourard is in the Department of Psychology; he also has a part-time practice as a consulting psychologist.

I became familiar with Art Combs more than a decade ago when I discovered his article "Seeing is Behaving" in *Educational Leadership*. He is an excellent speaker and a prolific contributor to learned societies and professional publications. The latest of his twelve books are *Helping Relationships: Basic Concepts for the Helping Professions* and *Helping Relationships Source Book*. Both books were written with Donald L. Avila and W. W. Purkey and were published by Allyn and Bacon in 1971. He has written more than a hundred articles, many of which appear in leading textbooks.

Art's undergraduate and graduate work was done at Ohio State University, where he received his Ph.D. in 1945. He has been

F. McLaughlin, "Conversation: Two Humanists," **Media and Methods,** 24-29, December, 1971. Reprinted with permission.

working as a teacher or counselor since 1930. He belongs to more than a dozen professional organizations and in 1967 was the president of the Association of Supervision and Curriculum Development. In talking with Art one senses that this gracious and quiet man can draw from an endless reservoir of lived experience, research, and writings in many fields to illustrate points he wishes to make.

Sidney Jourard is about twenty years younger than Combs. He was born and reared in Canada and completed his undergraduate education at the University of Toronto. His Ph.D. was awarded by the University of Buffalo in 1953. He has written more than thirty articles. Of his five books, *The Transparent Self* is best known and the one which this editor recommends as an introduction to his work. *Disclosing Man to Himself* is a more recent work that develops several of the ideas from the first book in greater detail. Both works are Van Nostrand paper backs. He too has delivered numerous papers at meetings, is in demand as a speaker and has also contributed chapters to many texts in the fields of medicine, psychology, education, and sociology. In addition to being a member of various psychological organizations, he is co-founder of the Center of Man, a growth center in Gainesville.

I discovered Jourard's work purely by chance about a year and a half ago, browsing through an issue of the *American Journal of Nursing*. The provocative insights he presented in "Suicide: The Invitation to Die" prompted me to read the two books mentioned previously. Both, by the way, are characterized by a clear vigorous writing style. There is a Zorbaesque quality about Jourard, a spontaneity that suggests that he is a fresh, original thinker, and the type of person who would make a delightfully unpredictable companion.

McLaughlin: This morning I spoke to a thousand teachers here in Alachua County (Florida). Uppermost in my mind was what I might say to teachers faced with teaching in the usual 30-desk classrooms and restricted by the usual administrative rules and regulations that stifle life in most high schools. What might I have said to help them develop more humane schools?

Combs: I don't know, but I think that's the wrong approach. I don't think we're likely to make much progress in humanizing education if we look at it from that point of view. What we have to do first of all, is to begin to raise some questions in teachers' minds. Charles Silberman points out in his book, *Crisis in the Classroom,* that one of the great problems we have is "mindlessness." There are so many things we do without questioning. To bring about change it is necessary to begin questioning some of the things which have been believed for generations, confronting teachers with the fact that their beliefs need examination. There are dozens of examples — the myth of the value of competition, the myth of the teacher as the fountainhead of knowledge, the myth of grade level organization, the myth of grades as important motivators.

The second thing I think we have to do is repair the terrible damage which has been done throughout the whole educational system by the attempt to industrialize it. We should have learned from industry. The application of industrial techniques to workers dehumanized the worker and the worker organized to beat the system. That's exactly what's happening to our students today; we haven't seemed to have learned anything. We are still trying to industrialize the whole school setup and, in the process, have practically demoralized both students and teachers.

McLaughlin: You mentioned the industrialization of education. As someone involved in putting out a magazine that works closely with publishers and producers of educational materials, I'm concerned about the tremendous pressure commercial people put on teachers by presenting them with packages that are construed as solvers of curricular problems. I'm even more concerned about those schools adopting the systems approach. They do so with the intention of giving the public the most efficient instruction for the least cost. This seems to me to fit with what you're suggesting about the industrialization of education. Administrators are being made accountable for their "school plants"; meanwhile the kids grow more and more frustrated and unmanageable.

Combs: Yes, I think this whole emphasis upon accountability which gets translated into behavioral objectives which in turn get translated into narrow kinds of instruction is another factor which leads to the whole dehumanizing process. The people who are pushing "accountability" also need to be held accountable for what they're doing to the education process. Let me hasten to say here that I don't have anything against the development of devices to make good teaching possible. Indeed, I think that one of the geniuses of the American people is that historically we have always found ways of developing laborsaving devices.

That's great. But there's a difference between developing a laborsaving device and having it control your objectives, goals, and processes; that's where we get into difficulty. I'm not discounting the value of what industry can give us in the way of gadgets and gimmicks.

McLaughlin: What can we do to counter the "systems" people and present a different case to teachers?

Combs: What we have to do is find a way of emphasizing the other half of the equation. Half the learning consists of providing information. That's a fairly mechanical, external kind of thing. The other half, however, is a very personal matter. It has to do with the discovery of meaning. That's where we're sick. We are experts at giving people information — we have all these new gadgets that can do it much better than we've done it before. For instance, the dropout is not a dropout because nobody told him anything — he's a dropout because he never discovered that what he was taught had any relevance for him. This is what the humanist is saying, "we have to pay attention to the *personal problem,* the affective, personal discovery question, the problem of relevance." This is what the humanist movement is about, I think. It is an attempt to redress the balance and to overcome the preoccupation which education has historically had with subject matter and the gadgets, gimmicks, devices, controls, systems to transmit it.

McL: Teachers are low men on the totem pole; they're not considered experts in anything — they're often looked upon as simply functionaries in the system to carry out an instructional program. What can we do to change their feelings about themselves, to sensitize them?

Jourard: I feel like I am being asked to function like an Old Testament prophet (*laughter*) — I don't mean in terms of forecasting the future, but pointing the way. I see the whole issue of education in this country in a slightly different perspective than Art does, partly because I'm really an outsider. I came to this country from Canada, so I can still look at things with a sort of oblique point of view. From my point of view we have, as they are now, teachers and not educators — they are trainers. They are functionaries, they are trained to be functionaries, they accept the training even when they have a lust or passion to wake a child's awareness and his curiosity. They are so strongly trained to administer a curriculum in various, technical ways that if they really want to engage individual students, one at a time, they can be penalized.

American education is an anachronism. As the culture goes through radical changes, the younger generation refuses to go in the paths of my generation. I don't know what the outcome is going to be.

McL: It seems to me when we're dealing with education's plight, we're dealing with the whole cultural drift of American society.

Jourard: Well, the young children, unless they're living in the boondocks, are so much more aware than their elementary and high school teachers. They've been smoking pot, they've been watching TV, they've been hitchhiking all over the country; they are self-sufficient. They're only pretending to be the kind of children whom conventionally trained teachers can teach. They have to impersonate some kind of human being in order not to freak out the teachers who are never trained to relate to these kinds of kids.

Combs: Let me return for a moment to how we might take a new view of systems. I have become keenly aware of two ways you can approach a problem. One, you can approach it logically: you decide what you want to do, you determine your objectives, you analyze the situation, the variables involved, then you go about trying to get people from here to there. That is a closed system. It's a system in which all the answers have been decided in advance. This is the method we use in dealing with problems almost everywhere we look. Earl Kelley once said "Logic is only a systematic way of arriving at the wrong answers." (*laughter*) I think what the humanist movement is saying today is that for the most important *problems* we face, the approach won't work! Instead we must learn to deal with events in which the ultimate outcomes may not be foreseeable when we start. That way we have to help people confront problems, then get in the problem with them and together discover solutions. That's an open-ended system.

I would say that one of our problems is that having been sold on the idea of systems, we define the system in terms of outcome, that is, closed systems. We must develop an approach in which you are interested in process systems rather than ends systems. That is to say, instead of being concerned that the students in my class should come out with the answers which I have decided they must have in order to pass the course — I approach the problem like a psychotherapist does with his patient, not being concerned to produce a specific outcome but creating conditions which will make it possible for the person to make an exploration and to arrive at the appropriate answers for *him*. In my classes I have learned not to be concerned about the specific outcome. What I'm concerned about is, can I create the conditions within which these youngsters will be set free to explore and discover whatever there is to be explored and discovered in the particular area in which I have some expertise. This involves sharing myself and my knowledge with them but does not require or direct them to come out with preconceived solutions. I think you can build systems to create processes. In psychotherapy, for example, the therapist could not care less about whether or not the client gets a divorce — what he's concerned about is creating the conditions in which the client can explore his problem and arrive at the solutions that are best for him. He's concerned about creating processes, not ends. I think that's the direction we have to move in. It also makes good sense in terms of curriculum for we now know that we'll never again be able to have a curriculum which we can require of everyone. The information explosion has destroyed that myth.

McL: This is one of the things that I have been suggesting through my own writing. If you hold that the teacher is an information dispenser, then your view of media sees machines as more powerful and efficient transmitters of information. But essentially what I'm interested in is getting kids involved in making magazines, making films, videotapes, and in the process, learning to think, write, and generally develop their communication skills. Student filmmaking is becoming a very popular mode of *process* education on both high school and college campuses. The problem right now is that most schools and colleges I'm familiar with have structures that resist the kind of processes that you're talking about.

Combs: We're scared to death that we might come up with the wrong answers. I think the same thing you're talking about applies to computers. Up until now we've been using computers to control people. Let's get to the place where we really know how to use computers to serve people, to set them free. Then, I think, we will have turned a corner.

McL: But we have to take an active role. As people who help train teachers, we must help teachers confront their own meaning and the meaning of how they work with children. If we don't do something, other people are going to do something we won't be able to live with.

Combs: Yes, you're right.

Jourard: Look, you're talking about grown men and grown women who are trying to fulfill the meaning of their lives — they want to make a living, they want to have some of the good things of American culture. in some ways, to be a teacher is to be a peculiar kind of martyr in a tremendously materialistic society. You are encouraged to see yourself as a professional person, but you don't get as good a salary as people do in other professions, you don't have the autonomy of a profession, and you're raising the question, "How can we (whoever we are), help them, the teachers (grown men and women), to please us (whoever we are), more." Well, who do we think we are? They're doing a job, I suppose, as well as they can, and as well as the taxpayers and parents and higher levels of economic interest allow it to happen. The teacher gets too big for his or her britches and he or she will be cut down and fired without a hell of a lot to protect him. You get a teacher who has views about politics and economics, and lets them be known, and they don't happen to fit the politics and economics of the community . . he'll be fired.

McL: All right, I don't want to get into the we-and-they thing, but many of the teachers I have talked to are concerned about help-ing kids become "authentic," and to understand what is happening culturally in this country. Where should such teachers turn for help for new techniques, for some support?

Jourard: I don't think it's technique. I think it's role-modeling and being a living exemplar, every teacher, a prophet, every teacher, who by the way he lives his life, a mixture of boldness, cunning, criticism, curiosity, fascination, love, concern, beliefs. His way of being rubs off, it's infectious. And the only way, I suppose, for teachers who aren't that way to become that way is to have heroes, leaders, principals, taxpayers, and others who are them-selves that way and invite them to be that way.

Combs: I think this is one of the places where the group process movement has something to offer to teachers. I am impressed with what Carl Rogers has been doing in helping teachers to consider more than the subject matter, to consider their feelings, attitudes, beliefs, and desires, and to do this in interaction with other people so they begin to value their own belief systems. This is a very valuable approach.

Jourard: Even beyond that, Art, I think encounter groups grew up because there's no encountering and open communication going on in everyday institutional life, everyday family life. The encounter group is almost like a spiritual toilet; it's a place to go and get relief, and then to go back to your life of sham and cosmetics. I think the value of encounter grouping is if, and *only if,* people who are in contact with each other will sit down, without the benefit of experts, and struggle to make their own perspectives known to the others, and open their ears and their hearts to the perspectives of the other persons who are there. And I think out of that kind of dialogue among people of all social classes may come the possibility of a new division of labor which will say, all right, it has become apparent we must help our children become human beings instead of functionaries. It's going to call for this, that, and the other thing. We, the taxpayers and parents, want you the teacher not just to present the straight, square, white upper middle class ideology that was called education, we want you to pluralize it and we'll back you up. That can only come out of some dialogue that isn't happening.

McL: Sid, you've written a great deal about the business of taking risks. Is there any point in your life when you discovered this and this marked a change in your behavior as a person? **Jourard:** I've never been as heroic as I suppose, at some childish level, I'd like to be. I was a sneaky experimenter, explorer when I was much younger and if I have had any progress, it's been to become more publicly experimental in some aspects of my life. I still have a robust sense of not taking risks with myself or somebody else. And, of course, I still retain a strong sense of my privacy.

There's two kinds of influence, it seems to me. Those who make a commitment to shape up people behaviorally, intellectually, ideologically, because they feel it's right and proper and they get financial backing to do it. Indoctrinating people in basic skills so that they can survive is very useful and very important. But equally important and more neglected in the West, is the *prophetic* function to challenge all that — to say what the hell is it all for anyway — not just to challenge it in words but to put your body where your mouth is and to explore other ways — there isn't a part of my life that I haven't challenged and explored and questioned. I question marriage, the way I raise my children. I raise questions about the way I do my work, how I play. A lot of it is scary. I haven't yet come up with any magical answers. To actually explore and test in more than words, it seems to me, is a very important educational function.

Combs: A good example is the basic idea of democracy. When men are free, they can find their own best ways, but damn few people are willing to put that to the test. They say "Yes, I believe that *but* not in this case. Yes, I think that's true *except* that . . ." It seems to me that that's related to the kind of authenticity we were talking about before. I think Sid is talking about that too — that there are an awful lot of people who are not really willing to behave in terms of their honest beliefs. I think that means, however, that we also have to give some concern not only to the fact that people *express* their values but to know somehow they've been able to explore them and determine whether they're effective values.

Jourard: But exploration is discouraged in American education and American life — it's a most peculiar thing. You probably have to be an historian to make sense out of it. It's a mania for security, the avoidance of economic risk-taking. Economic security is seen as the equivalent of the attainment of heaven. Younger people, in many cases, don't have that economic horror because they didn't grow up in the Depression. They're looking for adventure and sense an aliveness in their bodies, a curiosity, a wanting to try a large number of things to which a more security oriented person would respond, "I can't afford the time to experiment and explore because if I do I won't be doing what I should be doing, which is enhancing my earning powers and taking care of my fences." And, teachers, I think, unwittingly purvey this lust for security, for right answers.

Combs: One of the things we've been doing here for the last 3 years is training elementary teachers based on different assumptions as well as the conventional ones. In the new program, we see the production of a good teacher as a problem in becoming, in which we have to help a person find his way of operating. I think it's clearly seen in the term-end interviews we have been having the last few weeks. When we say to the old students, "Now you're gonna teach next quarter, what are you gonna do?" They'll tell you, "I'm going to do this, this, and this." They've already decided, they're already fenced in, they're already a closed system. The new students don't say that. You say "What are you going out to teach next quarter, and what are you going to do?" They say, "I don't know. I won't know until I get there, feel out the situation, see what the kids are like, see what the teachers and the principal are doing. Then I'll know!" They say it just like that. That's quite a different philosophical approach.

McL: You know, Art, the problem is we don't have any lobby to massively present some kind of counter approach to the American public. I recently quit my job and took a huge pay cut to return to teaching because I got involved in an institution that believed that the systems approach was *the* approach and no administrators there had the faintest idea of what these kids thought or felt or wanted to learn. I tried for a year and a half until I found I just could not make any accommodation with these people. But in the process of working there, I discovered to my dismay, that other "technocratic true believers," like those I worked with, are moving into state departments all over this country, and even in Latin and South America.

Jourard: If you want an even better example of behavioral objectives, and a state apparatus that carries them out, look, at Nazi culture which worked for a while. And then also look at George Orwell's *1984* and Huxley's *Brave New World*. If you have seized responsibility for "shaping up" the next generation, what better way to do it than with modern technology, bribery, and threats? In the last analysis, behavioral objectives are implemented by bribery and threats — if you don't do it, terrible things will happen. If you do do it, you'll get a reward. That's bribery and threats, anyway you look at it.

And it works. Except that there's always the saving remnant of people who either become martyrs who will be neither bribed nor threatened, or they're cunning and they impersonate the people who are bribed and threatened. But secretly they form a society which lives a different way of life. In some ways, I suppose you may even find some members of the teaching profession who pretend to be doing behavioral objectives just to keep people off their backs, but secretly are educating and inspiring students and finding the ones who don't want to be bribed and threatened into this or that but really want to study something.

McL: Sid, the interesting thing was, that was beginning to happen. But, more discouraging was the mania for creating an elaborate maze of learning packages, keyed by behavioral objectives, that students could plug into.

Jourard: So you end with a "systems" approach with "packaged learning" in order to turn out a product. Now, when I hear people talk like that I become very angry. I certainly don't want my children indoctrinated that way. They wouldn't put up with it anyway.

Combs: We've done quite a bit of research here in Florida on the helping professions and two fascinating things become clear, one — all the good helpers have broad rather than narrow objectives. If you ask the good ones what they're going to do they give you some broad beautiful generality. The poor ones say I want to do this "little bitty thing" today. The other observation is that objectivity correlates negatively with effectiveness.

McL: You talked about this when I heard you in Chicago. Would you elaborate on that?

Combs: Well, what I mean is when you do research, as we have on teachers, counselors, nurses, and Episcopal priests, the good ones have a subjective approach to their work, not an objective one. The good ones are empathically or phenomenologically oriented rather than being concerned with how things look from their point of view.

Jourard: "Objectivity" is another way of saying "I'm concerned that people fit into patterns." "Subjectivity" in that context means a respect for a variety of ways for the world to be experienced. A good helper is fascinated with someone who experiences the world in another way; he isn't upset by variety.

Combs: One of the things I think needs to come about if we are to humanize education is a different approach to payoffs. Teachers do what they're paid for. The coach is judged on how many teams he beats, the English teacher on how many kids write articles, and the reading teacher on how many kids learn to read. But nobody is asking, what about valuing? What about discovering? What about exploring? Those are *general* objectives and general objectives are generally ignored in favor of specific ones. I think we have to find ways of paying off the teachers who did a good job in developing a creative thinking, caring, valuing student. Until we do, it ain't gonna happen. People do what seems to them to be important. We have to make it important; otherwise, it won't occur. I think we're making some progress in this direction;

I think fascinating innovations are going on in places where teachers respect students and respect themselves. It's tough going though because we have to buck the whole industrailization pressure currently supposed to save our schools.

McL: Do you think the humanists will ever get it enough together organizationally to present an institutional alternative to say, the behavioral engineers? Or is it by nature a fragmentary movement?

Jourard: I don't know. Humanism is a very loose term. You get ten humanists together, and you will find it very hard for them to agree on anything but the necessity of pluralism.

Combs: This is one of the hard things about humanists. They don't take kindly to organization, and definition is organization. Trying to get a bunch of humanists to do something is like trying to decide where to go on a picnic, non-directively. Everybody sits around and says where do you think we ought to go and nobody comes up with any answers. We have that problem here. We've been trying to get some of our humanists together on this campus (laughter).

Jourard: Maybe God was trying to tell us something . . . (laughter)

Combs: We enjoy each other but we ain't about to enter into an organization with each other.

McL: Human beings need organizations, institutions, in which their energies are organized to work out problems that confront them. Without organizations, society would collapse, the species would not be able to sustain itself.

Jourard: I believe that. This is where I disagree with a lot of young people. The problem is to create institutions (and you notice here that I'm avoiding your question) — marriage, the family, or schools, etc. — that are run by people who don't have a commitment to keep the structure of the institution the way it was the day it was invented. I'm convinced the family structure, the way its been lived, is the main cause of disease in affluent America. Because as people live in tightly defined roles long after they are meaningful, it takes more and more out of them to stay in it. When you stay in something that is depressing you and stressing you long enough, you get heart attacks, cancer. The base line is not the way an institution looks but how the human beings feel as they live in it. It takes guts and imagination to change it so that one stays alive.

Combs: It seems to me, Sid, we're talking about form and essence. Sometimes you need to have the form before you can understand the essence. It was pointed out, for example, that Christ stated the essence of an idea and Paul gave us a church, and it's the church that's been causing us trouble ever since. I think the same is true about what you said, Frank, about needing organization — that's the form, and indeed we do. Sometimes we need enough organization so that we can get to the place so we can see what the essence is. But the problem is we oftentimes glorify the form and the form becomes institutionalized and develops values in its own right. That's what gets us into real trouble, it seems to me. Sometimes we have to break through and rediscover the essence of what we are trying to accomplish.

McL: Let me pose one final question. If either of you could bring about one change in the way adolescents are taught in high schools today, is there any one thing you would try for in a school situation? Let me phrase that another way. Is there any one thing that you would like to see happen or that you predict might happen to help schools become humane institutions?

Combs: I think your question runs directly contrary to what I'm convinced is the final solution. We keep looking for something, some gimmick that will make the difference, and I'm convinced that you're not going to change American education until you change the teachers. The change must occur in the hearts, understanding, thinking, beliefs, the values of the people who are running the business. We found in our research that there's no such thing as a good method or right method of teaching. I think there is no such thing as a good method or right method of organizing or administering or teaching. All that has to do with the forms. Much more important, the basic revolution has to be in the belief systems, in the consideration of what's important. It makes a hell of a lot of difference what a teacher believes is important. It shows in spite of her, and that's where the change has to be made. If you have a teacher who values giving kids freedom, she'll find ways of expressing it. If you find ways of having a teacher value what a child believes about himself, the teacher will find ways of building that. The difficulty is we haven't been able to concentrate on belief systems. That's where I'm looking for changes. I can't get excited about organizational systems . . .

Jourard: I think I would lower the age at which children can legally drop out of formal schooling to about 12. My stream of associations runs something like this: "Well, why don't we put education and training on a free enterprise basis, instead of letting the taxes do it. Governments can't leave such minimum indoctrination to chance. I think there's some wisdom in having compulsory education up to a certain level. I have a stereotype about the French. French education is strict as hell, and people who come out with a high school education there are very learned, skeptical human beings. They succeed in ways where we fail, despite cruddy classrooms, irascible teachers. Can you imagine John-Paul Sartre teaching high school in this country? Teaching philosophy? There's a case where I think, at least part of their required, public education works. Without any particular enlightened permissive this or that, or packaging. Thinking of educational alternatives, I know some young people who are trying to open up learning communites that don't have curricula, and I think it's grand to have such available against a backdrop of structure. I think if compulsory education limited itself to reading, writing, arithmetic, language, and thereafter people sought what they want, whether it's how to become a mechanic. . . . I think that would be an advance.

McL: Thank you.

The Cultivation of Idiosyncrasy

HAROLD BENJAMIN

That society which comes closest to developing every socially useful idiosyncrasy in every one of its members will make the greatest progress toward its goals.

In a tale given to American educators by George H. Reavis the wild creatures once had a school in the woods. All the animals had to take all the subjects. Swimming, running, jumping, climbing, and flying made up the required curriculum.

This was a school of no nonsense. It was a good, liberal educational institution. It gave broad general training — and instruction — and education too.

Some animals, of course, were better students than others. The squirrel, for example, got straight A's from the first in running, jumping, and climbing. He got a good passing grade, moreover, in swimming. It looked as though he would make Phi Beta Kappa in his junior year, but he had trouble with flying. Not that he was unable to fly. He could fly. He climbed to the top of tree after tree and sailed through the air to neighboring trees with ease. As he modestly observed, he was a flying squirrel by race. The teacher of flying pointed out, however, that the squirrel was always losing altitude in his gliding and insisted that he should take off in the approved fashion from the ground. Indeed, the teacher decided that the taking-off-from-the-ground unit had to be mastered first, as was logical, and so he drilled the squirrel day after day on the take-off.

Harold Benjamin, **Cultivation of Idiosyncrasy.** The Inglis Lecture, Cambridge, Mass., Harvard University Press. Copyright © 1949 by the President and Fellows of Harvard College. Reprinted by permission.

The flying teacher's practice in this case was in strict accord with the educational philosophy of the school. The teachers recognized that students would necessarily display great variations in their abilities. In the Woods Normal Schools, as a matter of fact, the teachers had learned a great deal about individual differences and the consequent tremendous ranges in human capacities. They set themselves doggedly, therefore, to the task of reducing these differences as best they might, that sane likenesses, safe unities, and noble conformities might prevail in the woods.

The squirrel tried hard. He tried so hard he got severe Charley horses in both hind legs, and thus crippled he became incapable even of running, jumping, or climbing. He left school a failure, and died soon thereafter of starvation, being unable to gather and store nuts. He was cheerful to the last and was much beloved by his teachers and fellow pupils. He had the highest regard for his alma mater, regretting only the peculiar incapacity which had kept him from passing the course in flying.

The snake was a promising student also. Being a combination tree-and-water snake, he was excellent in both climbing and swimming. He was also a superior runner and passed the tests in that subject with ease. But he began to show antisocial tendencies in arguments with the instructor in jumping. When he had been given the basic instruction in that subject and it came time for him to make his first jump, he coiled up and threw himself almost his full length. This was not jumping, said the teacher. It was merely striking — a snake skill — and not at all the general-education jumping which all cultivated creatures had to know.

"What kind of jumping is of any use to a snake," demanded the student, "except this kind?" Then he coiled up and struck again, or jumped, as he called it, with the beginning of a bitter sneer on his face.

The teacher of jumping remonstrated with him, tried to get him to jump properly, and used the very best methods taught in the more advanced demonstration schools, but the snake became more and more uncooperative. The school counselors and the principal were called in and decided to attempt to vary the snake's education by teaching him flying, but to their distress he flatly refused even to attend the preliminary classes in that subject. He did not say he was unable to fly — he merely scoffed at the notion of flying for a snake and said that he had no intention of ever bothering with the subject. The more the teachers argued with him the more he coiled and struck and sneered, and the more he sneered and coiled and struck the more bitter and introverted he became. He left school and made his living briefly as a highwayman, murdering other animals along the woods paths, until he struck at a wildcat one evening and was clawed to death for his lack of judgment. He died detested by all and mourned by none.

The eagle was a truly brilliant student. His flying was superb, his running and jumping were of the best, and he even passed the swimming test, although the teacher tried to keep him from using his wings too much. By employing his talons and beak, moreover, he could climb after a fashion and no doubt he would have been able to pass that course, too, except that he always flew to the top of the problem tree or cliff when the teacher's back was turned and sat there lazily in the sun, preening his feathers and staring arrogantly down at his fellow students climbing up the hard way. The teachers reasoned with him to no avail. He would not study climbing seriously. At first he turned aside the faculty's importunities with relatively mild wisecracks and innuendoes, but as the teachers put more pressure upon him he reacted with more and more feeling. He became very aggressive, stating harshly and boldly that he knew more about climbing than did the professor of that subject. He became very successful when he left school and he attained high position in the woods society. He was dogmatic and dictatorial, respected by all and feared by many. He became a great supporter of general education. He wanted the curriculum of his alma mater to remain just as it was, except that he believed climbing had no general cultural value and should be replaced by some more liberal subject, like dive-bombing, which in his view, gave the student a certain general polish superior even to that given by the study of flying.

The gopher parents thought that the school was very good in most matters and that all the subjects gave excellent results if properly taught, but they wanted their children to learn digging in addition to the general education. The teachers regarded digging as a manual skill, not elevated enough for general culture. Besides, they did not know how to dig and they resisted learning such a subject.

So the gophers withdrew their children from this institution and hired a practical prairie dog to set up a private school in which an extensive course was given in digging. The prairie dog schoolmaster also taught courses in running, jumping, swimming, and climbing. He did not teach flying. He said it was an outmoded subject. Digging, a more practical subject, took its place in the curriculum. So the ducks and geese and wild turkeys and prairie chickens all scoffed at the prairie dog's school. They set up schools of their own, very much like the other schools except that the ducks and geese emphasized diving and the wild turkeys and prairie chickens gave advanced courses in evasive air tactics.

At this juncture, Old Man Coyote, who had been studying the development of education in the woods, shrewdly observed, "All these pedagogical characters are going at this business wrong end to. They look at what animals and birds — a lot of animals and birds — do and need to do. Then they put those needs and those doings into formal schoolings and try to make the little pups and cubs and fledglings fit the schoolings. It's haywire, wacky, and will never really work right."

Tom Gunn's Mule, a sour-visaged individual, ready to criticize all theories, heard Old Man Coyote's remark and demanded harshly, "If you're so smart, how would you do it?"

"Why, I would turn the whole thing around," explained Old Man Coyote modestly.

"Turn it around?" scoffed Tom Gunn's Mule. "What d'ye mean, turn it around?"

"These school people start with things that birds and animals do — or even more often what they did some time ago," explained Old Man Coyote. "Then the teachers hammer these doings — or as much of them as they can handle and as they think high-toned enough — into schoolings, courses, curriculums, and subjects. Then they hammer the pups into the schoolings. It's a rough and dopey process, and the teachers have had to invent good explanations to defend it. Discipline, culture, systematic training — things like that — are what the teachers use for this purpose. I don't know what they mean and I think the teachers don't know what they mean, but I do know they make a lot of cubs and pups and fledglings mean and rough and dopey when they could and should make them good and slick and smart."

"Sure, sure," snorted Tom Gunn's Mule, "But you still haven't told me how you would do it."

"Turn it around," said Old Man Coyote. "Start with the pups. See what the pups do. Then see what the school can do for the pups. Then see what the pups and the school together can do for all the creatures in the woods. Simple — forwards instead of backwards — right end to instead of wrong end to."

Old Man Coyote turned triumphantly and started to trot away.

"Hey!" shouted Tom Gunn's Mule. "Wait! These teachers have schools now. They have to run those schools. They are practical people. Just how, specifically and precisely, would you tell them to change their schools so as to get their education right end to, as you call it?"

Old Man Coyote patted a yawn with the back of his forepaw. "I lay down general principles," he said. "These schoolteachers have got to figure out some of the minor details themselves."

This is the end of the story, but I am a schoolteacher myself, and so I have been trying to figure out a few of the details upon which Old Man Coyote touched. . . .

It has been almost a quarter century since Truman Lee Kelley presented evidence to show how nurture operates upon children to reduce certain of their most socially useful idiosyncrasies. He observed parenthetically in this connection that school men appeared to resent oddity in their pupils, that too often they were pedagogical plainsmen, lovers of the dead level and organizers of mediocrity, and that under an egalitarian banner they flouted democratic equality by plying a Procrustean trade of forcing the weak and stunting the strong. Hugging their precious averages and norms, said Kelley, they spent their professional lives in a process of weary shoveling to fill valleys and steady erosion to remove mountains of human capacity. He asked that the policies and practices which produced this kind of education should be rigorously examined and drastically modified.[1]

. . . I believe that the central question is one which a democratic society may ignore only at its deadly peril.

The question is double-barreled:

1. How much uniformity does this society need for safety?
2. How much deviation does this society require for progress?

The insight with which the line of safety is drawn and the skill with which the conditions of progress are embodied in an educational program determine in large measure whether a particular society will be a great society or a mean society, whether it will be strong or weak, whether it will be enduring or evanescent, whether it will be a creator and bearer of high meanings or a purveyor of the insignificances of ignorance and brutality.

The first steps in determining an educational program, whether for an entire national group, for a particular profession, or for a small number of students in a classroom, are the steps that are most commonly slighted. They are often assumed to have been taken when in fact they have been by-passed.

What are these first steps? Let us look at an example. Because the defenders of educational plainsmanship are often especially worried over a lack of the uniformities which they consider necessary for national security, let us take our first example from the area of military education . . .

We Americans often put . . . young officers into battle after we have so trained them on a thorough plainsman's level and are lucky enough to have stout old human nature — tough, resilient, and resistant of uniformity — come to our rescue. Many times in our history it has been this triumph of native difference over a dead level of training which has enabled us to win our battles. Individual idiosyncrasy, brilliant nonconformity, and daring disregard of the tenets of military plainsmanship have consistently dragged victory from defeat which has been prepared by faithful copying of standard models.

"Whenever I met one of them generals who fit by note," said Nathan Bedford Forrest accurately and without false modesty, "I always whipped him before he could pitch the tune." If Forrest could have been sent to West Point in his youth and trained into being a more faithful copy of Braxton Bragg or Samuel D. Sturgis, if General George Washington had been commissioned in the British Regulars at an early age and made much more like Lord Howe or Charles Lee, if Chief Joseph of the Nez Percés and Crazy Horse of the Oglala Sioux could only have had the advantages of a military education to model them after Captain Fetterman and Colonel Custer, the history of the United States' wars would be considerably less marked by peaks.

It is an ironic testimonial to the power of the educational plainsman's philosophy that in the very field of human endeavor where cultivated idiosyncrasy pays off most spectacularly and in clearest-cut physical terms, the doctrine of the approved doctrine, the uniformity of the uniform practice, and the massing of mediocrity should have held such undisputed sway. Here if anywhere it might perhaps seem that educators would revolt against the practices of pedagogical plainsmanship and become educational mountaineers. Here was where mountaineering would give results which nations commonly assess at high value. But the strength of conformity-enforcing agencies was too great. The shadow of Frederick of Prussia with his stiffly aligned peasants-in-arms moving in unison was too much even for men who saw demonstrated almost every year the battle superiority in American woods of non-alignment and non-unison. No matter; the principle of the pedagogical plainsman still triumphed. It was never more brilliantly expressed in action than on that memorable day on the Monongahela when Major General Sir Edward Braddock lined up his exhausted men as they staggered from the woods and gave them a stiff dose of manual-of-arms and close-order drill in preparation for the coming attack of the French and Indian skirmishers. Almost two centuries later, his spiritual and professional decendants still keep his memory green by an improved manual-of-arms and an improved close-order drill which are just as effective today as their predecessors were in the middle of the eighteen century. . . .

Would you then not have a standard education for infantry officers? Would there be no minimum essentials for second lieutenants? Gad, Sir! I can see the veins turn purple in the colonel's neck. I can hear his fist hammer on the desk.

But not all colonels would so respond — not nearly so many as you might think; not even so many colonels, perhaps, as presidents and chancellors, deans and professors, superintendents and principals, teachers and headmasters, regents and trustees, parents and clergymen, legislators and those men-in-the-street who sometimes retire to their homes and write letters to the editor.

All of us tend to echo these doubting cries. All of us are prisoners of our schooling — a schooling based on some combination of the concepts of the uniform and level noble-traits or specific-skills. The first article in our pedagogical faith is the *credo* of minimum standards. That *credo* lies flatly athwart the law and the gospel of Old Man Coyote's theory of education.

Old Man Coyote insists that the boy whose mathematical, linguistic, geographical, or other peaks of ability are built to great heights will have his valleys of ability in other areas pulled up towards his peaks until the sum of his achievements will be far above the minimum essentials ever set by plodding plainsmen. Old Man Coyote insists further that the learner must go above his present peaks and valleys as a free, daring, and enterprising individual and never as one herded under the lash of a minimum standard.

This is a hard doctrine for us to accept. It is hard for us because we have confused our minimum standards with our objectives.

Our objective, in the case of military education, for example, is to keep the peace as long as possible and, when wars break out, to stop them as quickly and as efficiently as we can. The minimum essential is a lazy plainsman's device for shortcutting the objective. The sturdy mountaineer looks keenly across the land at the goal as he ascends every peak.

The observed facts of human development support Old Man Coyote's doctrine. Few if any men ever became great historians or great citizens by studying the outlines of history required in the freshman year. Few if any men ever became great infantry leaders by concentrating on the dead level of infantry fundamentals. Few if any great jurists, painters, industrialists, or musicians ever attained their heights of uniqueness by drill on the minimum essentials.

"But Gad; Sir!" repeats my hypothetical colonel or professor or Tom Gunn's Mule, "We are not educating great generals, unusual soldiers, geniuses — we are just aiming modestly and in a common-sense way to train ordinary, dead-level, good infantry officers — interchangeable-standard-uniform. You'd have them at least speak English, wouldn't you? You'd have them know how to load and fire an M-I, wouldn't you?"

"Ah!" says Old Man Coyote, "I would have no ordinary, dead-level officers — they would all be great officers in terms of their abilities — because that's a better way to win wars — and certainly some of them might not speak English or know how to load and fire an M-I rifle. Some of them might speak only Spanish, for instance, in the San Martin Corps of the United States Foreign Legion, and some of them might command only mortar platoons."

"A likely situation," snorts Tom Gunn's Mule.

"It would be a lot more likely in the American Army," softly observes Old Man Coyote, "if the present brass had been educated forwards instead of backwards."

I have used these second lieutenants as examples in part because the objective of their education is relatively easy to see. Let us now consider examples of a kind of education which perhaps does not have such easily seen objectives.

Suppose it is teachers rather than infantry officers whom we are educating. Suppose we need one thousand new teachers in Massachusetts or Maryland next fall. Shall we seek in the teachers' colleges of these states to turn out a thousand more or less faithful copies of a model teacher? Shall we give marks of *A* to those most nearly approaching the approved pattern and marks of *C* or *D* to those furthest away from the pattern but still not so far away as to deserve being failed? Do we really want them all to act, look, talk, teach, and think alike? Are the deviations from the model which they display merely the measures of our inefficiency in teaching them, in bringing them up to the straight-*A* standards of near perfection?

"Ah! No, no!" we say hastily. "We who educate teachers have studied individual differences. Most of us who are old enough to affect the policies of teacher-training institutions studied individual differences in Volume III of Edward L. Thorndike's *Educational Psychology,* first published in 1914. We have known about individual differences for a long, long time. We try to develop the individual differences, the idiosyncrasies, of these teachers. We want to develop their idiosyncrasies in groups. We want blocs of idiosyncrasy. We need fifty different kinds of teachers next year, English and Social Studies teachers for small high schools, boys' physical education teachers who can also take a section in biology, mathematics and physics teachers, girls' counselors who can teach French, vocational agriculture teachers, home economics teachers, and so on. Certainly we want idiosyncrasies — in standard groups, that is."

The Old Man Coyotes murmur that we want developed useful idiosyncrasies. Useful for what? Useful for our objectives? Are those objectives standard, minimum-essential objectives? They should not be. They should be as varied as the children whose learning these teachers are to aid. We want one thousand uniquely educated teachers. We want teachers whose idosyncrasies have been nurtured for unique learnings in schools.

Here is a prospective teacher whose interests and abilities in the nature and processes of child growth and development are exceptional. We shall not try to hold him back in this idiosyncrasy in order to flatten his ability peaks. We shall work with him to build up those peaks.

Shall we ignore this prospective teacher's valleys of ability in written communication, in science, in mathematics? Not at all, but we shall try to haul them up only by tying them to his rising peaks of ability. If we build his peak of understanding and skill in child growth and development high enough, his lower abilities in speaking, writing, computing, and biology can be brought far above the modest levels set by a plainsman's minimum essentials.

Suppose it is a citizen of the United States that we are educating in the secondary school, for example. Is not this situation fundamentally different from one in which we are trying to produce Army officers or schoolteachers? Can we not make a better case here for the plainsman's education? Do not all citizens have to vote intelligently; read newspapers and listen to radio commentators critically; write letters to friends; make a living by applications of science, mathematics, economics, and manual skills; be an amiable member of a family; and perhaps even create and enjoy beauty in line, form, color, tone, melody, and rhythm?

Do we not have in these activities of the good citizen the bases of the general standards which education must meet? Are not these the doings we must use to construct schoolings through which all good citizens must pass? Is not this, the secondary school, the real yoke of general education to which all proper citizens must learn to bow? Must not all educated men and women pass under that yoke in true subjugation of spirit and intellect to make a society strong? . . .

Questions like these provide the real test of adherence to a theory of education as the cultivation of idiosyncrasy. The educational mountaineer replies to them by saying that no subject is pedagogically sacred, no matter what its patriotic, religious, or utilitarian status may be; that only the individual personality is an end in itself, and that education must therefore be a process of developing individuals by means of schoolings rather than a process of bringing learners up to a standard of schoolings.

The plainsman does not often say just the opposite of this, but he has to act thus or betray his plainsmanship. He is forced into a series of acts which constitute much of the business of many modern systems of education.

There is first and always the business of curriculum construction. In general education, it is a process not only of determining what is a sacred subject but also of assessing degrees of sacredness and indicating where in a child's life the subjects should be learned. Thus the Gettysburg Address is obviously sacred and must be memorized by all sixth graders. What is the verdict on Washington's Farewell Address? It is not quite so sacred perhaps and does not need to be memorized. Let it be studied by all ninth graders carefully and respectfully. What of Franklin's Autobiography? Of Hamilton's and Madison's essays? Of Grant's Memoirs? Of Franklin D. Roosevelt's speeches?

If Cervantes is to be studied by everyone in high school, where are Goethe, Dante, and Racine to be met? If the multiplication tables to twelve times twelve are needed by everybody fourteen years of age, twelve times thirteen, fifteen times nineteen, and many other combinations as far as twenty times twenty must be good general education for many if not all persons who are eighteen years of age.

This is the first mark of the pedagogical plainsman, therefore; that he is continually constructing curricula, sorting subjects, fussing over facts, determining the significance of dates, tampering with time allotments, and computing percentages of sacredness.

He can be seen most clearly when he is working on very simple materials.

"Ah, 1492," he mutters, "there's a must for Americans; and 1776 — no doubt about that one — it goes in the *all-100 per cent* compartment; so do 1812, 1861, 1898, 1917, and 1941. Those are easy, but some of these others are difficult; 1789, 1848, 1912, and 1933, for example; 1789 can't be quite so sacred — put it in high school European history where it is not required; and 1933 is college stuff and not really a foundation of Americanism — it is New Dealish besides."

The most popular exemplification of the pedagogical plainsman's curriculum theory is found in the radio quiz program; its most high-toned manifestation is in current lists of great books. It was never more dramatically displayed in action on this continent than when the Ghost Dance craze swept over the Western country in the eighties of the last century. Here was a sacred schooling for a defeated, starving people. The Indians must dance, the ghostly teachers said, and Tauka Wakan would then wipe out the white men and bring back the buffalo. There was just one subject — the sacred dance. It made its graduates immune to white man's weapons. It was the greatest single educational short cut ever offered to Americans but its vogue ended abruptly on December 24, 1889, as a battery of four Hotchkiss guns poured explosive shells into a huddled group of Indian men, women, and children.

The quiz-program masters are just playing at education for a sheltered people's escapism, and thus they have need for only play counters in their game. The great-books professors have a closed game, very serious, and, since they pay all bets in great-books chips, they can operate happily so long as they stay inside the charmed circle. The unfortunate Sioux ghost-dancers at Wounded Knee Creek were forced to count their scores with their lives; their subject was not sacred enough for Hotchkiss guns.

A corollary activity for the pedagogical plainsman is the drawing of curricular distinctions. He traces the boundaries between general education and special education, between liberal studies and vocational training, between pure science and applied science, between the arts and the humanities, between philosophy and religion, between psychology and sociology, between history and anthropology, and so on and on into the academic night.

The more boundaries he surveys, the more new ones he discovers. He finds subjects within subjects, heaps classifications upon dichotomies, and uncovers new fields for education in never-ending labor.

In the plainsman's practice, the duty of the individual learner is clear. He must acquire, adjust, and conform. He must acquire subjects, knowledge, skills, in proper blocs and sequences and at the proper time. He must adjust to the teacher, to the class, and to the community in terms of his knowledge and skills. He must conform in those adjustments to the dictates of society, vocation, government, religion, and other ruling systems of behavior and thought.

The acquire-adjust-conform combination has seldom been so well exemplified as in the pre-1945 Japanese system of education and culture which began with bowing to the Emperor's portrait and ended with thought police. It is a matter for sober reflection that a very similar education could be initiated with flag idolatry and developed, through avoidance of disloyal acts, to a complete rejection of any ideas which might be held by subversive groups.

I say *could be*, since it is hard for us Americans to conceive of a situation in which our thoughts would be policed. Unconsciously we rely upon a type of mountaineering in our education to protect us in the free exercise of idiosyncrasy in thought, at least. We should ask ourselves, however, whether the official thought-control process is not already at work when a committee of the Congress through the newspapers accuses a government scientist of disloyalty, and then refuses for months to give him a hearing. How much freedom of thought, under such conditions, remains to government workers or to young men and women aspiring to be employed by the government?

Not long ago almost any student of American education would have said that thought policing by applying the doctrine of guilt through thought association would be impossible in the United States of America. Today [1949] he could not be so sure. The year 1949 marked the issuance of a document by the headquarters of the Supreme Commander for the Allied Powers in Japan in which American citizens were solemnly told that the history of a Soviet Spy ring in Japan prior to World War II shows us that we cannot trust the loyalty of our closest friends or even relatives, and that persons who have sympathized with Communist causes, even though not themselves Communists, must be prevented from occupying security positions.

Upon this basis, of course, the Commander-in-Chief of the United States Armed Forces would be called by any Dixiecrat a very poor national security risk. He should not be given access even to restricted and much less to confidential or secret materials. He has proposed a civil-rights program for Negroes which the Communist Party supports. Every public-school man in the United States who believes in free and compulsory education is a poor security risk. Every Communist government in the world preaches the same doctrine. The president of the University of Maryland has been assailed by a local news sheet on the chief grounds that he is trying to give higher education to young men and women whose parents cannot afford to pay private college tuition fees. According to the guilt-by-association theory, the paper has an open-and-shut case against the president. Every Communist in Maryland agrees with him. So do many of the clergymen of the Roman Catholic Church, and the president might well be accused, therefore, of subservience to a foreign power, the Holy See.

These are not merely straws in the wind — they are more like haystacks in the cyclone. The loudmouthed declaimer of the correct thought, the patrioteer who screams most passionately of loyalty while stealing from the tax payers . . . these are signs of a culture passing in some parts under the tutelage of pedagogical plainsman.

The defense against this drift towards pedagogical plainsman-ship cannot be bought by arms, by law, or even by exhortation. It can be purchased only at the price of a mountaineering education of democratic power and scope.

The creed of the educational mountaineer provides that force to do democracy's work. It contains two main articles of faith. The first is that of equality of opportunity; the second is that of equality of efficiency.

To give equality of opportunity, the mountaineering educator starts with a maximum of understanding for every child. That means that every child will be studied as precisely and extensively as present techniques allow. The crippled, six-year-old girl of modest intellectual ability will get just as much understanding as research and practice can provide. The physically perfect six-year-old boy of highest intellectual capacity will also get just as much understanding as research and practice can provide.

Why not give more understanding to the child with the higher ability?

It cannot be done. There is no more understanding available than the educational mountaineer gives to every one of his learners.

To give equality of efficiency, the educational mountaineer develops the crippled six-year-old's personality, let us say, by teaching her tap-dancing. She can move her right foot only by dragging it on the floor, but she can lift her left foot off the floor and move the toe and heel. She learns to tap-dance with her left foot.

"Tap-dancing a first-grade subject?" screams the plainsman. "If it's good for one child, it's good for all of them. Democracy demands that they all learn the multiplication tables. If democracy demands tap-dancing at all, it demands it for all."

The mountaineer says, "I am not teaching tap-dancing. I am teaching a shy child to be more confident. I am taking a tiny peak of ability and trying to make it a tower of idiosyncrasy by which one who may be some day a great woman in her own right can get her first secure moorings."

The educational mountaineer develops the six-year-old of high intellectual capacity by encouraging him to study osmosis.

"Osmosis in the first grade?" cries the plainsman. "Osmosis is a high-school subject. That's where we teach it for everybody in good democratic fashion."

But the mountaneer says again, "I am not teaching osmosis. I am teaching one who is a great genius to be in truth the great genius that he is."

Here I pause to point out the inescapable fact that the mountaineer must know how to teach tap-dancing and osmosis if he is going to use them as means of developing personalities and characters. In a reasonable long lifetime of observation of educational plainsmen and educational mountaineers in many kinds of schools and in many parts of the globe, I have seen no slightest evidence that those teachers who believe that education starts, proceeds, and ends with a developing individual have as a group any less erudition and command of subject matter than have those teachers who believe that education starts with a required curriculum and ends with mastery of a minimum essential. I have indeed seen evidence to indicate that a truly profound command of a field of knowledge inclines men toward the pedagogical peaks. How else can we account for the prevalence of mountaineers in the great graduate schools?

Whether the mountaineer is in the graduate school or in the first grade, whether he is educating citizens in the high school or officers in the Army, his answers to the double-barrelled quesiton raised earlier in this lecture are clear, concise, and unequivocal.

How much uniformity does this society need for safety?

It needs only that uniformity which the achievements of its greatest goals require. It demands security of life and health for its people. It demands wide opportunities for its people in work and play, in song and prayer. It must provide each individual with maximum aids to the development of his powers to contribute in every way possible to the great goals of his people.

Are there necessary restrictions on the individual's development? Of course there are. Should there be guidance, direction, in the building of his abilities? Of course there should be. The child with an idiosyncrasy of aggression cannot be permitted to develop it into an idiosyncrasy for brutality, mayhem, or murder. He must instead be helped to develop it into an idiosyncrasy for fighting disease through the practice of medicine, battling hunger by farming, breaking down isolation by blasting highways through mountains, or doing some other aggressive job commensurate with his pattern of abilities.

How much deviation does this society require for progress?

It requires just as much deviation, just as many uniquely developed peaks of ability, just as much idiosyncrasy as the attainment of its goals will allow and need. All societies are wasteful of the capacities of their people. That society which comes closest to developing every socially useful idiosyncrasy in every one of its members will make the greatest progress toward its goals.

The key decision on both the matter of minimum safety and the matter of maximum progress is this decision concerning the amount of caution needed to protect the society's goals and the amount of daring required to advance the society toward those goals.

Who makes that decision?
In a democracy, the people make it.
In this democracy, I have heart and faith that our people will not make the decision very wrong. . . .

REFERENCES

[1]T. L. Kelley, **The Influence of Nurture upon Native Differences** (New York: The MacMillan Company, 1926).

The Monkey on the Bicycle

HANS P. GUTH

. . . when the measurement people come to us with their instruments, my answer is: "Don't make a monkey out of me. I refuse to get on your bicycle."

. . . I'd like to start out with a broad generalization of this matter of defining . . . objectives. It seems to me that there are two large groups in the profession who have a position on this subject. First, there are those that I'm going to call the "vocal minority," and I mean "vocal" in the sense that they do verbalize freely about the matter of objectives. When they do a unit on place names, it is preceded by seven stated goals. They publish forty-eight approved objectives for teaching . . . [their particular subject matter]. On the other hand, there are the people that I am going to call the "inarticulate majority," the group to which I belong, because when I am asked to define objectives [as an English teacher] . . . I always feel somewhat uneasy. All I really want to do is take my ditto sheet with the sample sentences from Stephen Crane, or the poem by Robert Frost. I want to go into the classroom, close the door softly behind me, and do my thing.

For instance, I take a ditto sheet into the classroom that has some sentences in pidgin English that I collected in Hawaii last summer. I present those sentences that I collected, and we talk about them. In class, I don't particularly theorize or argue. I simply take these along and read a few of them. They go like this:

> My car went broke down. You can give me ride?
> Yesterday she like go leech one ride from Dennis, but Dennis

Excerpts from Hans P. Guth, "The Monkey on the Bicycle," **English Journal,** 785-792, September, 1970. Copyrighted © 1970 by the National Council of Teachers of English. Reprinted by permission of the publisher and author.

no like give her one.
Hurry up! We going home. You no like go or what?
He been work too hard.
Ugly dat one!
"Daddy, where you?" "I stay here."

Now suppose the assistant principal sitting in the back of the room came up to me afterward and said, "What are you doing this for? What's the point of taking this kind of thing in?" I suppose if backed into a corner, I would try to get at some of the things that I've tried to do with this ditto sheet. For example, one thing this exercise does is to help make students aware of language as language. Everyone uses language all the time, never really thinking about it or becoming aware of it. To the student, language is much the way water is to the fish in the sea. And contrast is a great educating agent. When we see something done differently, when it doesn't fit the mode, when we look at some of these pidgin sentences and they sound like English but not quite, we say, "Now what's the difference between this and the way we say it?" And then all of a sudden we become aware of some of the things that make our language work.

. . . Another thing I'm trying to get at is that the students using this kind of dialect are people, not just with parents from Korea and China, but from the Philippines, Samoa, mainland USA, and what not. Yet these people are living together in the islands, and they have to communicate in English. I want my students to realize one important fact that stares us in the face once we think about it: Many Americans — not just in Hawaii, but all over the country — are bilingual. And even if they aren't bilingual, somewhere in their background they have some contact with some kind of language other than English. They have some aunt, or grandmother, or friend, or somebody who, in fact, probably speaks a sort of working pidgin still, after twenty years or fifteen years or thirty years in this country. And this puts quite a different perspective on American English as a *common medium,* as something that people from many different backgrounds had to adopt or are still adopting as a means of communication. And we realize then that American English is one of the things that hold our country together. In our diversity of backgrounds and interests it provides the common medium.

Another thing I am trying to get at through these sentences is that language is basically intended to be responded to positively, to be fascinating. We don't go through these pidgin sentences in order to say, "Look at these ignorant people out there in the Pacific who can't even speak their own language properly." That's not the point of the assignment. The point of the assignment is to say, "Look at this use of language. Marvel at it. Be fascinated by it. Be entertained." This is something where we say, "Look at this kind of thing. Study it. Learn something from it."

. . . Now, the trouble with trying to list these worthy objectives, the trouble with trying to formalize these worthy goals, is two or threefold. First of all, it's a lot to ask of these eight little sentences. It's a lot to ask to get all of these things out of this one sheet. In fact, even as I state these goals, we realize that these are not the objectives for this particular assignment. These are the *long-range goals* that . . . teachers always work toward. These are the kinds of things that are implied in everything we do. For instance, fostering a positive interest in language, and showing that we approach language as a marvelous, flexible instrument, and that we are interested in what language can do — we do that all the time, even when we are off duty. . . .Just the other day, for example, I was listening to some talk between two English teachers. In California these days evolution versus Genesis is again a big topic. These teachers are talking about the Monkey Trail — the Scopes trial, and one fellow said to the other, "You know, my father was at the Scopes Trial in Tennessee." So the other one looks at him and says, "As a witness — or as an exhibit?"

The second problem we have with these so-called objectives is that we write all of them down in our lesson plans — this is what we want to do — and then half of it comes off in class, and the other half doesn't. In other words, these things that I described are *opportunities*. If we have a good class hour, some of these things will come out, we hope. Some of this will come through. But we wouldn't want to be judged by results that say, "You've done Items 1 and 3, but did you slip up on Item 2!"

Finally, and most importantly, the whole thing is too *verbal*. It's so easy to state these goals that make us feel good and make us sound good, but it's so easy for these words just to be words. We are confronted in this country now with a whole generation that is suspicious of big words, brave words uttered by people over thirty. In fact, the assistant vice-principal, if he is still listening to me, by now is saying, "Hans, you are quite a talker, aren't you? In fact, now I realize why on campus they call you 'Talk-talk Guth.' "

If we talk about objectives at all . . . we must be careful to make sure that these aims — these objectives — are not just words, that we talk not just about what people *say*, but especially what they are going to *do* in their classroom; [that we don't just talk about what people think but] . . . also very much about what they feel; that we don't talk just in terms of official aims, but that we very much talk in terms of hidden promises, tacit assumptions, habits, customs, preferences, likes and dislikes. And in the short time I have left, I would like to verbalize perhaps two or three basic long-range goals . . .

The first long-range goal in teaching . . . is making the student branch out emotionally and intellectually and opening something up through imaginative experience. And the important point about that is that this is not behavior in the overt sense. This deals with *internal experience*. And even though there are . . . external symptoms of glistening eyes and of going to the bookshop afterwards and saying, "Do you have that collection of poems by Dylan Thomas?", those are just the symptoms. We don teach . . . just to produce the symptoms. I don't teach literature to teach the students how to make purring noises when I read Thomas to them.

Let me go on . . . [and illustrate] another basic goal of English. I have already hinted at the fact that in California we are again in one of these censorship quarrels where the textbook authors are busy going through their books changing all the *damns* to *darns,* and changing all the *My Gods,* to *My Gosh,* and changing all the *Hell no's* to *Hell yes.* In fact, one of the authors now concludes his letters "Gosh Bless." And it's a futile and degrading thing. We encounter a four-letter word, and we try to explain that this word in context is not really obscene. And we don't really know how to handle this matter successfully. Ultimately, this is a matter of how well we ourselves use language. Here you stand: you are an English teacher. You are supposed to make language work for you and be persuasive and eloquent and have the public accept your version of the thing. But we realize that this is very difficult. We seem ourselves defeated in what is actually our second major assignment as teachers: to work in this area of using language for a purpose, as an instrument in human relations, in organizations, in politics. . . . One thing we should try to do for the student is to say, "Well, here is language. You can make it work for you, rather than *against* you."

. . . [The third long-range objective is that learning is truly significant when it is personally meaningful to the learner. I recall] . . . a little exchange that someone recorded in a fourth-grade class, from an article called "Poetry in an Elementary Classroom." Apparently the person had taken in a Robert Frost poem, the one about the horse and the man in the woods on a winter evening, the dark lonely woods, covered with snow, the man lingering there and the horse wanting to go home to the stable. So at the end of this the teacher turned to the group and said, "Now what is the basic difference between the horse in this poem and the man?"

And one student says, "Well, the horse has four legs, and the man has two." And the teacher says, "Good." And then someone else says, "One of them is happy and the other one is sad." And the teacher says, "Fine." And then another students says, "The man knows he's going to die and the horse doesn't." And the teacher doesn't say anything. He lets it sink it. And the point about that response by the student is that it is *true*. It is significant. It's worth taking in. It's worth pondering. And when composition ceases to be skill that's taught, and becomes expression — communication — in the true sense, then we read it not as an exercise, but then we read because we want to see what the student has to say.

This perception of relations is what we aim at when we say that we want our students to think. Thinking establishes relations within the content of the students' experience. That content builds up slowly, and from a hundred sources, many of them not funded by the school board. A good teacher tries to broaden the students' experience. But he is not so foolish as to take a bow when the student's experience quotient goes up from 68 to 92.

Summing up these three goals . . . I think we can label them roughly: first, *imagination,* the area of extending feeling and thinking on the part of the student; second, *power,* the ability to use language, for a purpose . . . third, *understanding,* the ability to relate a piece of poetry to your own experience, to relate one piece of poetry to another and talk about a common theme or something of that sort. I call these humanistic goals, because they all have to do with the basic goals of humanistic education, which are to develop more fully and to bring out more fully whatever human potential there is in the student.

Where does this leave then people with the tests and the measurement items, the learning modules, the clearly defined, limited objectives? They come to us, and they say, "Here, you do six units of this or that, and in the statistics the performance rate goes up 25 per cent, and that is so much per dollar per pupil." All this kind of talk reminds me of the monkey we see on the Ed Sullivan show. Ed Sullivan once in a while has three trained chimpanzees who ride the bicycle. They do three laps and the audiences goes wild, because the Ed Sullivan audience just loves to see a monkey do his three laps on the bicycle. In terms of overt behavior and of measurable results, and of something we can demonstrate to the taxpayer, those monkeys are a tremendous success. When they started out being educated, they knew nothing about riding a bicycle. And now that they've been trained, they ride that bicycle and they do the three laps. But when you watch the monkey a little more closely, you realize that the monkey's heart is not really in it. And all the while that he's on that bicycle, his mind is somewhere else. His attention wanders. And you realize there's more to this monkey than Ed Sullivan will ever understand. There is a great unused potential for monkey business, and for monkeyshines. So my suggestion is — and I try to word it as rationally and calmly as I can — when the measurement people come to us with their instruments, my answer is: "Don't make a monkey out of me. I refuse to get on your bicycle."

Accountability From a Humanist Point of View

C. A. BOWERS

I should like to suggest that we begin to think of accountability in terms of what the student needs in order to realize his fullest potential as a person, rather than what it is the public wants — which is often defined in self-serving economic and social terms.

There is increasing reference in the literature and public speeches to the importance of accountability in education. President Nixon, in his Education Message (March 3, 1970), stated that teachers and administrators should be held accountable for their performance. The Superintendent of Public Instruction in Oregon, Dale Parnell, has a commission working on the task of developing a master plan for the public schools that incorporate the principles of teacher accountability and management by objectives. A writer, commenting on the Texarkana experiment, suggested that perhaps the most far-reaching implication of performance accountability is its potential use in regular classrooms. "In the future," he wrote, "teachers might be required to show measurable evidence that their students are learning at a prescribed level in a prescribed amount of time."[1]

At one level of analysis I find myself in general agreement with the concerns which underlie this emphasis on greater accountability in education. I can even see where accountability and management by objectives might have value in upgrading the teaching of such basic skills as reading and arithmetic. But at the risk of seeming to oppose what is becoming another folk value, I would

C. A. Bowers, "Accountability From a Humanist Point of View," **Educational Forum,** 479-486, May, 1971. Reprinted by permission of Kappa Delta Pi, an Honor Society in Education and owner of the copyright.

like to argue that when people extend the idea of accountability to all areas of learning in the schools, as is done in the three examples I cited earlier, they are obscuring fundamental questions that are vital to the performance of the competent teacher and to what I conceive to be the purpose of education.

If one examines the literature on accountability in education, he will find that the term is generally used in a highly abstract manner that suggests a hidden political purpose. When the advocates attempt to be specific about what they mean by accountability they invariably identify the quantitative aspects of education: rate of learning, finding the ratio between "inputs" and "outputs," and the unit cost. Later, I shall say more about reducing educational issues to quantitative terms. For now, I would like to analyze the consequences that would result for the student and teacher, if the idea of accountability were actually to be applied in concrete situations.

That the idea of accountability is used in a highly abstract manner can be seen in the fact that the "public" is always identified as the entity to whom the educator is to be held accountable. For example, Leon Lessinger, a former Associate Commissioner in the U.S. Office of Education and a leading advocate of accountability in education, asserts that the "public expects greater relevance in what we teach."[2] Who is this public? Does it have a common point of view, value system, and set of expectations so that everybody represented by the term "public" would agree on what is meant by "relevant education"? Lessinger, like other advocates of accountability, makes the mistake of treating the public as a unitary entity that shares a common set of values and expectations. This is surprising because most knowledgeable teachers, school administrators, and school board members know that their communities are composed of interest groups that have different and often opposing expectations. They also know that these interest groups wield differing amounts of power. When one takes the idea of accountability out of its rhetorical context — where it is often used as a political slogan — and attempts to implement it in a pluralistic community, it becomes obvious that it is not as clear and as workable a concept as its advocates claim.

The principle of accountability, when it is applied in a community composed of diverse interest groups, has the effect of politicizing the educational process. The decisions and performance of the teacher may become a social issue that arouses intense political activity — much of which is directed at the board members and school officials. Even when the issue is not likely to arouse the controversy that results from sex education, or a discussion of whether pacifism is not more consistent with American ideals than militarism, there is still the question of which interest groups are being served by the teacher's actions. By claiming that the teacher must be held accountable to the public the teacher is being placed in the impossible situation where his method of discipline, assigning homework, recommending outside reading, etc. may be approved by some individuals and groups in the community but disapproved by others.

If we were to follow the principle of accountability to its logical conclusion, the person who believes in prayer in the classroom would have as much right to expect the teacher to conform to his wishes as the person who believes that the teacher should maintain the separation of church and state by omitting religious instruction. Similarly, the trade unionists in the community could legitimately ask that American economic and social history be presented in a light that serves their cause, just as the business group could demand that this same history be interpreted in a way favorable to business interests. The teacher would also be as accountable to minority groups — both economic and racial — as he is to values of the white, Protestant majority. I suspect, however, that the advocates of accountability would not want to have the principle interpreted so literally that every interest group in the community would feel they had a right to control the schools for their own ends.

In addition to serving as an invitation to all individuals and social groups to assess the adequacy of the school's program in terms of their own needs, the current discussion of the virtues of accountability implies that everybody has the right to pass judgment on the teacher's performance regardless of their own competence. For example, the parent who is a school drop-out and an anti-intellectual would have the right to pass judgment on the teacher who holds a master's degree in his teaching subject. The idea of accountability is part of the populist ethos to which politicians and educators appeal when they want to win over more supporters. T. S. Eliot identified the limitation of this position when he wrote in Notes Toward the Definition of Culture, "A democracy in which everybody has an equal responsibility in everything would be oppressive for the conscientious and licentious for the rest." In view of this problem, it would be useful if the advocates of accountability would clarify whether they really think everybody, regardless of their qualifications and responsibility for the outcome, should be allowed to pass judgment on the teacher's competence.

The academic freedom of the teacher is a related issue that has been totally ignored by the advocates of accountability. Few of us would regard the teacher as competent if he used the classroom for the purpose of indoctrinating students with his own ideas or with the ideas of a powerful special interest group in the community. It can be argued that one of the characteristics of a competent teacher is that he attempts to foster independent and responsible thinking among students by encouraging them to consider conflicting evidence, ideas, and values. This process is essential to developing the student's self-confidence in the power of his own intellect, and to developing his ability to assess the evidence and to formulate his own conclusions. For example, in a social studies class where the settlement of the West is being discussed, unless the viewpoint of the Indian is presented along with the white person's explanation of events, the student would get a distorted interpretation of this period in American history. A presentation of the Indian's side of the story would undoubtedly include the long list of broken treaties, the Trail of Tears, and the battle of Wounded Knee where Indians were senselessly massacred. According to the principle of accountability, a parent could intervene in the classroom if he felt that the teacher in presenting the Indian's interpretation of these events was being unpatriotic in teaching about the settlement of the West. Such intervention would jeopardize the teacher's academic freedom, just as it would be threatened by the parent who thinks that the teacher should be accountable to his point of view by not teaching the theory of evolution. In both examples the freedom that must exist in the classroom if we are to avoid having the truth determined on the basis of which social group can exert the greatest pressure on the school board is being sacrificed for a political slogan.

No matter how the issue is argued, the idea of holding teachers directly accountable to individuals in the community is incompatible with academic freedom. It is ironic that those individuals who are advocating greater teaching accountability, presumably out of a genuine concern for improving public education, have not realized that they are threatening the very thing that is necessary for the teacher to function properly and to keep the classroom free of partisan politics.

There are some other pertinent questions about how the idea of accountability will be interpreted and applied to education. Will the teacher be held accountable for teaching students, in addition to the basic tools of communication, to raise their own questions, to make their own synthesis of ideas, to trust their own insights, and to understand their culture so they will no longer be influenced by its unexamined premises? These intellectual qualities are the ones usually associated with the mature and responsible citizen. Yet, I suspect that teachers will not be held accountable for fostering these traits. This approach to education would involve an intellectual treatment of the subject matter, as well as academic freedom for the teacher. That the advocates of accountability have been silent on this aspect of education suggests that either they have overlooked its importance — which indicates that they do not really understand the mental traits of a mature and responsible person — or they have been unable to reconcile the intellectual process which academic freedom is designed to protect with their populist interpretation of accountability.

I suspect that another reason the advocates of accountability have not talked about education as an intellectual experience is that they have committed themselves to a quantitative system of measurement. There is some usefulness in knowing the rate at which a person can perform a skill. But I am not sure that we can measure objectively and quantitatively what a student learns in the social sciences and humanities unless they are rendered lifeless by being reduced to names, dates, and places. The true-false and the fill-in examinations — which provide the quantitative score — necessitate transforming the complexities of the phenomena being studied into an overly simplified view of reality where it can more easily be labeled as true or false. Educational measurement encourages teachers to offer a simplistic view of life, conditions students to look for the right or wrong answer without doing the hard work of thinking and wrestling with ambiguities, and allows the educator to maintain the illusion that he is conducting his enterprise on a scientific basis. Perhaps this is the only approach to education that our present system of accountability in education will tolerate. Here I am referring to control of education by local boards that must be responsive to diverse and often conflicting interest groups.

In reading the literature on accountability, especially such documents as the recent report of the Society of Educational Engineers, a group in Oregon composed mainly of superintendents, one has the feeling that history indeed repeats itself. The values of efficiency, scientific measurement, and accountability, which seem so new and full of promise to some of these educational reformers, have been tried before, and, it must be added, without the great success that was hoped for. In the early nineteen hundreds attempts were being made to measure and increase the efficiency within the schools. In his book, *Education and the Cult of Efficiency,* Raymond Callahan reports that by 1915 there were special "efficiency bureaus" set up in major cities where "educational efficiency experts" worked full time developing rating procedures to measure the teachers' performance, and to apply the principles of scientific management to public education. Then, as now, the ideas came from the areas of business and industrial engineering. Perhaps if we were better aware of the history of

American education we would be able to place the following statement by Leon Lessinger, which he made to the Society of Educational Engineers, in its proper context. Lessinger told his audience
that

> Clearly, a new educational movement is under way. We seem
> to be entering the age of accountability in education. This
> is a most radical departure from present-day practice. It
> attempts to put us in a position to tell the public and ourselves
> what we accomplished by the expenditure of a given amount
> of the funds. It permits us to judge our system of instruction
> by the results we produce. There is hope that it will lead to
> cost-benefit data and insight.[3]

The principles and techniques that are being heralded as new
are the same ones that dominated public education between 1900
and the Depression, although the labels have been updated. Callahan summed up the consequences of applying business-
industrial procedures and values to that period of education by
noting:

> that educational questions were subordinated to business con-
> siderations, that administrators were produced who were not,
> in any true sense, educators; that a scientific label was put
> on some very unscientific and dubious methods and practices;
> and that an anti-intellectual climate already prevalent, was
> strengthened.[4]

There is a certain tragic irony in the fact that while many
educators are attempting to transform education into a technology
that will make the control of students more efficient, the students
themselves are turning against the technological view of reality
because of its dehumanizing effects. Theodore Roszak, the author
of *The Making of a Counter Culture: Reflections on the Technocratic Society and Its Youthful Opposition,* found that many of the
youth are seriously addressing themselves to the question of "how
shall we live?"[5] They are asking questions about what constitutes
personally and socially meaningful work, whether excessive
reliance on technology and the world view it promotes are partly
the source of our alienation, whether our social priorities are morally sound, and what constitutes an adequate sense of personal
and social responsibility. If the student looks to the educator for
help in clarifying the assumptions and values that underlie these
pressing issues, he will find that the "efficiency" oriented educator
can only respond by talking about systems analysis, management
by objectives, accountability, performance contracting, and the

technology of modifying behavior. It should not be a great surprise to anybody when the students reject the educators for attempting to turn them into technologists, rather than assisting them in clarifying the assumptions they wish to live by. I am afraid, however, that as the students increasingly rebel against the spiritual emptiness of their technologically oriented educators, the efficiency hungry educators will respond by calling for more and better techniques for controlling behavior rather than examining their own assumptions and goals.

I should like to suggest that we begin to think of accountability in terms of what the student needs in order to realize his fullest potential as a person, rather than what it is the public wants — which is often defined in self-serving economic and social terms. The problem can be stated in a way that makes clearer the danger of looking to the public for the answers to the purpose of education. Determining the purpose of education is the same as determining the potential and purpose of man. It is an important philosophic question, and thus it cannot be answered by finding out what the consensus is in the community or state nor can the answer come from individuals and interest groups who attempt to settle educational questions by using economic, social, or religious criteria without considering their implications for education.

One way to answer the question is to determine those characteristics that are associated with maturity, and I think we know enough to identify some of these characteristics. We would all agree, I believe, that the mature person is one who is aware of his own freedom and has a well developed sense of values that enables him to use it in a personally and socially responsible manner. Moreover, he has a positive self-concept that is derived from a feeling of self-mastery of his own rational and physical abilities, rather than from the crowd that gives approval in exchange for blind conformity. He would certainly be proficient in using the symbolic and communication skills of his culture, and he would be knowledgeable about his culture and its underlying assumptions. While he would not represent the final answer to the question of man's potential, his life-style and creativeness might cause those interested in the question to see new potentials that were not seen before.

The educator has to make a decision about whether he is going to use his talents and energies to help each student develop in the direction of his own maturity or whether he sees himself as being accountable to interest groups who may want the classroom to be used for such varied ends as maintaining the community's status system, providing a compliant work force, or indoctrinating students with the beliefs and values held by the dominant interest groups in the community. Those educators who think they can serve both the needs of the students — and I am not talking about needs students themselves can identify — and the interest of local groups are engaged in a game of self-deception. For in order to limit the student's understanding and abilities to what can be tolerated by interest groups it is often necessary to manipulate the student's self-identity so that he feels confident about himself only when his behavior conforms to the norms of the interest groups. The teacher would also have to condition him into believing that the range of his freedom is circumscribed by the expectations of others. This is really what socialization is all about, but when it is carried on in the unexamined manner demanded by many interest groups, it becomes debilitating for the person undergoing the process.

If, on the other hand, the teacher feels himself accountable to the long-range needs of the students, he will attempt to create an atmosphere of trust in the classroom where genuine inquiry can take place. In this atmosphere the student does not have to earn a positive self-image by meeting somebody else's terms. He can begin to develop a positive self regard as he learns to trust his own intellectual and emotional responses as he encounters different aspects of his culture. The teacher must also have the ability to teach him the information gathering skills without turning off his interest in learning by using fear and guilt as a means of controlling his behavior. Equally important to the student's future development is the teacher's knowledge of the culture and his awareness that he cannot know what, among all the ideas, assumptions, and values he teaches, will prove dysfunctional at some future point in time. When the teacher is sensitive to the risks the student faces in learning from others, he will discourage the students from uncritically accepting as real what are actually the notions, imaginings, and longings of a particular people at a particular point in history. For when the student unquestionably accepts the truths of other people he may be trapped into reliving the problems connected with their form of cultural blindness.

We are reminded almost daily that some of our most basic cultural assumptions about the environment, meaningful work, the nature of scientific technology, our view of progress, and our Protestant attitude toward the nature of time, need to be re-thought as we face a deepening crisis with our environment, and in our relations with each other in urban centers. These inescapable facts should make educators more conscious of being accountable to students for insuring that their education does not become simply a matter of training for a job that may shortly be eliminated by advances in technology. The students need to learn about their culture, particularly about those assumptions and values that are at the root of current social and ecological problems. They also need to learn how to deal with social issues at an intellectual rather than an emotional and fearful level — as many adults now do. If the current advocates of accountability were genuinely concerned with this form of education, they would be talking about the importance of academic freedom, the problems of recruiting more intellectually mature and socially representative people into the field of teaching, the kind of education that teachers need in order to be culturally literate, and the kind of education that administrators need in order to understand the educational process and their role in protecting it from fearful and anti-intellectual elements in the community. Instead, we hear them talking about input-output indicators, auditing the teacher's performance, applying systems analysis and design to education, and the need for establishing an Educational Engineering Institute in Oregon so that all schools may be controlled more efficiently.

The language of the educational engineer has a great power for mesmerizing people, but it does not tell us anything about the vital issues in education. Before we can talk about accountability we must first clarify the issues that relate to the purpose of education. Otherwise, the technological aspects of education will become ends in themselves.

REFERENCES

[1]Dale Bratten, Corline Gillin and Robert E. Rousch, "Performance Contracting: How It Works in Texarkana," **School Management,** (August, 1970), p. 10.
[2]Leon Lessinger, "Evaluation and Accountability in Educational Management," **Academy of Educational Engineers** (published by the Society of Educational Engineers, 1970), pp. 7-8.
[3]*Ibid.*
[4]Raymond Callahan, **Education and the Cult of Efficiency** (Chicago: The University of Chicago Press, 1962), p. 246.
[5]Theodore Roszak, **The Making of a Counter Culture** (New York: Anchor Books, 1969), p. 233.

The Humanities and the Schools

MARTIN ENGEL

*Humanization of learning is the microcosm of the humanization of
our culture and our life.*

As we set out to reform education, we focus upon the subject.
We tamper with the materials of the discipline or the skills in
manipulating that discipline. We work to fix and improve the content. However, curriculum or teacher skills with that curriculum
are only one dimension of the total learning experience. The fact
is that the school system as a whole is a value communicating
institution. It controls, or seeks to control, the minds and behavior
of its students. As a total milieu, it is far more successful in this
manipulation of mind and attitude than any instructional content.
Most schools and school systems are authoritarian and repressive.
Children learn quickly what is valued and what is despised; for
example, conformist behavior for the former and individual initiative
for the latter. The real total content of a school involves what
is permitted and what is supressed in the child's behavior.

Today school reform is dominated by those scientific educators,
researchers, and psychometricians who subscribe to operant conditioning, behavioral objectives, and measurable changes. Such
changes are achieved, they believe, through the intervention and
control that their materials, techniques, or curriculum impose. In
fact, of a much larger magnitude of behavioral control is the total
school experience. For example, its repressive regulatory mode
reaches far beyond the brief classroom limits of any consciously
controlled behavior model. Imagine a new curriculum devised to
stimulate verbal communication within a school milieu which in

Martin Engel, "The Humanities and the Schools," **Teachers College Record,**
239-248, December, 1970. Slightly edited and reprinted with permission of the
publisher and author.

fact encourages competition, isolation, silence, and self-containment. In other words, the organization of the school system is the real medium, and the students get the message loud and clear!

Schools as Controlling Institutions Let me state the case much more strongly. This is not a new message, and it has been broadcast recently with great fervor, yet it is still very unpopular. Schools, as controlling institutions, are systematically destructive to the mind and soul of children. They are aesthetically, emotionally, spiritually, morally, and intellectually sterile. They drive the sense of joy and pleasure in learning out of their students. They are the cause, not the victim of student rebellion. They are the merchants of irrelevance, trivia, irrationality, and a sense of competitive hostility among teachers and students alike. They bore the creative, eager, confident spirit of the young, usually destroying it. The desire to learn, which exists in all children, is methodically sealed off forever. Students from the first grade to the last quickly learn to turn-off when they enter the school and to turn-on when they leave. Schools seem to be very careful to keep reality, the vital sense of life, feeling, and joy out of the educational experience.

Schools are prisons in the sense that they isolate the student from the lively confusion and complexity of the outside world. They are training camps which seek to stamp out the child that lives within all of us. They drill the young to be old — to be adult, to stop being a child. O. K. Moore contends that the adult is the norm of the species. Schools process the young to become that norm. What willful destruction! Having lost the sense of total, integrated living which is the natural property of the child with his mind, body, and feelings all of a piece, whole and organic, we have actually lost the most precious part of ourselves. In such an environment, there may be learning, but there is no growth and there is no pleasure in learning. In such an environment, the arts and humanities are no more than arid packaged disciplines, objective and meaningless. Of what use is it to talk about the humanitites in schools which fragment the individual, forcing him to suppress his feelings and body, teaching him to behave, to conform, to obey, to accept, to consume, and to submit?

As long ago as 1916, Randolph Bourne said: "There is something remote and antiseptic about even our best schools. They contrast strangely with the color and confusion of the rest of our American life. The bare classrooms, the stiff seats, the austere absence of beauty, suggest a hospital where painful if necessary intellectual operations are going on."[1] It must be obvious by now that it is not the children who fail. It is the schools which fail the children. Every child who is not a creative, self-expressive individual who loves to learn, has been denied the opportunity by the schools. Schools corrupt the virginal sense of play, enthusiasm, and pleasure which is the prime value of life, replacing it with a sense of drudgery, guilt, anxiety, fear, and inferiority.

Aesthetic and Anesthetic Schools prevent the growth of the sense of responsibility insofar as the word means the ability to respond. Instead of generating the *aesthetic* vision of life, they produce the *anesthetic* numbing of the feelings, the deadening of the rich sensorium which all children bring eagerly to the schools. Soul is not only for the blacks. Soul is what most children have and most adults have lost. Soul is what you lose in schools.

Our repressive and authoritarian culture suffers from the misconceived fantasy that it is in desperate need to assert control over itself. We suffer from an obsessive anality. We fear that if we relax just a little bit we will cause a big, uncontrolled mess. We can see this unconscious anxiety determine the character of our schools. They always explain their strictness and order as the necessary means for preventing chaos and confusion. Yet as any physician can tell you, it is the repressed, excessively-controlled individuals who suffer all sorts of illnesses. Furthermore, the idea that the opposite of order is chaos is erroneous and uniquely Western. Chaos literally means empty space. Confusion means, obviously, to fuse together. Are both concepts so repugnant to us? Is not the opposite of order really complexity? Is not chaos merely an order which we do not understand? Does the external imposition of discipline and control really generate internal control and self-discipline?

The great national crisis in the urban schools now points at, among other things, "below normal" reading skills levels. However, the preoccupation with testing, measurement, verbal criteria, behavioral skills and the entire anal, manipulative, quantifying rationality of the sciences may very well be the cure that is killing the patient.

We now understand such bureaucratic manipulation to be an outgrowth of the nineteenth century technological/industrial mindset, and we have come to identify this attitude as hostile to the development of the authentic, self-actualizing, creative personality. In human growth and learning, systems and efficiency are not always very efficient.

Humanization of Education Does the school system encourage sensitivity, creativity, or individual initiative? Does the organization — the supervisors, principals, guidance counselors, teachers, physical plan — encourage self-expression, an aesthetic vision of life, a sense of compassion? Does the institution of American education honor the qualitative over the quantitative? Does it respect the intimate and the interpersonal development of the children?

Eliot Eisner explains the apparent "success" of the physical and social sciences. He states: "One will note that the vast majority of curriculum development projects in the sciences and mathematics have demanded no structural change on the part of the institution. These programs, like interchangeable parts, were designed to fit into the existing structure. Can humanities and arts programs succeed in such a structure or will they demand a reconceptualization of how schooling proceeds?"[2] We may ask, in broader terms, if not *all* learning programs would succeed upon the heels of a humanized and personalized restructuring in the schools.

Even those schools which have a great deal of art and humanities in their curriculum tend to be repressive, authoritarian, and stultifying. A swelling bibliography of radical school reform argues against this impersonal, dogmatic, and demeaning system — and it is the educational system which is the culprit — supported by self-aggrandizing bureaucracies, administrators, teachers, and, too often, ambitious or indifferent parents. Let me cite only one passage from this vast literature, from George Dennison's *The Lives of Children* which emblazons my point with banner clarity:

> I would like to say why . . . our school professionals, taken as a class, an institutionalized center of power, are fundamentally incompetent and must be displaced. My purpose is not to castigate the bureaucrats, but to recall parents and teachers to an awareness of one crucial truth . . . : that in humane affairs — and education is *par excellence* a humane pursuit — there is no such thing as competence without love.[3]

By now it must be apparent that meaningful learning does not rest upon the content or the methodology of courses or programs. Rather the issue hinges upon what may be called the *humanization of education*. It is quite possible that all the arts and humanities courses in the world, no matter how well aimed, structured, or intentioned, are of little avail within a school or school system which in its very conception and process is antihumanistic.

Not only the sciences, but even the humanities are not humanistic as presently taught in the schools. The fact is that neither has contributed to man's humanity, neither has altered the quality of modern life for the better. Science has increased the quantity of our material well-being, but the arts and humanities have not filled the vacuum left by the technocratic culture hell-bent upon drowning itself in an ocean of ennui polluted by late-model cars, appliances, early retirement, and a vacuous old age.

Lasch and Genovese stated it this way in the *New York Review of Books:*

> It is absurd to seek a reconciliation of science and the human-
> ities — the constant refrain of our leading educationists —
> when those who teach the humanities have so little to con-
> tribute to such a merger, having accepted the physical
> sciences' own misguided canons of objective truth. Civilized
> conditions of education cannot be achieved by closing a non-
> existent gap between science and the humanities, but only
> through a resurgent humanism that informs both.[4]

The failure of the humanities in modern Western culture can be articulated in nearly absolute terms. I need not remind you that many of that generation of Germans responsible for unspeak-able horrors against humanity were well educated in the human-ities. They were far more familiar with the arts, languages, and history than the kids in our schools. Elie Wiesel calls the greatest discovery of the second World War the fact that Adolf Eichmann was cultured, read deeply and intelligently, and played the violin. The assumption that more humanities courses will make students more humane is erroneous, and if they fail to make stu-dents more humane, then whatever else they do is insignificant.

To Learn and To Be We are, I think, historically past the point of sustaining subject matter as discretely articulated, but isolated disciplines. We are past the point of regarding knowledge merely as skills, information, and concepts which exist under the steward-ship of scholars and teachers, and to be acquired by students equally under that stewardship.

We can no longer compartmentalize the humanities from the physical sciences or the human sciences. We can no longer regard knowledge as objective and neutral. We must stop asking how we can improve teaching, just as we must stop asking how we can improve the schools. Rather, we must ask how we can help the young to learn and to be. George Dennison says: ". . . that the education function does not rest upon our ability to control, or our will to instruct, but upon our human nature and the nature of experience."[5]

By the way, the universities, while I have not focused upon them, are not exempt from this same criticism. There we can find all of the forces which hamper free and humane inquiry: authority, professionalism, tradition, rituals of certification all the way up to the Ph.D., and most gross of all, the confusion between *search* and *re-search,* with the latter rewarded on a quantitative basis. As long as we persist in conducting education upon a nineteenth century industrial model, as long as we stress the academic, European, cultivated tradition and deprecate the indigenouse, experimental, vernacular tradition, as long as we value the product of the mind and intellect apart from and above the body and the feelings, our schools will fail to meet the needs of the whole person.

A book that has had considerable influence upon me recently is Theodore Roszak's *The Making of a Counter-Culture.* In it the author argues for a humane life style in opposition to the technocratic and totalitarian mass culture which has so effectively captivated us. While not referring to the process directly, Roszak clearly is making a case for the humanization of learning, especially if we believe that the schools are a microcosm of the culture they reflect and support:

> It is not of supreme importance that a human being should be a good scientist, a good scholar, a good administrator, a good expert; it is not of supreme importance that he should be right, rational, knowledgeable, or even creatively productive of brilliantly finished objects as often as possible. Life is not what we are in our various professional capacities or in the practice of some special skill. What *is* of supreme importance is that each of us should become a person, a whole and integrated person in whom there is manifested a sense of the human variety genuinely experienced, a sense of having come to terms with a reality that is awesomely vast.[6]

In such a life style, all learning is humanistic because it is a nonutilitarian and nonproductive process which teaches that getting there is not only half the fun, it's the whole trip. Gertrude Stein said: "And when you get there, there is no there, there." Subjects, professional educators, institutions of learning, etc., must diffuse themselves into pluralistic, total communities devoted to learning as a part of living. The senses of the body, emotions, feelings, fantasy life, warm, interpersonal relationships and mental health will be restored their rightful place, from a subordinate position vis-a-vis the manipulative, rationalistic, quantifying scientific methods, to one of pre-eminence. The innocence and enthusiasm of childhood will be preserved rather than institutionally destroyed. A-rational and non-intellective awareness will have equal stature with cognitive knowledge.

Humanization of learning is the microcosm of the humanization of our culture and our life. In this context, we confront the dichotomy between the pleasure principle and the reality principle as discussed, after Freud, by Marcuse and Norman O. Brown. Only in a nonrepressive, Dionysian culture can a humanized life be enjoyed. Harvey Cox conceives of the problem of the interaction between the needs of our culture and a humanized perspective in these terms: "Western man has purchased prosperity at the cost of staggering impoverishment of the vital elements of his life. These elements are festivity — the capacity for genuine revelry and joyous celebration; and fantasy — the faculty for envisioning radically alterative life situations. . . . Man is esentially festive and fanciful. To become fully human, Western industrial man . . . must learn again to dance and dream. . . . Unless the industrialized world recovers its sense of festivity and fantasy, it will die or be destroyed."[7]

REFERENCES

[1]Randolph Bourne. **The New Republic,** August 5, 1916.
[2]Eliot Eisner, "The Humanities: Is A New Era Possible?" **Educational Leadership,** April, 1969.
[3]George Dennison. **The Lives of Children.** New York: Random House, 1969.
[4]Chrstopher Lasch and Eugene Genovese, "The Education and the University We Need Now," **New York Review of Books,** Vol. 13, October 9, 1969, p. 21.
[5]Dennison, *op. cit.*
[6]Theodore Roszak, **The Making of a Counter-Culture.** Garden City, N.Y.: Doubleday and Company, 1969.
[7]Harvey Cox, "In Praise of Festivity," **Saturday Review,** October 25, 1969.

Behavioral Objectives and Humanism in Education: A Question of Specificity

ASAHEL D. WOODRUFF AND PHILIP G. KAPFER

The threat potential of behavioral objectives exists in the tendency of some modern behaviorists to limit objectives to overt visible behaviors, thus excluding the important behavioral processes of perception, concept formation, thinking, feeling, synthesizing, creating, and so on.

The behavioral objectives movement clearly sets out to shape the behavior of students. The question, of course, is *what* behavior? If a narrow concept of behaviors is adopted, then a narrow instructional system will develop. If a broad-gauge learning program is to be developed, then a broad concept of behavior must be its starting point. The use of behavioral objectives in curricular and instructional development carries both promise and threat to education, depending on the concept of behavior that is adopted.

Behavioral objectives are a powerful tool for making educational goals precise, for identifying relevant media and learning activities, and for knowing when goals have been achieved. The threat potential of behavioral objectives exists in the tendency of some modern behaviorists to limit objectives to overt visible behaviors, thus excluding the important behavioral processes of perception, concept formation, thinking, feeling, synthesizing, creating, and so on. The atomistic specification of behavioral objectives also excludes the highly significant decision-making and decision-executing areas of human behavior, which represent the most

Asahel D. Woodruff and Philip G. Kapfer, "Behavioral Objectives and Humanism in Education: A Question of Specificity," **Educational Technology Magazine,** 55-59, January, 1972.

significant aims of education. The claim often made that these more humanistic behaviors can be cultivated by reinforcement schedules within the paradigm of operant conditioning is not being demonstrated and is not very convincing.

In this article we will attempt to sketch a more broadly conceived behavioral approach which places a priority on the higher humanistic behaviors and subsumes the smaller instrumental abilities under them. We also will view this approach within the framework of the most prominent curriculum models and current developments in the matter of objectives.

Three Curriculum Models

Three principal curriculum orientations can be seen in the schools. These are summarized in Figure 1 and are discussed below.

Effective Living

The life-relevant curricular and instructional model is found in varying degrees in vocational and other applied subjects. This model has the power to provide an effective humanistic education when it is adapted to significant decision-making and decision-executing behaviors. This model will be developed later in this article.

Scholarship in a Discipline

This model, which received renewed emphasis following Sputnik, is found in many of the acronymed science and, more recently, social science courses. The pattern is advocated by discipline-centered educators, and ranges from a focus on the processes of inquiry in a discipline to the memorization of concept statements and principles that make up the verbal structure of a discipline.

Social Conformity

The social conformity model is found to a greater or lesser degree in most subjects taught in the public schools. It is advocated by those who believe schools should shape the motives of students, and it is subtly but powerfully operative within the conformity pressure of both the community and the school. It is most

Figure 1

Three Curriculum Orientations

Effective Living

The Aim:
To satisfy personal wants.

Personal Conceptual Knowledge:
A working familiarity with the behavioral properties of objects in the environment.

Life Behavior:
A series of acts consisting of manipulating concrete objects to satisfy personal wants, during which the person develops mental concepts incidental to the personal decisions he makes concerning his own behavior. These concepts then accumulate incidentally into a body of generalized knowledge.

A Concept:
A memory of some of the perceived properties of an object encountered in the environment. Such perceptions of recollections of environmental phenomena are carried within a person and reactivated at decision-points that involve the phenomena.

Basic Modes of Encounter with Environment:
Utilization in seeking wants.
(1) Inquiry used to support utilization.
(2) Integration to enhance breadth of understanding.

Scholarship in a Discipline

The Aim:
To accumulate and organize information.

A Disciplined Body of Knowledge:
A body of factual information organized in an orderly structure for storage and retrieval.

Academic Behavior:
The systematic search for information required to fill in the cells of an outline. This involves the development of verbal summaries of information about sets of phenomena for the purpose of further inquiry to construct an exhaustive body of such information.

A Concept:
The statement of a key idea that is central to an organized body of information. This involves independent packages of data in a file as contrasted with behavioral memories in a person.

Basic Modes of Encounter with Environment:
Inquiry and integration. Systematic processes of data collection and processing to build a disciplined body of information.

Social Conformity

The Aim:
To produce an "acceptable" person.

Knowledge of the Social System:
Familiarity with the society, its institutions, its heroes and its norms.

Social Behavior:
The acceptance of dominant patterns of thought, action and taste, as expressed in daily behavior.

A Concept:
The key modes of thought of a given social system. A person will have knowledge of the behavioral norms of the institutions of the society.

Basic Modes of Encounter and Environment:
Imitation of prevalent patterns in either inquiry behaviors, integration behaviors, or utilization behaviors.

apparent whenever any controversial subject is taught, such as evolution, human sexual behavior, Communism, religion, or the war in Vietnam.

Some Background About Objectives

The curriculum has always been aimed at behaviors, although not necessarily in the same sense as that used by Roger Mager and others when writing on the topic of "instructional" objectives. The behaviors can be seen in the curriculum in three ways.

First, broad behavioral goals have been prominent for many years. The Educational Policies Commission was the chief source of such goals, and similar pronouncements can be seen in state level and local school board documents. Curriculum guides and teacher and student curriculum materials typically have presumed to serve such behaviors, although most of the materials used in the public schools actually have been derived almost entirely from outlines of the subject matter fields. Lest we obscure the point, however, broad behavior goals are behaviors.

Second, behaviors similar to or identical to those in which people engage outside of school can be seen in some parts of the curriculum (e.g., the vocational areas). Functional behaviors, such as producing an object, staging an event, or completing a form, are stated and directly pursued in applied types of learning experiences.

Third, behaviors of a verbal nature have been promoted in the bulk of the curriculum, although more by default than by design. Curricula in the humanities, the language arts, the social studies, and to a large extent in the fine arts have been designed without reference to specific behaviors stated in the form of objectives. Verbal learning activities have been adopted on the implicit assumption that the acquisition of verbal information about those aspects of life would somehow transfer to life itself and produce desirable economic, political, social, aesthetic, and other valuable behaviors. Based on this assumption, educational effort has been aimed directly at the learning of the verbal information. The implied objective for the student has been the ability to pass verbal academic tests (which is, of course, a behavior — but not necessarily a useful in-life behavior).

Because we will discuss in the next section the behavioral objectives movement, it is useful here to summarize the above background discussion for easy reference. Behaviors have always been a part of the public schools curriculum in three ways:
   (1) Broad behavioral goals have been stated, but have not been translated into component behavioral goals.

(2) Functional behavioral goals have been stated in applied curriculum areas.
(3) Verbal behavioral goals, either actually stated or implied by test performance requirements, have been used in the remainder of the curriculum.

The Behavioral Objectives Movement

The recent rigorous movement toward precise behavioral objectives was not initially a movement to substitute behaviors for learner goals. As pointed out in the preceding section, such learner goals were already behaviors. Rather, the movement had one major thrust — to state the behaviors precisely and in specific and concrete form. Then, given such statements, the intent was to translate the behavioral objectives directly into relevant learning experiences, and to recognize learning when it had occurred. The primary emphasis, however, was on the latter — precise measurement. The effort to state goals explicitly was a means to that end.

The greatest measurement difficulties have always been in the cognitive curriculum areas, not to mention the affective component of behavior.. These areas have also been generally assumed to be the most basic for producing an educated person. It is not strange, therefore, that the main effort in the behavioral objectives movement thus far has been focused on producing objectives in the cognitive curriculum areas, nor that the behaviors chosen for attention have been largely overt verbal behaviors of the test-performance variety.

The emphasis on measurability led to a level of specificity that seemed to some observers to transform education into a mechanistic program devoid of real human value. Also, the focus on verbal test-type behaviors has led to the charge that behavioral objectives have little relevance to life beyond the school. One of the most compelling of the current critics of behavioral objectives is Charles Silberman in his popular book, *Crisis in the Classroom*. He states, "Indeed, the approach to instructional technology that most researchers are following [based on precise, measurable behavioral terms] is likely to compound what is wrong with American education — its failure to develop sensitive, autonomous, thinking, humane individuals."[1] Silberman supports his criticism of the behavioral approach with examples of CAI systems and an analysis of the Individually Prescribed Instruction (IPI) materials developed in Pittsburgh. These two types of approaches, he feels, are the results of limiting the term "behavior" only to actions that are measurable. Silberman's criticisms should not be taken lightly.

Rather, his reservations, and those of many similarly concerned individuals, should be taken as cause for reexamination of some of the major current thrusts of the behavioral objectives movement.

A Humanistic Reorientation of the Behavioral Objectives Movement

Behavior exists along a generality-specificity continuum. For example:

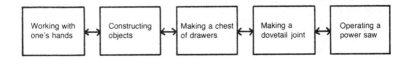

However, instructional activities can deal with behaviors only at some specific level. In the above example, the third through fifth behaviors are specific enough for good instructional planning. Of course, these three behaviors do differ markedly in the kind of planning they require. The fifth is largely a procedure-following behavior with a fairly simple and invariant pattern. The fourth requires much more conceptual understanding and several specific motor patterns. The third involves all that the other two involve, and in addition it encompasses a large amount of cognitive understanding of all the materials, tools, and processes involved in making a chest of drawers.

The temptation to which too many advocates of the behavioral objectives movement succumb is to stay at the fifth level of the behaviors indicated above. Writing behavioral objectives at this level is easier than at other levels, and the objectives meet all the generally suggested criteria of precision; but staying at this level has one serious, if not fatal, flaw. It is so atomistic that it is meaningless to a learner all by itself. Although a typical boy would enjoy for a short while learning to use power machinery, the isolated nature of such an objective does not provide sufficient motivational power on which to build an entire curriculum. In addition, transfer of atomistic behaviors to behaviors at the more humanistic levels does not occur automatically. Also, there could be no significant way of ordering the thousands of such discrete objectives in a curriculum area into an effective curricular scope and sequence.

One obvious solution to this problem is to focus on behaviors analogous to the third one in our example. Behaviors at this level are the kind of purposive goal-seeking behaviors in which people are engaged most of the time in their out-of-school lives. Moving to this level along the generality-specificity continuum requires a model of behavior to match these larger behaviors. Out of such a model, then, must be derived curricular vehicles that enable students to use life-like projects at the third level with supporting vehicles that provide for learning about the component phenomena and processes involved at the fourth and fifth levels.

Although the foregoing illustration is in the physical area of life, the same analysis and process of derivation can be used in the domains of self-interactions, interpersonal interactions, institutional participation, and the aesthetic domain. Note the following continuum developed within the institutional participation domain:

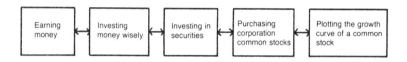

An additional example illustrates the interpersonal interactions domain:

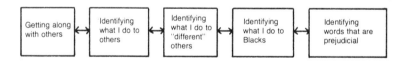

A Comprehensive Model of Behavior

Goal-directed or want-serving behaviors and the manner in which they are shaped are most accurately represented by the biological model of adaptation, supplemented by several component forms of learning from established psychological models. The synthesized model (shown in Figure 2 in abbreviated form) consists of a cybernetic cycle within the person[2] (rectangles in Figure 2) tied to an interlocking cycle of interaction with the environment (circles in Figure 2).

People freely engage in two kinds of activities and interactions in life. First, as illustrated in Figure 2 at Step 1.0, they explore things out of curiosity and, as a result, form percepts with subsequent organization of the percepts into concepts as shown at

Step 1.1. Second, they pursue in a purposeful way a series of specific goals to satisfy their needs. The selection of those goals is illustrated in Step 1.2. The activities necessary for achieving the goals are shown in Step 1.3 and in the interlocking loop labeled 2.0, 2.1, and 2.2. Perception of the consequences of the actions used for achieving the goals (Step 1.0) completes the cycle.

Figure 2

Model of Want-Serving Behavior Within the Environment

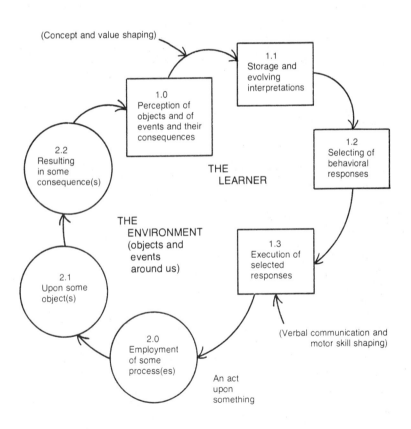

The two behaviors just described, namely, exploring the environment and pursuing goals, activate the following "laws" of what may be called "psychic adaptation" (or learning):

(1) Behavior is shaped by its immediate, perceived consequences.

(2) The shaping is specific to the particular bit of behavior going on, and does not generalize or transfer.

(3) The shaping takes effect by altering the concepts, habits, and skills that were mediating that particular instance of behavior.

(4) The shaping is involuntary and occurs whether the person is aware of it or not.

(5) The efficiency and magnitude of the behavioral shaping described above is greatly increased when the person's attention is focused on the critical properties of the processes and objects with which he is interacting.

Objectives Within a Comprehensive Model of Behavior

As pointed out in the preceding section, some objectives fall in the area of curiosity satisfaction and some in the area of purposive goal pursuit behaviors. We will look at both of these types of objectives in this section.

When learners are engaged in perceptual intake as they explore phenomena out of curiosity (Step 1.0 in Figure 2), their interests and wants are extended, thus solving the motivational problem of limited student interests. In this case, the only behavioral objective possible could be written as follows: "You (the learner) will be able to demonstrate in whatever manner you choose what you have learned." This objective is stated in a form that allows for different perceptions among learners and thus recognizes the psychological fact that each learner perceives different properties of any given phenomenon.

When behavioral objectives are written at the level of purposive goal-seeking or project-type behaviors (Steps 1.2 and 1.3 in Figure 2), want-serving behavior on the part of the student is activated. This solves the motivation problem that accompanies atmostic behavioral approaches to instructional design. In addition, learning strategies are simultaneously initiated based on the laws of psychic adaptation. Behavioral objectives written at this broader level encompass the smaller instrumental abilities and thus give purpose to the instrumental abilities and thus give purpose to the achievement of these behaviors. The more specific behavioral objectives, when subsumed by the broader project-type objectives, are used for their original intent — namely, measurement of concept development, vocabulary development, verbal information acquisition as needed, and motor skill development. They need not be used for instructional planning because the project goal and the phenomena involved in the project direct that process.

The search for an adequate set of project-like behavioral objectives is guided by the following set of intents:

(1) To include both consuming and producing behaviors.
(2) To encompass the complex cognitive-affective behaviors of a mature life as well as the more atomistic and instrumental behaviors popularly identified with limited versions of behavioral objectives. This includes concepts and values, creative freedom and ability, motor skills, verbal communication patterns and essential operant habit patterns.
(3) To put the emphasis on the development of competency, not on the shaping of preference.
(4) To work for competencies that flexibly serve personal goals and urges, not that foster or preserve any particular style of life.
(5) To focus on competence at a meaningful level in life — the level of holistic behaviors that includes both the expression of feeling and the exercise of judgment. This contrasts with mechanistic competencies that are meaningless in themselves.
(6) To lay out a list of behaviors as possibilities, within which all interested people can express their priorities.
(7) To establish a set of production steps that screen subject matter content through the desired behavioral goals, and allow the content that is relevant to those goals to enter the curriculum.

Conclusions

The social conformity curriculum model discussed earlier strongly permeates the curriculum of the so-called academic subjects in most schools, in spite of massive attempts to substitute discipline-oriented curricular models. These two orientations do, however, have one thing in common. They both depend in large measure on verbal behaviors. This is entirely defensible in the case of the discipline-oriented model. As long as the student (typically at the upper division and graduate levels of college) is preparing himself to be a professional scholar in a discipline, he most certainly must learn the inquiry processes and the verbal conceptual structure of his discipline. However, very few students, even at the college level, intend to become lifelong discipline scholars.

When these two verbal curriculum orientations are translated into instruction, an extremely unpalatable environment results in which students spend a good deal of time auditing verbal input without prior perceptual experience and therefore with very little comprehension and much memorization. Where good teaching of what otherwise would be strictly verbal data and concepts does occasionally exist, the use of considerable transfer, motivation, retention, and reinforcement pedagogy is evident as a means of propping it up. Certain elements of such pedagogy are, in fact, more evident than would be necessary or desirable in a curricular and instructional program designed for effective living.

Many educational technologists have attempted to escape the transfer and motivational problems of verbal curricula by favoring action terms that call for non-verbal executions such as "construct," "order" and "demonstrate" rather than verbal behaviors such as "identify," "name" and "describe." Such emphases do indeed meet with greater success than strictly paper-pencil approaches. In large measure, this success results from the curriculum becoming more phenomenal because it deals with real objects, processes, and consequences through non-verbal objectives, thus taking advantage of the inherent interest that we all have in phenomena; but the possibility of a more basic problem remains. The student may not be involved in real-life, want-serving behaviors (curiosity-satisfying behaviors, in this case). Rather, he may be involved only in achieving teacher-dominated terminal behavioral objectives, in which case the learning he has attained may not satisfy *his* curiosity. Certainly such learnings would not be used *at the time they are learned* for satisfying the *student's* wants. As a result, the potential for transfer from in-school learning to out-of-school behavior would be greatly reduced.

The British open classroom approach has in large measure avoided the problem of atomistic behavioral objectives. Many of the learner activities included in open classrooms involve phenomenal materials (Steps 2.0, 2.1, and 2.2 in Figure 2) and are perceptual-conceptual in nature (Steps 1.0 and 1.1 in Figure 2). The "open" or "informal" character of the classroom refers to allowing learners to freely select materials and activities based on their own interests rather than on autocratic demands of the teacher. The teacher maintains control by providing inherently interesting phenomenal materials, focusing learner attention on those materials rather than on himself, and eliciting highly individualistic learner response to the materials. The skill of the teacher in carrying out this off-stage-center role makes the difference between a chaotic environment and an effective learning theater. Some instances of purposive goal-seeking or project-type behaviors (Steps 1.2 and 1.3 in Figure 2) also can be seen in open classrooms. When this does occur, the full cycle of want-serving behavior shown in Figure 2 is activated and maximum in-life relevance is attained.

In summary, the most beneficial and practical approach is to (1) focus curriculum and instruction on life-like, want-serving behavioral objectives, (2) provide for the discrete learning that is necessary to perform these humanistic behaviors, and (3) make sure that specific overt behavioral objectives are written for that discrete learning so that measurement for mastery can occur.

REFERENCES

[1]Silberman, Charles E. **Crisis in the Classroom.** New York: Random House, 1970, p. 196.
[2]Further explication of the personal cybernetic cycle may be found in "Cognitive Models of Learning and Instruction" by Asahel D. Woodruff. In Laurence Siegel (Ed.) **Instruction: Some Contemporary Viewpoints.** San Francisco: Chandler Publishing Company, 1967, pp. 55-98.

What is Success?

IRA J. GORDON

If by accountability we mean measurement, how do we measure the success of the school in moving children, as much as the school can be responsible, toward inquiry, toward respect for self and others, toward a sense of competence and commitment and responsibility? . . . We can measure these and we can become just as careful and "respectable" as those who measure minutiae.

My topic is a rather grandiose one, "What is Success?", and as a subtopic, if we can define it, in what way are we accountable for achieving it.

I have heard from some of my colleagues, who look at life a little differently than I do, that one ought to have in mind, any time you do anything, what it is you want to achieve and how you measure it. I have a plan of what it is I want to achieve with you, but I assure you I have no system for measuring it. First, I would like to present to you some long range goals as I see them, but they are also immediate, because you cannot separate means and ends that easily. Second, to indicate to you what may be some of the factors which affect the ability of children to attain these goals, and, therefore, what we should be held accountable for both as teachers and as parents. Third, to provide you with some ways to measure both what we are doing and the results, that is, some child performances which indicate movement toward or arrival at our goals.

If I asked you for two sets of letters or initials which would characterize education, what would you say? The ones that would come immediately to mind are "the three R's" and "the ABC's." But a recent conversation I had with the superintendent of schools

Ira J. Gordon, "What Is Success?" Paper presented at the National Association for the Education of Young Children Conference, Atlanta, Georgia, November 17, 1972 and published by permission of the author.

in Yakima, Washington, really got me very excited about going beyond the three R's and the ABC's. He was concerned in our Follow Through Program and in early childhood education, in general, about how we could demonstrate the worth of such programs to very skeptical people. And the first thing he said to me is "Don't give me IQ scores and don't give me achievement test scores; what I want to know is what are the commitments these youngsters have when they become adolescents. Do they hang in there, are they organized, do they think about jobs? What are they like when they are adolescents? Don't tell me about this other kind of minutia." He used the word minutia. This set me off. If the three R's and the ABC's are insufficient, what can we come up with? So I have invented the QRS, which will no doubt become infamous after this article! The mnemonic system is one Q, two R's, and three S's, for those of you who need help in remembering. They are not profound, you know them all, but let us go over them anyhow.

The first goal is to develop a *questioning, open attitude and an inquiring mind*. I want to create in children and in ourselves the kind of orientation toward the world that is full of curiosity, wonder, exploration, and search; in which the assumption is not made that the final answers are in, and all you need to do is rote your way through them. So, "Q" is the opening, questioning attitude.

The first of the two R's is *respect for self*. We can break it out into two pieces, the first being the establishment, in each of us and in the children we work with, of a sense of dignity and a sense of self-esteem. I had an interesting experience with this sense of dignity a few weeks ago while visiting a nursery school in Port Jefferson, Long Island. The children were just arriving about nine o'clock in the morning and pouring off the mini-buses. I opened the door to help them, and a little four-year-old stood outside the school while everybody else went tearing in. He stood there until there was no more traffic and then he looked at me and said, "You don't have to hold the door for me, I can do it for myself." So I promptly shut the door. I watched him for five minutes struggling to get that heavy door open. He finally managed it and you never saw a prouder kid march himself into the center. You can see a sense of dignity, a sense of self-esteem in four-year-olds. But is any of that going to be left by the time he is eight or nine or ten after what we characteristically do to him when he gets into kindergarten, like my son was in, in which you have to put your thinking caps on before you went out on the playground, pick a piece of equipment you were going to play on, go out and Lord help you if you shifted from that piece of equipment to another piece of equipment when you got there? More than that, the classroom doors opened right on the playground, but you had to line up on the inside in order to get on the outside because, afterall, lining up is a fundamental first-grade skill! So, what do we do to children's dignity and self-esteem?

There is a second part of respect for self that ties back into the "Q". Some of us are not very elegant, we do tend to be sloppy and our categories are not mutually exclusive, so a little bit of the R falls into the Q. It is *the sense of initiative and drive and direction.* We would like kids to be self-starters. We would like them really to set out for themselves, establish their own goals, and learn how to pursue them effectively. So respect for self includes not simply a feeling about one's self, a sense of dignity, but also it should be evident in behavior in terms of initiative, drive, push, direction, and self-starting.

The second part, or R₂, is *respect for others.* That is not new to any of us. Part of my shame about my country is the evidence, beginning in the primary grades, of a fundamental failure of our school system and of our society at large to instill in us a respect for others. While we still use code words such as busing, we have got a long way to go. We need as a basic goal, if we are not going to completely shred the fabric of this society, to develop in ourselves and in the children with whom we work a respect for others of different backgrounds, from different racial groups, from different religious groups, from different nationality and regional groups. If we want to be held accountable, on this one we all strike out. When we can continue to spend billions for bombs and pennies for people we are a long way from respect for others. When we function in terms of "I don't want to go to school with so and so", we are a long way away. So we have to build this respect or all else will fail in a fundamental way. But there is another facet. We need to enable children to have a respect for people of different status and different authority. I do not see respect for others as just others of your age who are different than you. This may be a picture of myself at middle age teaching in a University, but I am concerned about the whole business of respect across generations, across authority levels. For us who work with children, as well as for the children then, there is not simply the ethnic respect, the racial and religious respect, but a fundamental respect for the people with whom you have to work who possess different authority statuses and different age statuses and job statuses, and ability statuses and so on.

Let us move then to the three S's. The first one is *a sense of competence.* This is the need for children, and again all of us, to have a belief in our ability to do, a belief in our own powers, a belief that what we do individually, personally, does make a difference and that each of us can accomplish some fundamental good. But this too has to be tempered a little bit with reality. Those of us who have messed around, and I use the word advisedly, with self-concept research, know that on very simple kinds of scales which we have administered at different times, you find children who report the best picture of themselves — "Anything you can do, I can do better" — if you remember that old song. And yet when you watch them behave, it isn't there. I am not talking about a false sense of competence which may really be a defense, but about enabling children to have the kinds of opportunities and experiences so that they can really sort out what they can do well, their areas of skill and contribution and ability. What are the things I can justifiably say, "Yea, I'm at the top of the pile", as well as the fundamental recognition there are some things I cannot do very well. Now I have no hesitation in admitting quite frankly that I am a total illiterate when it comes to anything to do with an automobile, outside of turning the key and pressing the accelerator. The Army invested a considerable amount of time, money, effort, coercion, and what not, trying to make a motor mechanic out of me for a short period. And, I am happy to say, it failed. Some things I know I cannot do. There are days when I am out on the highway and the car conks out and I wish I could, and all I know how to do is take my AAA sticker out and hang it on the aerial. Each of us needs to enable children and ourselves to recognize that a sense of competence is not a total thing. There are areas of competence and areas in which we recognize our lacks.

The second "S", which we have not stressed enough, is *a sense of responsibility for one's own conduct*. There are times in the third force movement, a humanistic psychology movement (of which I am not a member), in which people so concentrate on the "I", and so concentrate on the self as the fundamental and final judge that they lose sight of the fact that we live in a social world, that we have obligations to others, we have responsibilities to others, and that we must be held accountable for our own personal behavior. Children need to learn what the consequences are of what they do. Sometimes these consequences are pleasant, but sometimes in the real world they are not. They have to learn to examine the potential consequences of what they are going to do before they do it, so that they engage in a thought process of saying, "What will this do to somebody else if I simply live out whatever I think I should do?" They have to tie together the inner and the outer. They also, as part of this, need to learn to delay gratification. We are caught up in a society which lives far too impulsively and far too moment by moment. If you examine some of the research on achievement in the usual sense of the word, we know that children who cannot delay gratification have a good deal of trouble in achieving. If we still recognize that we are helping children to make it in a very complex technological society, and they are all not going to be moving back out into the woods, then they do have to learn that I've got to do something today, but my payoff may not come until next week or next year. All of us need to learn to set goals that we are not going to get to tomorrow, to not live so impulsively off the top of our heads. I think we confuse spontaneity with creativity. Creativity, at least for those who have ever been creative, is damned hard work. We need to enable kids to see that you have to stay with something and that the payoffs are not immediate. M and M's or tokens of immediate social reinforcement may actually be working against us here.

The Last "S" is *a sense of commitment.* I am very proud of the fact that in 1972, at least through November 7, my children were majoring in McGovern. I think we have been blessed that we do have a generation in their late teens and early twenties who, in spite of all we did to them in school, somehow or other (maybe because some of them had very good teachers; we know there are a great many very good and dedicated teachers) have developed a sense of responsibility for someone other than themselves. They have a commitment to serve, a nonself-centered view. This is essential. Those of you who are interested in self-concept need to include this in your definition and not see it only as the "almighty I." This means not just when you are an early adolescent or late adolescent or under twenty, but this means throughout all life. This means occasionally, maybe often, thinking more about your duties and responsibilities to others than your own immediate self-gratification. I have been troubled recently by experiences of people who have forgotten this, who have turned to self-gratification and in the process have deeply hurt other people to whom they should have had a commitment of many, many years. It does happen, and yet I think it reflects again a failure somewhere in our way of teaching, our way of learning, and in our way of life.

These are our goals. One Q and two R's and three S's. How do we get to what might affect how children might arrive at these goals? Two recent books, one of them edited by Moynihan and Mosteller (1972), a re-review of the Coleman study on Equality of Educational Opportunity, and a new book by Christopher Jencks (1972) which already is controversial, have both pointed out, although Moynihan and Jencks do not agree with each other, how much of the variability in children's learning and in children's achievement in the academic and income sense of the word is due to nonschool factors. In Moynihan and Mosteller, for example, David Armor suggests, with rather good evidence, that two-thirds of what accounts for the differences in children in their achievement is due to factors over which the school has little or no control. Recent studies by Miller (1971) in England, Keeves (1970) in Australia, Rupp (1969) in Holland, and really from throughout the world support the notion that we should not be holding the school totally accountable for the relative success of children in arriving at academic goals. These various studies indicate that the first institution which must be held accountable is the home. A good deal of "QRS" gets started and organized before arrival at school and this is why I am in the pre-school business I guess — but also continues throughout the school years. So, we as educators, cannot take total responsibility. Yet we are now developing a new definition in many places of our own role and our own responsibilities. We are beginning to recognize that we have a role in working with the family, in helping it achieve and strengthening it to achieve its fundamental central role in the education of the child. We need to see that we play a role in influencing what happens in homes as well as being influenced by the arrival on our doorstep of children from various homes.

You are familiar with the variety of home-oriented, pre-school programs of the past half-dozen years. The work of Gray (1966), Karnes (1970), Levenstein (1970, 1971, 1972, 1973) and others, as well as our Florida efforts, have demonstrated successful approaches to working with parents of pre-schoolers.

May I refer you now to the new grant made by the Office of Child Development and the Office of Education to the Educational Development Corporation in Cambridge of a half-million dollars to develop films and filmstrips and a variety of kinds of curriculum materials for high school youngsters in what they call parenting? Many high schools have set up programs for adolescent girls, but I certainly would not exclude adolescent boys. It still takes two in spite of some changes in the world. Parenting is a complex role and schools are now beginning to accept in many places a responsibility for teaching parenting as well as teaching other skills.

What specifically in the family affects "QRS"? What are effective parenting skills? Most of these ideas come out of the general research literature, not simply in the United States, but throughout the world. First, you cannot get a child to be curious and open and questioning if he comes from a shut down home. If he comes from a home that does not value and encourage questioning, open discussion, exploration, argument and debate, and all of these kinds of things, it becomes extremely difficult to reverse that in the school situation. The data are fairly clear that parents who engage in what is called spontaneous teaching, who do not sit down and say, "From 9 to 10 on Monday morning I will drill my child on a reading lesson," but who in the course of traveling in the car, shopping in the supermarket, walking down the street, watching a television program, any of the normal events, pick up the Q's, raise a question, start a debate — these parents do something that enhances that experience and converts it from simply what may be part of an ongoing stream into a highlight. One such highlight is helping youngsters to have a variety of experiences with nature itself. I was eleven years old before I knew that there was dirt under the concrete of the sidewalks of New York. It was not until they started to build the Eighth Avenue subway that I discovered there is something besides pipes under there. My daughter had to go to Israel to learn how to milk a cow. Many of our youngsters have virtually no experiences anymore with nature. I do not know how many of you are Peanuts fans, but I noticed this cartoon. Snoopy is sitting on his usual perch with his little bird friend Woodstock and he is saying, "Woodstock has never seen a fireman, a firetruck, or a candy store. He's never heard an opera or a symphony, he's never seen a movie or a play. On the other hand, he's seen the sky, the clouds, the ground, the Sun, the rain, the Moon, the stars, a cat, and several worms. Woodstock feels that he's led a very full life." I would like children to have both, the symphony and the Sun. I do not think that they could experience them in the same way Woodstock does, but nevertheless, the development of "Q" requires a wide range of exposure to the world.

The "R" develops for the child with the exhibition of parent respect and love for each other. Further, only rarely do we hear parents say, in somewhat structured teaching situations, a really warm, kind and encouraging word now and then; they rarely get an enthusiastic tone in their voices and say, "You're right on! Great! Good!" How easy it is for all of us to forget how important that is. How rarely do we do it to each other in our daily lives. Further, it needs to be done in relation to the person's areas of concern. For example, if you were to comment that's a nice suit I have on today, my professional ego is not very tied up in clothes. I really want to know that somebody thinks I am a good teacher rather than how I look. We do not do very much of this in the home and we do not do very much of this generally.

The involvement of children in family affairs, in both the chores that have to be done and the decisions that have to be made, seems to me to be fundamental. There was a marvelous cartoon about Lyndon Johnson several years ago which showed Lady Bird saying to Lyndon, "On your way to the state department take out the garbage." We need to say that to children too. All of us can be garbage-taker-outers, room-cleaner-uppers, not because we learn responsibility that way, that is a myth, but simply because the darn thing has got to get done. The child as a member of the family has to help to get the things done. In many families we have abandoned this or we have attached it to payment or we have done all kinds of things with it that get away from the basic idea that part of one's self-respect comes from seeing oneself playing a positive, necessary, fruitful role in preserving the family and helping it move along.

Children need to see their parents as able and competent at playing a role. One of the fundamental goals of many of our programs for youngsters is to involve parents in decision-making, not only because parents have a basic right to be involved in decision-making, but also because then their children can see that society as an institution recognizes the parent is competent and able. Note how often not only poor but also middle-class and even well-educated parents feel alienated and incomplete and out of it in their ability to affect the school. When children hear parents say, "There's nothing I can do about it", this detracts from the development of their self-respect.

Basically, in terms of what Maslow would have called the basic physiological needs, we have to be sure the child has enough to eat and he is healthy and his physical needs are being met. You can have a great many other things, but if you do not have an adequate diet lots of other development will go down the drain. As Herbert Buck said, "Love is not enough; you've got to have a full belly, too." Therefore, we cannot look at the family and our role in relation to helping the family on Q and R without getting into a more comprehensive view of what needs to go on.

The second "R" is *respect for others*. All of us know that in homes we talk about others. But we need to talk about others in a non-Archie Bunker fashion. "All in the Family" is great to watch for half an hour on Saturday, but I wonder how his daughter made it. She must have gotten it someplace else. She sure did not get it from Archie. She probably got it from her mother. We do know that in many homes, people of different groups, different backgrounds, different classes, different incomes are referred to in extremely derogatory terms. People come to the door, people come to work, people do all kinds of things around the home. The child sees the way his parents deal with the variety of people with whom they come in contact. We need to remember that the parent, then, is a fundamental model in enabling the child to arrive at respect for others. Along with that the child needs considerable experience in relating to others on the street, in the recreation program, at school and the scouts, and wherever. Now, I would be foolish if I said to you that all the experiences are going to be pleasant. Children are going to fight, have fought from time immemorial about anything, from whose father was stronger than whose father, what block you live on, race, religion, and everything else. We should not assume that simply placing children together in a group and saying to them love each other, means they are going to do it. But they will work their way through. The solution is not to reseparate them; the solution is to assist them in working their way through.

We need to have in the home authority with reason rather than with threat. There is the story that Basil Bernstein tells for other purposes, in terms of language development, about the mother who gets on the bus in London with a four-year-old. The child stands on the seat and she proceeds to tell him why he should sit down, "It's not polite to stand up, the man in back of you can't see out the window, you're getting the seat dirty," on and on and on, and the child is still standing up. Finally she swats him and down he goes. The next child gets on the bus with another mother and he stands on the seat and she just starts with a swat and down he goes. The second mother in one sense of the word is more efficient; the child sat down. But the first mother is really, in terms of development of understanding, and respect, and everything else (and in terms of language development incidentally), the far more effective mother. We do an awful lot of the authority-without-reason thing in school. We may not do the physical swat but we sure do the verbal one. Children only can learn to respect others if they in turn have been treated with respect.

Now we move to those S's again. The sense of competence comes out of experiences with objects and people and situations in which the child gets some positive response. We can think of innumerable examples at all age levels. In terms of the sense of responsibility for his own conduct, the child needs to live with real consequences. I am not advocating teaching the child that the stove is hot by burning his hand, but very often we shield children from the realities of the world. We do not have an if-then orientation toward them; we set some kind of an if-then and we do not follow through. They need to learn that behavior has its consequences, sometimes pleasant and sometimes not. They must be faced with reality and not so protected that they think that they can control everything, that they themselves are truly the center of the universe. All of us has faced the child coming home and saying, "Everybody else is doing it," and you know the difficulty you have in saying, "That's great for them but in our family we don't." As you explore you find out it is not everybody else, it is just one other that is doing something . . .

We should shift a child from saying life is complete when I have my own room, my own television set, my own hi-fi, my own guitar, my own this, my own that, or whatever it happens to be, to realize that life is more than this indulgence. We need to model a sense of commitment. Only by demonstrating by our activities our commitment to the causes and beliefs that we hold, by getting out and doing, by voting, by working for others, by contributing, by getting up and speaking, do we show the worth of a sense of commitment. Only as we demonstrate, in our own personal lives and in our behavior to each other as family members, that our committment transcends sometimes our own personal self-centered needs and recognizes our concerns for other members of the family, can children see the value and worth of this sense.

All the QRS's need to be conveyed within a climate of love, joy, laughter, and open expression. It is not a matter of a curriculum in which we sit down and say, "Today I am going to do spontaneous teaching and at ten o'clock I am going to involve the kid in family affairs. We know it is not that kind of thing at all. We do not need a new course. It means an opportunity to talk about anything, a sense of backup and support, an honest flow of information, a clear demonstration of standards. But what else does the family require? It requires a belief on parents' parts that what they do early and often makes a difference, that you cannot begin to communicate with the child at thirteen years if you have not communicated with him at thirteen months. We see so many of our friends in different places around the country who say, "I can't talk to my kid anymore." When my wife and I talk it over later, we say, "Hell, they never did." We need a commitment, then, to parenting as a vital role. It is a dignified role and it requires effort, and one does not arrive at it purely by biology.

But accountability is predominantly a school problem, and you can say, "This is interesting about parents, but what do I do about my job as a teacher, administrator, or other professional in relation to those Q's and R's and S's?" First, have we encouraged families to believe in their worth? I am continually struck by parents who say to me, "Teachers have told me not to, to not dare do that at home because they're going to take care of that in school." The horror, of course, is when ghetto parents tell me that not only did the teacher not let them do it or not encourage them to do it at home, but the children really did not get it in school either.

Reading is a very good example of this. Generally the attitude that educators have taken is that learning is one private preserve of the school and that nobody else knows how to do it or ought to do it. I would suggest that learning goes on every minute, everyday. It stands to reason that we find two-thirds of what counts is outside the schools because two-thirds of the child's life is outside the school. Therefore, one of our jobs as school people is to understand this, to translate, to work with the other kinds of agencies, especially the family which has the fundamental role.

But we can look just at school. First, is the school itself set up for inquiry and discussion? That is an awful standard to be held accountable for. You can walk into school buildings, and all of you have at different times, and you do not need a very elaborate forty item questionnaire to know what's happening. You can sometimes stick a wet finger in the air and sense something is going on in this building that looks interesting, exciting, and you can walk into another building and know it is shut down, that people are there but nothing is happening. Does the school itself create an environment that fosters inquiry and debate? Take a look at your next faculty meeting; it is rare if there is any inquiry and discussion and debate.

Second, in terms of respect for self, if teachers do not have respect from administrators, if school systems, school boards, superintendents, curriculum experts, principals, and parents do not see the teacher as worthy of respect, then it is extremely difficult for the teacher in turn to demonstrate respect for children. You cannot hold the teacher accountable for the development of self-respect, self-esteem, and dignity if he or she is treated as a hired hand with no respect, self-esteem, or dignity. That applies whether it is the kindergarten teacher or the college professor. The encouragement of the teacher's initiative and self-direction, the setting of the kind of school or university stage in which the teacher is free to grow, to inquire, to wander, to explore, are essential if we are going to be able in turn to teach children to learn, within some orderly set of bounds. Gardner Murphy (1958) once beautifully expressed the thought in reference to fostering children's creativity: "It may be necessary to encourage a long period of grasping and gloating, messing and manipulating . . . He [the child] must richly experience, richly interweave, richly integrate while the mind glows in earnest contact with these delights . . ." This applies to teachers as well.

Let me give you an example of part of another way of looking at R_1. Do we as adults treat children with respect? I had the delightful opportunity to be in London last spring to visit an infant school for five-, six-, and seven-year-olds. We cannot, of course, generalize that this is *the* British infant school; this was *a* school. Four of us from the States met with the head mistress in her office. She closed the door to stop and talk with us. There was a knock on the door and the door broke open and five little ones were standing there. She asked, "Yes, can I help you?" Aside she said to us, "You know, the door is never closed. They don't know what to do with a closed door." They said, "Well, we'd like to talk with you." She said, "I have some visitors here. Is it very vital?" They said, "No, it can wait." She said, "Why don't you came back in a little while when I'm finished here and I'll be glad to talk with you." The children said okay and turned around and left. I would like to see that happen in PS 132 in New York where I grew up, I would more likely be "Who are you?, what do you want?, get out of here!" as the basic kind of response to the children. I talked later in the afternoon with one of the children who said, "I just had coffee with the Head." Having once been stationed on Navy ships, I had a different connotation, but I said, in my best, cool fashion as I once learned as a counselor, "Oh, would you care to tell me more about that?" He said, "Yeah, some of us just felt it had been a long time since we had a chance to chat. And so we went to the Head and said, you know, we'd like a tea and chat, and she said well I don't have any tea now, I have some coffee, so I had coffee with the Head." The whole climate of access in a school with several hundred children, where a little five-year-old who felt quite free to say, "I'd like tea and chat," is a climate that builds self-respect and is something that we can do in school.

When we look at what we can do in school in terms of respect for others, we can look at it in two ways. First, the encouragement of real integration. You cannot basically learn to respect others if you have no dealings with them. As I said earlier, I deplore what I see as a movement away from a fundamental commitment. Second, we need in the curriculum to have music, art, social studies, science, geography, and literature which emphasize the multiple roots from which our people came, and the contributions and values of all. We should not do this superficially. I remember going to a second grade around Christmas time and they had piñatas up. The children were having a delightful time with the piñatas. The teacher told me she was teaching them about Mexico. Now if all the children know about Mexico and Mexican culture is piñata, forget it. It is a long way from a real understanding of the roots of a great many of the people who live in this country. Similarly, I attended a playday in one of our Follow-Through schools in Philadelphia which was over 90% black. This is where each class puts on something on the stage and all the proud parents sit in the audience. It is one way of getting the parents there because their children are performing. What enthralled me was the children did Dutch dances, Elizabethan May Pole things, sang Scandanavian songs, put on a little piece of Mikado, but there was no reference in the art, in the music, in the songs, in the dances, in anything that took place that day, to the black experience of these parents and these children. What really astounded me was that the teachers were black and were negating their own rich heritage. We need to explore how to represent positively, not just for the black children but for all children, the contributions of the Black, the Chicano, the Jew, the Pole, the Italian, the Chinese, and maybe even the Wasp. How do we set up this respect for others?

To develop a *sense of competence,* children need opportunities for success, the use of noncomparative judgments, evaluation in terms of their movement and their performance, and not in terms of their standing in a group. We have a lot of evidence to support this from all kinds of research.

Movements toward S_2 *(responsibility for action)* can be aided by the involvement of children in real decision-making, in setting limits, in a sense of responsibility for the operation of the classroom. All of us have engaged in pupil-teacher planning. All of us know that it is often a farce, and that pupil-teacher planning is the manipulation of children to come out where teachers wanted them to come out. What I am talking about is an honest commitment, that if we involve the children we really do not quite know what will come out. Whatever comes out is grist for the mill, is useful, can be converted into the Q and the R and the S.

Commitment to others can be fostered by developing the kinds of curriculum and experiences in which children get out of the building, explore local affairs, find out why that creek is polluted, participate in local government, or, as adolescents, work in the crisis center, help man the day care centers, or ring the doorbells to help get people out to vote. It requires a recognition that a good deal of learning takes place outside the classroom, but that it is still part of the school.

If by accountability we mean measurement, how do we measure the success of the school in moving children, as much as the school can be responsible, toward inquiry, toward respect for self and others, toward a sense of competence and commitment and responsibility? I have no quarrel with performance measures. We can and should develop performance measures. We can see whether or not we have set up the kinds of schools that encourage these goals, whether children are moving toward them, and we can use performance measures to do it. In the late 1950's and

218/Educational Accountability

early 1960's, a series of studies under the direction of Vynce Hines, Kimball Wiles and Maurice Ahrens of the College of Education, University of Florida, were conducted in Tampa, which analyzed principal attitudes and principal behavior and the effect of these attitudes and behavior on teacher morale, teacher performance, and, in the long run, on pupil behavior. These studies are a mine of information of ways you can carefully and systematically look at the climate of a school and get at what the principal believes by what he puts into practice. We can examine, through systematic observation, the Day Care Center, as Prescott (1967) and her associates did, or the classroom, as we at the Institute for Development of Human Resources, among other groups around the country, have done. We have developed a series of measures which can be used to indicate whether the room and the school are setup for these goals to happen, and also whether actions of children demonstrate they are achieving these goals. Bob Soar's work (1971, 1972), for example, using the measures he himself developed and those developed by Bob Brown (1968) and Dick Ober (1968) have been applied in Follow Through classrooms and have demonstrated their worth.

Let me be very specific as to what I mean. Take the business of the inquiring mind. On Bob Brown's Teacher Practices Observation Record (TPOR) you can pick up such things as, does the teacher:

1. Involve the pupil in uncertain, though incomplete situations?
2. Lead the pupil to a question or problem which stumps him?
3. Ask the kind of question that is not readily answerable by a study of the lesson?
4. Permit the pupil to suggest additional or alternative answers?
5. Encourage the pupil to guess or hypothesize about the unknown or untested?
6. Entertain even wild or far-out suggestions by pupils?
7. Ask the pupil for support for his answer or opinion by the provision of evidence?

The Florida Taxonomy of Cognitive Behavior, an observational schedule built on Blooms' Taxonomy, includes such items for either teacher or pupil as:

1. Seeks information
2. Asks and gives reason
3. Asks who, what, or where
4. Infers feeling or motive
5. Infers causality

6. Cites evidence for conclusion
7. Proposes plan or rule
8. Compares with criteria rule or plan

An observation schedule I am working on, growing out of anecdotal records of classroom teacher-pupil behavior, contains the following items for the teacher in addition to items covered on the TPOR and the Cognitive Taxonomy:

1. Provides material and time for the pupil to develop ideas
2. Asks "How would you predict?" questions
3. Asks pupils for their questions
4. Makes "if, then" statements

All of the above items can be used to assess pupil behavior. In addition one can observe pupils who:

1. Find their own information
2. Use reference materials independently
3. Implement or develop their own ideas
4. Engage in the decision-making process
5. Ask questions about the subject
6. Pose problems

In a series of studies conducted by Mary Budd Rowe (1972, 1973), the phenomenon of "wait time" was investigated. These studies investigated what happens to classroom inquiry in elementary science when teachers move from their usual pattern of (1) asking a question, (2) waiting less than a second for a response before cuing, and then, when a child makes a response, (3) waiting less than a second before responding. She and her colleagues found that when teachers waited about 3 seconds and engaged in low overt verbal reward schedules the (1) length of student responses increased, (2) the number of unsolicited but appropriate student responses increased, (3) the number of student/student comparing increased, (4) more evidence followed by or preceded by inference statements occurred, (5) the number of questions asked by children increased and (6) the number of experiments they proposed increased. Children also engage in more structuring, soliciting, and reacting behaviors. Further, the number and kind of teacher questions changed from the usual information type to including more leading and probing questions.

We see then that we have a beginning technology for the examination of inquiry behavior in the classroom, but that is perhaps the most cognitive and, therefore, the easiest. What about our R's and S's?

Soar's FLACCS, the Florida Climate and Control System, yields a number of observables for *respect for self*. First, looking at teacher behavior:

1. Does the teacher move freely among the pupils?
2. Does she engage in positive redirection, attend pupil closely, give individual attention?
3. Does she praise, smile, laugh, nod?

On the negative side:
1. Does she ignore and refuse to attend to pupils?

Other items from our anecdotal material are, does the teacher:
1. Admit error in content and schedule?
2. Listen to the pupil's opinion?
3. Ask for pupil's opinion?
4. Use group discussion to allow feelings to be expressed?
5. Have the pupil write stories about himself?
6. Have the pupil make tape recordings?
7. Tell the pupil about his work?

On the negative side, does the teacher:
1. Humiliate?
2. Yell at pupils?
3. Punish pupils for showing expressions of anger?
4. Put her hand over the pupil's mouth or even in some cases use scotch tape?
5. Require pupils to line up for everything?
6. Require pupils to work only on specific instructions from the teacher?

Some positive evidence for pupils can be:
1. Trying again after failure
2. Initiating an activity or experience
3. Sharing a personal triumph as well as problems with teachers and pupils
4. Telling teachers negative feelings
5. Expressing positive moods.

Alan Coller has pulled together for ERIC/ECE the variety of assessment methods used to get at self-concept in young children. His review indicates that we are still a long way from effective measurement, but that observation and inference is probably our best bet at the moment.

We can examine *respect for others* through Bob Soar's FLACCS which contains such items as:
1. Pupil is helpful and shares

2. Pupil chooses another
3. Pupil pats and hugs another
4. Offers to share and cooperate
5. Initiates contact
6. Agrees with another
7. Sounds friendly towards another
8. Praises another
9. Helps another

It is also possible to pick up the negative effect of:
1. Making disparaging remarks
2. Threatening another
3. Making a face at another
4. Being uncooperative
5. Interfering or threatening
6. Taking or damaging the property of another
7. Picking at another child
8. Hurting another child

We have been able to see and code the following from our anecdotal approach. Teachers who:
1. Tell pupils not to disturb others who are working
2. Tell pupils to keep hands to themselves
3. Tell pupils not to disturb by moving around
4. Ask pupils to help others
5. Reward pupils who help others in their work
6. Tell pupils not to belittle others who cannot do the work
7. Tell pupils to share materials and information with others
8. Compliment pupils for good sportsmanship when it occurs
9. Compliment the class when they show care and concern
10. Talk to the class about others' limitations as a means of helping them understand each other
11. Use stories and films to explore the culture of ethnic groups
12. Verbally disapprove of derogatory remarks about race, religion, nationality
13. Ask the class about how they think others might feel
14. Verbally disapprove of pupils who are belittling other class members
15. Ask the class to discuss differences in people
16. Discuss controversial issues with the class

We have seen pupils who:
1. Give credit to another pupil
2. Work cooperatively in a group
3. Share information and materials

4. Listen to others
5. Can discuss controversial issues
6. Engage in effective group discussion

There are, of course, the usual socio-metric techniques and social reputation techniques for assessing pupils' acceptance of others. We can observe how they relate after school, the language they use, and the way they play on the playground.

So even in this so-called difficult area of the self, we have an emergency technology which allows us to use performance-based items to see whether schools are setting the stage and pupils are indeed exhibiting respect for self and others.

Our three S's are also observable. For S_1, the *sense of competence,* we have a number of measures of self-esteem, both self-report type and observational. Here let me again stress the observational. There is obviously overlap with our inquiry area and with the respect for self, but one can see a teacher who:

1. Has pupils find their own information
2. Provides the time and opportunity for the pupil to use special aids, language aids, language master, tape recorder, listening center
3. Tells the pupils when they have done a good job
4. Displays pupils' work
5. Gives alternative ways of working when a pupil shows a lack of interest or frustration
6. Keeps a record of work accomplished (a visible record)
7. Gives extra time to those who need it

On the negative side:
1. Makes all the decisions about curriculum and behavior

One can see pupils who:
1. Admit errors
2. Ask teachers for help
3. Ask other pupils for help
4. Move freely to get materials without correction
5. Volunteer
6. Seek independent work
7. Stay with great persistence at tasks
8. Seek the hardest of things to do
9. Actually do perform well on product measures of school achievement

When we look at *the sense of responsibility for one's own conduct,* we find that schools have been working on this for a long time, but usually from the negative direction of coercive and authoritarian means. We can see, and can encourage teachers who organize classes into committees and work groups, who provide time for class meetings, and who on Bob Brown's TPOR:

1. Have pupils make own collection analysis of subject matter
2. Have pupils find detailed facts and information on their own
3. Have pupils work independently on what concerns the pupil
4. Encourage self discipline on the part of the pupil
5. Withhold judgment on pupil's behavior or work
6. Encourage the pupil to put his ideas to a test
7. Evaluate the work of different pupils by different standards

Soar's FLACCS also has relevant items. You can observe pupils who work and play with little supervision, who follow routines without reminders, who engage in task-related movement around the room.

Our anecdotal records reveal the following as negative influences:

The teacher who:
1. Allows no discussion
2. Makes all the rules and decisions
3. Tells pupils to raise their hands and wait their turn and stay in their seats
4. Helps pupils only when they raise their hands for help

Last, we come to *the sense of commitment* which obviously relates to the above. A study by Severy and David (1971) yielded the shocking finding that mentally retarded children, especially preschoolers, engaged in far more helping behavior than did normal children, especially those in the middle grades. One could relate this to what behaviors are modeled and encouraged in special classrooms as opposed to those in our regular school. They coded the following as helping behaviors and saw them divided into psychological and task oriented help:

1. Showing concern
2. Advising, suggesting, or interpreting
3. Comforting or reassuring
4. Fixing something
5. Protecting, warning, defending
6. Getting help for somebody else, helping another accomplish a task, or helping out in distress
7. Offering needed help

The FLACCS has a number of similar classroom observation items. We saw some teachers who rewarded helping behavior,

discussed the problem of helping, talked about leadership responsibility, but generally we found that most of the classrooms we
observed seemed to discourage this pattern in favor of the "do
your own work" pattern. From my perspective, children need to
learn both, how to work independently and how to help and share.
We need a better balance.

Both the conditions and achievement of success in the area
of the sense of competence, responsibility, and commitment have
a beginning technology. Behaviors can be stated carefully and
can be observed.

If we adopt the notion that QRS's are as important outcomes
of home and school as ABC's and reading, writing, and arithmetic,
we cannot abandon the definition of success and the measurement of it only to the latter domains. While our instruments are
still crude, the beginnings of them do exist and we can and should
be held accountable for achievement, for what we do. We can
measure and we can become just as careful and "respectable"
as those who measure minutiae. Success and accountability need
not be dirty words or code words for narrow goals. We should
not abandon the field to those who define achievement only as
reading skills. We should seize the opportunity to use our own
inquiring minds, our own respect for self and others, and our
own senses of competence, responsibility, and commitment to
demonstrate both effective teaching and the establishment of
learning climates in home and school, and effective learning which
enables children to answer, "Who in the world am I?" We should
then demand real accountability from our peers and our parents
as we seek to achieve this broader definition of success.

REFERENCES

Brown, B. B. **The Experimental Mind in Education.** New York: Harper and
Row, 1968.

Coller, A. R. "The Assessment of 'Self-Concept' in Early Childhood Education."
Urbana, Ill.: ERIC Clearinghouse on Early Childhood Education, 1971.

Gordon, I. J. "Early Child Stimulation Through Parent Education." Final Report,
June, 1969, University of Florida, ED 033-912, Children's Bureau.

Gordon, I. J. "A Home Learning Center Approach to Early Stimulation. Progress
Report, June, 1972, University of Florida, Grant No. 5 ROI MH 16037-04, National
Institute of Mental Health.

Gordon, I. J. "The Florida Parent Education Early Intervention Projects: A Longitudi-
nal Look." Modified from a paper presented at the Merrill-Palmer Conference
on Research and Teaching of Infant Development, Detroit, February 8, 1973.

Gordon, I. J. and Jester, R. E. "Instructional Strategies of Infant Stimulation, JSAS. **Catalog of Selected Documents in Psychology,** 1972, **2,** 122.

Gray, S. W., *et al.* **Before First Grade: The Early Training Project for Culturally Disadvantaged Children.** New York: Teachers College Press, 1966.

Hines, V. A., Wiles, K., and Ahrens, M. "F Scale-Gamin and Public School Principal Behavior." **Journal of Educational Psychology,** 1956, **47,** 321-328.

Hines, V. A., Wiles, K., and Ahrens, M. "As Others See You." **Progressive Education,** 1957, **34,** 126-128.

Hines, V. A., Wiles, K., and Ahrens, M. "Democratic Administration: Passé, Cliché, Touché?" **High School Journal,** 1959, **42,** 106-112.

Hines, V. A., Wiles, K., and Ahrens, M. "Good Principal, Effective Leader." **Overview,** 1961, **2,** 31-32.

Jencks, C. **Inequality: A Reassessment of the Effect of Family and Schooling in America.** New York: Basic Books, 1972.

Karnes, M. B. "Educational Intervention at Home by Mothers of Disadvantaged Infants." **Child Development,** 1970, **41,** 925-935.

Keeves, J. P. "The Home Environment and Educational Achievement." Unpublished manuscript, Australia National University, Ocober, 1970.

Levenstein, P. "Cognitive Growth in Preschoolers Through Verbal Interaction at Home by Mothers of Disadvantaged Infants." **American Journal of Orthopsychiatry,** 1970, **40,** 426-432.

Levenstein, P. "Learning Through (and From) Mothers." **Childhood Education,** 1971, **48,** 130-134.

Levenstein, P. "But Does It .Work in Homes Away From Home?" **Theory into Practice,** 1972, **11,** 157-162.

Levenstein, P., *et àl.* "From Laboratory to Real World: Service Delivery of the Mother-Child Home Program." **American Journal of Orthopsychiatry,** 1973, **43,** 72-78.

Miller, G. W. **Educational Opportunity and the Home.** London: Longman Group, 1971.

Moynihan, C. and Mosteller, F., Eds. **On Equality of Educational Opportunity.** New York: Random House, 1972.

Murphy, G. **Human Potentialities.** New York: Basic Books, 1958.

Ober, R. L. "Reciprocal Category System." Gainesville, Florida: Florida Educational Research and Development Council, 1968. Reprinted in **Journal of Research and Development in Education,** 1970, **4,** 34-51.

Prescott, E., Jones, E. and Kritchevsky, S. "Group Day Care as A Child Rearing Environment." 1967, Pacific Oaks College, ED 024-453, Children's Bureau.

Rowe, M. B. "Wait-Time and Rewards as Instructional Variables: Their Influence on Language, Logic and Fate Control." Paper presented at the meeting of the National Association for Research in Science Teaching (NARST), Spring, 1972.

Rowe, M. B. **Teaching Science as Continuous Inquiry.** New York: McGraw Hill, 1973.

Rupp, J. C. C. **Oprveding Tot School-Weerbaarhend (Helping the Child to Cope With School).** Groninger, Netherlands: Woltens-Noordhoff, 1969.

Severy, L. J. and Davis, K. E. "Helping Behavior Among Normal and Retarded Children." **Child Development,** 1971, 4, 1017-1031.

Soar, R. "Research Findings from Systematic Observation." **Journal of Research and Development in Education,** 1970, 4, 116-122.

Soar, R. "Empirical Analysis of Selected Follow Through Programs: An Example of A Process Approach to Evaluation." **National Society for the Study of Education Yearbook,** Chicago: University of Chicago Press, 1972.

Humanistic Goals of Education

ARTHUR W. COMBS

We need good citizens, free of prejudice, concerned about their fellow citizens, loving, caring fathers and mothers, persons of goodwill whose values and purposes are positive, feeling persons with wants and desires likely to motivate them toward positive interactions. These are the things that make us human. Without them we are automatons, fair game for whatever crowd-swaying, stimulus-manipulating demagogue comes down the pike.

Modern education must produce far more than persons with cognitive skills. It must produce *humane* individuals, persons who can be relied upon to pull their own weight in our society, who can be counted upon to behave responsibly and cooperatively. We need good citizens, free of prejudice, concerned about their fellow citizens, loving, caring fathers and mothers, persons of goodwill whose values and purposes are positive, feeling persons with wants and desires likely to motivate them toward positive interactions. These are the things that make us human. Without them we are automatons, fair game for whatever crowd-swaying demagogue comes down the pike. The humane qualities are absolutely essential to our way of life — far more important, even, than the learning of reading, for example. . . .

Self-Actualization — Primary Goal of Education

Social scientists in recent years have given increasing thought to the problem of self-actualization. "What," they ask, "does it

Arthur W. Combs, **Educational Accountability: Beyond Behavioral Objectives.** Washington, D.C.: Association for Supravision and Curriculum Development, 1973. pp. 23-40. Reprinted with permission of the Association for Supervision and Curriculum Development. Copyright © 1973 by the Association for Supervision and Curriculum Development.

mean for a person to be truly operating at the fullest extent of his possibilities?" The answers they find to these questions are helping us to understand what self-actualizing persons are like and how it is possible to produce them. These studies are in many ways among the most exciting currently occurring on the psychological scene. To this point, four basic qualities seem to be central to the dynamics of such personalities. Self-actualizing persons are:

1. Well informed
2. Possessed of positive self-concepts
3. Open to their experience, and
4. Possessed of deep feelings of identification with others.

Informed educators have taken their cues from this work.

Self-actualization is not just a nice idea — whatever we decide is the nature of the fully-functioning, self-actualizing person must also be the goal of education, as of every other institution for human welfare. The production of such persons is, after all, what it is all about. In 1962 one group of educators tackled the problem of trying to define what the basic principles of self-actualization might mean for education. This work has been published in the ASCD 1962 Yearbook entitled *Perceiving, Behaving, Becoming*[1], a volume which is among the most popular in educational history and which, though it is now ten years old, continues to be an educational best seller.

The authors of this book began with a series of papers by four outstanding psychologists who defined the nature of self-actualization. From that beginning the educators asked, "If these things are so, what does this mean for education?"

In the course of their examination they found innumerable aspects in the current educational scene which actually prevent the development of healthy personalities. They were also led in their discussions to point the way toward new objectives for education more likely to achieve the production of self-actualizing persons than those to which we have been accustomed.

Many people believe that there is no place in our educational structure for "affective" concerns. They ask, "Do you want education for intellect or adjustment?" As though it were necessary for us to make a choice between the production of smart psychotics and well-adjusted dopes! Affective, healing aspects of behavior are not something separate and apart from cognition. Modern psychologists tell us that affect or feeling is simply an artifact of the degree of personal relevance of the event perceived. We have no feeling about that which is of no concern to us. The greater the degree of personal relevance, the greater is the degree of feeling or affect or emotion which is likely to be experienced by the behaver. The attempt to rule out the humane aspects of life from the classroom is thus to make the classroom sterile. If affect has to do with relevance, then we are either going to have affective education or none at all. If the human qualities we expect of education are important, they must be given their proper place in the perspective we take on accountability. We cannot afford to be so preoccupied with the cognitive, behavioral aspects that we later find we have "thrown out the baby with the bath water."

Unfortunately, humane qualities are already relegated in our public schools to "general" objectives — which means they are generally ignored — while teachers concentrate their efforts on what they are going to be evaluated on. English teachers concentrate on English, coaches concentrate on winning football games, science teachers concentrate on getting students into national science competition, and elementary teachers are evaluated on how well children learn to read, write, and figure. But no one evaluates teachers on whether their students are becoming good citizens, learning to care for each other, work together, etc. Everyone knows that people tend to do those things they are being evaluated for. Indeed, it is an understanding of this fact that has brought about the pressures for accountability. If humane qualities are to be achieved, such qualities must be given front rank in importance and schools must be held accountable for their nurture.

If the four qualities of self-actualization previously mentioned are accurate, we need much more than behavioral objectives as criteria for their achievement. Such questions as a positive self-concept, openness to experience, and identification do not lend themselves to behavioral measurement. Aspects of self-actualization can be assessed, but rarely in precise behavioral terms. Indeed, the attempt to do so may even impede their effectual development. The humane qualities we seek in education, such as positive self-concepts, feelings of identification, responsibility, openness to experience, adaptability, creativity, effective human relationships are, like any other behavior, outcomes of *personal meaning;* and it is here that we need to look for answers to our problems of accountability.

The Assessment of Personal Meaning

To deal effectively with the internal qualities of personal meaning and the humane objectives of education, a new approach is needed. Called for is a psychology that differs from the limited concepts available to us in the various forms of S-R psychology with which we traditionally have lived. What is needed is a humanistic psychology expressly designed to deal with the human aspects of personality and behavior, a psychology which does not ignore the student's belief systems but makes them central to its concerns. Fortunately, such a psychology is already with us.

The past 30 years have seen the appearance of "humanistic" psychology on the American scene. This approach has a holistic character capable of dealing quite directly with many of the more general objectives of education.[2] Psychologists attached to this new frame of reference call themselves by many names: self psychologists, transactionalists, existentialists, phenomenologists, perceptualists, and the like. By whatever name, however, these psychologists are concerned with more than the specific, precisely designed behaviors of individuals. They are deeply concerned with questions of values, human goals and aspirations, feelings, attitudes, hopes, meaning, and perceptions of self and the world. These are the qualities which make us human, and it is because of these concerns that this point of view has come to be known as the humanistic approach. Humanistic approaches to psychology, it should be clearly understood, do not deny the tenets of behavioral approaches. Quite the contrary, they include such approaches, but extend beyond them to deal with more holistic matters not readily treated in the older behavioral system. This is precisely what is needed in modern approaches to educational accountability.

Behavioral objectives provide too narrow a basis for proper assessment of educational outcomes, and our concepts of accountability must be expanded if they are properly to match the broadest goals and requirements for our educational system. Humanistic approaches to psychological thought provide us with theoretical guidelines to effective practice consistent with these broader goals. It is high time that these new conceptions be made an integral part of the training of educators and given wide dissemination throughout the profession. Interested readers may find an introduction to this position in the work of such writers[3] as Carl R. Rogers, Abraham Maslow, Arthur W. Combs, Earl Kelley, Gordon Allport, and William Purkey.

What is needed now is a systematic attempt to give principles and contributions of humanistic psychology wider understanding at every level of our educational structure. This is a point of view specifically designed to deal with the problems of personal meaning. As a consequence it is able to provide important guidelines for thinking about our broader objectives, for finding better ways to achieve them, and for assessing whether or not our educational processes have truly achieved their objectives.

If behavior is symptom and meaning is cause, then if we could somehow assess meaning we would not need to be so concerned about measurement of behavior. Meanings, however, lie inside persons and, at first glance, it would seem impossible to assess them. It is true that meanings cannot be observed directly, but neither can electricity, and we have managed to measure that pretty effectively by inference. The same thing works for personal meaning. While meanings cannot be read directly, they can be inferred by a process of "reading behavior backward." If it is true that behavior is the product of perception, then it should be possible to observe a person's behavior and infer the nature of the perceptions which produced it.

Actually, this is what all of us do in interpreting the behavior of those who are important to us. In our research at the University of Florida on the helping professions, we find it also the approach to students, patients, and clients which distinguishes effective counselors, teachers, nurses, professors, and Episcopal priests from ineffective ones.[4] Such inferences are not made by seeking one-to-one concomitants. The process calls for a holistic rather than an atomistic approach to understanding human behavior. Instead of cataloging specific behaviors, the observer uses himself as an observation instrument and observes all he can by immersing himself in the situation. By a continuous process of observing, inferring, and testing his inferences over and over, he is able in time to arrive at accurate understandings of the peculiar meanings producing the behavior in the persons he is observing. Meanings can be assessed.

The problem is not one of learning to do something entirely new. It is a matter of learning to do what all of us already do occasionally with persons who are important to us. We have little trouble being sensitive to and interpretive of meanings existing for those above us in the hierarchy, such as principals, supervisors, and superintendents. What is needed now is to learn to do these things more often, more precisely, and in more disciplined fashion with persons in positions subservient to us, such as students. These are skills that can be learned. Indeed, many fine teachers already have them.

The assessment of meaning has an additional advantage. It focuses the attention of educators on the causes of behavior directly. The attempt to catalog behaviors with too great specificity may actually take us further and further away from the basic meanings producing them. Assessing outcomes through global behavior is likely to be somewhat closer to the basic causes of behavior but may still be far less exact than we might desire. As a matter of fact, too much attention to the observation of specific behavior can seriously interfere with understanding the causes of behavior, by concentrating attention on symptoms rather than causes. Like hundreds of other teachers of "Human Growth and Development," I used to send my young teachers-in-training to observe the behavior of a child in the classroom, insisting that they should record precisely what the child did from moment to moment. These instructions were intended to discipline the student into being a careful observer.

This is still standard practice in many colleges of education. Unfortunately, what it does is to concentrate the student's attention on the behavior of the child instead of on the causes of that behavior. In recent years I have found it more helpful to send students into a classroom, not to observe it, but to participate in it. They are instructed to "get the feel" of the classroom. "See if you can figure out how the child is thinking and feeling about himself, his classmates, his teachers, the work of the school. See if you can figure out his purposes, what he is trying to do, then tell me what you saw that made you think your inference was accurate." This procedure concentrates the student's attention on making and supporting inferences about the causes of children's behavior rather than on simply observing the symptoms. I find that since we have adopted this system my students have become far more effective than previously.

If such procedures for assessing meaning seem imprecise and vague as we have described them here, they need not be. It is quite possible to make inferences with high degrees of accuracy and reliability by application of the usual tests for scientific [validity: 1) feelings of subjective certainty, 2) conformity with known facts, 3) mental manipulation, 4) predictive power, 5) social agreement, and 6) internal consistency.] . . .[5] Inferential techniques are already widely used in psychological research, especially in the study of such personal meanings as attitudes, beliefs, self-concept, and purposes. The assessment of meaning outcomes of education can be made with whatever degree of precision is desired, from informal observation to highly controlled and systematized procedures.

The exploration of highly personal meaning, of course, does not lend itself well to study by standardized techniques. There are, however, procedures in fairly wide use for the assessment of meanings of a more general sort. With a comparatively small diversion of funds and human talent currently assigned to behavioral approaches to the problem, many more could be developed within a comparatively short time. If the heart of learning is the personal discovery of meaning, the proper assessment of educational outcomes should be the most accurate possible understanding of the personal meanings being produced by the system. Use of behavioral objectives is a highly inaccurate approach to that problem. If the goals of accountability are to be achieved, we are going to have to find ways of assessing personal meaning more accurately and simply.

Traditional psychologists of S-R, behavioristic persuasion are often aghast at inferential procedures which seem to them to be grossly unscientific and subjective. Their commitment to the behavioristic approach to psychology makes it impossible for them to accept inferential techniques, even though these have long since been adopted in many of the physical sciences for solution to some of their knottiest problems. The formulation of inferences *can* be made highly accurate by use of the very same techniques as those used in any of the other sciences.

The attempt to approach accountability through assessment of personal meaning is not only likely to be more effective, it has additional advantages of great practical value in the classroom. This approach is far simpler for teachers to manage than are highly specific lists of behavioral objectives, because with such an approach there are fewer concepts to master. Attention can be given to basic principles rather than to limitless details. The teacher preoccupied with manipulating behavior is likely to find himself dealing with classroom problems through various forms of reward and punishment, or such controlling devices as force, coercion, exhortation, or bribery. Such approaches are very likely to produce their own resistance in the students whose behavior he is attempting to change. It is a part of our American heritage to resist being managed, and it should not surprise us if such techniques call forth in students ingenious and creative devices for sabotaging the system.

The teacher who is concerned about personal meanings of students is much more likely to find that his relationships with students are warmer and more human. Human aspects are not rejected but actively sought and appreciated. Empathic teachers, honestly concerned with understanding how students think, feel, and perceive are far more likely than other teachers to be liked by their students, have less problems with motivation and discipline, find themselves more successful in carrying out their assigned tasks — to say nothing of being more relaxed and happy on the job.

A major objection to inferential approaches to the study of behavior proposed by behavior modification-performance criterion advocates is that inferences can only be made from behavior, and thus this approach is no different from the goals they seek. "We are willing," they say, "that you should make inferences about behavior if you wish, but what is the point? Why not simply observe behavior?" Of course it is true that humanists must begin their studies of student behavior from careful observation of it. Every psychologist, no matter what his allegiance, must begin from that base. A major point of this discussion, however, is that sole reliance on observation of behavior is but a symptomatic approach to assessing outcomes of teaching. Approaching accountability in that fashion thus concentrates attention on the wrong dynamic, and the attempt endlessly to catalog specific desired behaviors creates an unnecessary and complicating detour for understanding.

The holistic-inferential approach to assessment offers a much more direct and efficient approach to the causes of behavior. It does not attempt to itemize all behavior or gather it up in great masses. Instead, it uses the observer himself as an effective screen for observing those aspects of behavior providing the most efficient clues to the causes he is seeking to understand. . . .

Precise answers to the assessment of personal meaning extend considerably beyond the scope of this essay. Many techniques have already been worked out, either informally over the years by persons engaging in the various helping professions or, more recently, in the work of humanistically oriented psychologists. Since a great many persons today believe the problem is important, almost certainly we should be able to make tremendous strides in this form of assessment in the future. The immediate need is to go to work on a three-pronged effort directed toward:

1. *Making meaning important.* Since people only do what seems important to them, the first step in improving our capabilities for the assessment of meaning is to regard it as an important question. This calls for encouraging teachers, principals, supervisors, administrators, and everyone else engaged in the educational effort to understand that their inferences are important and helping them at every level to sharpen their skills in this regard. This will not be an easy task in view of the current preoccupation with strictly behavioral approaches to educational problems. The extraordinary pressures being placed on educators everywhere to emphasize such objectives leave little room for much concern with the development of skill in the assessment of personal meaning. A major first step in the encouragement of attention to personal meaning will, therefore, need to be the development of a more adequate perspective on assessment problems and deceleration of the current tallyho for behavioral objectives, behavioral modification, and performance-based criteria.

Beyond that, educators at every level of operation need to be encouraged to experiment with the assessment of personal meaning and to sharpen their own skills toward these ends. As we have previously stated, the process of inference is a matter of reading behavior backwards, and this is a process that all of us naturally use in dealing with people who are important to us. The problem for people on the firing line is to learn to do this more often, more systematically, and more effectively in their professional roles.

2. *Collection and evaluation of already existing techniques.* People have been making inferences about other people since time immemorial. As a consequence, we already have in existence ways of assessing personal meaning of an informal character accumulated through the experience of persons in helping professions over generations. A serious attempt should be mounted to gather these, assess their effectiveness, and make them more readily available to others throughout the profession.

In addition to such informal techniques, psychologists, sociologists, anthropologists, and others in the social sciences have developed an ever increasing number of more formal techniques over the past 30 or 40 years for assessing human attitudes, values, beliefs, and perceptions of self and the world. There is, for example, a very large literature on projective techniques and the use of personal documents for assessing personal meaning. Such studies need to be exhumed from wherever they are buried in the literature, examined and assessed, and made more widely available to persons who are interested in measuring personal meaning in more formal terms.

3. *The development of new techniques.* Vast sums of money are currently being poured into the effort to improve America's schools by the application of behavioral objectives approaches to assessment and by the injection of industrial techniques into every aspect of our educational effort. These tremendous capital outlays are matched by vast expenditures of human energies focused on behavioral approaches to educational accountability. We have already mentioned how this preoccupation can actually inhibit or destroy the search for viable alternatives to educational assessment.

Most of our financial and human resources are currently focused on doing more of what we already know very well how to do. What is badly needed now is the diversion of very large chunks of these financial and human resources to the exploration of problems we have so far sorely neglected. A redistribution to concentrate efforts on the study of personal meanings and their assessment in educational settings would provide education with enormous dividends within a comparatively short time.

Who is Responsible for What?

In the final analysis, whatever success or failure education achieves will be dependent upon how effectively teachers carry out their professional responsibilities. Teachers surely must be accountable, but what can they truly be held accountable for? Current attempts at accountability recognize this principle and seek to make teachers accountable for the behavior of their students. Is this a tenable position? To answer that question we need to answer a prior one, namely, to what extent can *any* person, teacher or not, be held accountable for another person's behavior?

Since behavior is never the exclusive product of any one stimulus or set of stimuli provided by another person, it follows that no human being can ever be held responsible for the behavior of another except under three possible conditions:

1. *If the other person is too weak or too sick to be responsible for himself.* Adults have to be responsible for some aspects of children's behavior, especially acts which might prove harmful to the child or to others. The same rule applies to persons who are too sick to be able to care for themselves and who need the help of others. Acceptance of the responsibility to aid them has long been a basic tenet of our Judeo-Christian philosophy. Such conditions of responsibility are comparatively short-lived, however, existing only until the individual can care for himself. Generally speaking, the older a child becomes, the more it is necessary for him to assume responsibility for himself. The principle is clearly recognized in our courts. It is also the goal of human development as the organism strives for freedom, autonomy, and self-actualization. It ought to be the goal of education as well.

2. *If one person makes another person dependent upon him.* Whoever takes upon himself the responsibility for making decisions for another person has also assumed responsibility for his behavior. A person who, for whatever reason, has induced or seduced another to surrender his autonomy has at the same time assumed responsibility for his actions. This may occur in the case of some physicians who accept the principle of "total responsibility for the patient." It may also occur in the case of the psychotherapist who permits his client to develop a deep transference, or in the case of a teacher who seeks to assume the role of a child's mother. Such dependent relationships may sometimes be desirable in the doctor-patient relationships.

In most of the other helping professions, not dependent on the helper *doing* something to his client, the development of such dependency is generally regarded as unfortunate and undesirable. Most modern approaches to psychotherapy, for example, carefully eschew the development of dependent relationships because they

believe strong dependence of the client on the therapist saps
the client's capacities to solve his own problems and unduly pro-
longs the therapeutic relationship. Certainly the development of
dependency can have little place in education, an institution whose
basic objective is the production of intelligent persons, capable
of acting autonomously and freely with full responsibility for themselves.

3. *If responsibility is demanded by role definition.* Sometimes
responsibility for another may be imposed on an individual by
virtue of his peculiarly assigned role. An example might be the
responsibility of the prison guard to make certain that prisoners
do not escape. Such role-defined responsibilities for the behavior
of others, however, are ordinarily extremely limited and generally
restricted to preventive kinds of activities. So a teacher, by reason
of his role, might be held responsible for keeping children from
fighting with each other. Holding him responsible for whether or
not a child does his homework is another question. One cannot,
after all, be held responsible for events not truly within his control,
since few of us have much direct control over even the simplest
behaviors of other persons.

The basic democratic philosophy on which our society rests
holds that "when men are free they can find their own best ways."
Citizens are regarded as free and responsible agents. Each is
held accountable for his own behavior, very rarely for the behavior
of others. Educators share these common responsibilities.

But what of professional responsibility? For what can teachers
be held accountable simply because they are teachers? Surely
not for the behavior of students five years from now; too many
others have had their fingers in that pie. The teacher's influence
on all but the simplest, most primitive forms of student behavior
even in his own classroom cannot be clearly established. As children get older, the less can even those few items of behavior
be laid at the teacher's door. The attempt to hold teachers responsible for what students do is, for all practical purposes, well nigh
impossible.

Even if this were not so, modern conceptions of the teacher's
role would make such an attempt undesirable. Increasingly, teaching is understood not as a matter of control and direction, but
of help and facilitation. Teachers are asked to be facilitators rather
than controllers, helpers rather than directors. They are asked
to be assisters, encouragers, enrichers, inspirers. The concept
of teachers as makers, forcers, molders, or coercers is no longer
regarded as the ideal role for teachers, a position firmly buttressed
by evidence from research. Such shifts in our thinking make the
act of teaching a process of ministering to student growth rather
than a process of control and management of student behavior.

We are accustomed to thinking of the proper model for teaching in medical terms, of the doctor, who *knows,* telling the patient, who does *not* know, what the problem is and what must be done. Such an approach to dealing with human beings works fine when dealing with their bodies, which can be manipulated by some outside force. Applied to teaching, learning in this sense is seen as the interaction of a teacher who knows and a student who does not know.

Actually, when dealing with human affairs the reverse of the medical model is far more often required. When changes to be produced must be made inside the individual where they cannot be directly manipulated, it is the student who knows and the teacher who does not know. Counselors and psychotherapists have come to understand this relationship, and almost all new concepts of psychotherapy are based in one form or another upon an open system of operation. In my own experience as a psychotherapist I have long since given up trying to guess how my clients will solve their problems. They always find much better solutions than anything I ever thought of, and with good reason. After all, it is their problem, they are living with it, and all I know about it is what they tell me in an hour or two a week. Since they are possessed of far more data than I, it is small wonder they find better solutions than the ones I might have thought of. I find the same principle is true in working with students in the classroom, and my teaching has immensely improved since I gave up deciding in advance the precise outcomes in terms of which my students should behave.

Teachers can and should be held accountable for behaving professionally. A profession is a vocation requiring some special knowledge or skill; but the thing which distinguishes it from more mechanical occupations is its dependence upon the professional worker as a thinking, problem-solving human being.[6] The effective professional worker is one who has learned how to use himself, his knowledge, and skills effectively and efficiently to carry out his own and society's purposes. Professional teachers, therefore, can properly be held accountable for at least five things:

1. Teachers can be held accountable for being informed in subject matter. This is so self-evident as to need no further discussion.

2. They can also be held responsible for being concerned about the welfare of students and knowledgeable about their behavior. It cannot be demanded of teachers that they love children. Love is a human feeling and cannot be turned on and off at will. Besides, some children are sometimes not very lovable. Professional responsibility, however, requires concern for the persons involved in the process, and such concern can and should be demanded

of teachers and made an important aspect of assessment procedures.

3. Educators, whatever their titles, can also be held professionally responsible for their understanding of human behavior. Since people behave in terms of their beliefs, the beliefs teachers hold about what children are like and how and why they behave as they do play a crucial role in their influence upon students placed in their charge. Professional educators need the most accurate, sensitive, effective understandings about children and their behavior that it is possible to acquire in our generation. This also seems self-evident but is all too often violated in practice.

The beliefs many teachers hold about what students are like and why they behave as they do are sometimes little short of mythology. False and inadequate concepts abound throughout the profession and find expression in practices that are not only hindering, but are often downright destructive. One reason for this may be the inadequate behavioristic psychology which has served as the basic foundation for American education for more than 50 years. Whatever the reason, the beliefs teachers hold about the nature of behavior are crucial for their behavior toward students; and the character of these beliefs can and should be explored in any comprehensive attempt at assessing professional accountability.

4. Teachers may be held professionally responsible for the purposes they seek to carry out. Human behavior is purposive. Each teacher behaves in terms of what he believes is the purpose of society, of its institutions, of the schoolroom, of learning a subject, and, most especially, in terms of his own personal needs and goals. . . . So many things are done with no clear understanding of the purposes behind them. Too often the question "why" is not even asked.

The purposes held by educators play a vital role in determining what happens to students everywhere. They provide the basic dynamics from which practices are evolved. They are basic causes of teacher and administrator behavior and determine the nature of what goes on in classrooms and the schools and systems in which they exist. Yet purposes can also be explored, evaluated, and, when necessary, changed. As a consequence, any system of accountability must give the exploration, assessment, and continuous review of educators' purposes an important place in its attempt to help education achieve its fundamental objectives.

5. Professional educators can be held responsible for the methods they use in carrying out their own and society's purposes. This does not mean that educators must be required to utilize some previously determined "right" kinds of methods. So far as anyone can determine, there are no such things. Methods, in

themselves, are neither good nor bad. They can only be judged in terms of the purposes they were used to advance and the impact they had on the persons subject to them.

The methods teachers use, we are beginning to understand, must be highly personal. They must fit the teacher, the students, the subject, the school, and the circumstances in which they are employed. This is likely to be a highly unique and individual matter, difficult or impossible to measure in terms of any previously concocted criteria. The essence of good professional work calls for thinking practitioners able to confront problems and find effective solutions. Often these solutions may be highly unique and incapable of measurement by standard techniques.

Professional responsibility does not demand a prescribed way of behaving. What it does require is that whatever methods are used have the presumption of being good for the client. The emphasis is not upon guaranteed outcomes but on the defensible character of what is done. Doctors, for example, are not held responsible for the death of the patient. What they are held responsible for is being able to defend in the eyes of their peers that whatever they did had the presumption of being helpful when applied. Teachers, too, must be prepared to stand this kind of professional scrutiny of their information, beliefs, purposes, and the adequacy of the techniques which they use. Whatever they do should be for some good and sufficient reason, defensible in terms of rational thought, or as a consequence of informal or empirical research. This is an area of accountability sadly overlooked in most educational thinking.

In research on good and poor teachers at the University of Florida, good teachers stand up very well under these five criteria. The good ones seem to have developed positive perceptions of their subject matter, themselves, children, purposes, and methods in the course of their growth and experience without anyone consciously attempting to instill such perceptions. One wonders what might be done to improve the quality of teaching by a systematic process of helping teachers explore and discover more adequate conceptions in each of these areas. A program of accountability focused on such goals might prove to be far more significant for the production of positive change.

In the preoccupation with behavioral objectives and performance-based criteria as approaches to the problems of accountability, the factors involved in professional competence which we have mentioned have been given little attention. If one could be assured, however, of high levels of professional responsibility in school personnel many of the problems of accountability would solve themselves. Speaking as a parent, I would be quite content to entrust the education of my children to professionally responsible teachers who understood behavior, were concerned

about youngsters, knew their subjects, ascribed to positive purposes, and were willing and able to discuss and defend the practices they engaged in. If I had that I would feel little need to
assess their productivity. I could rest content that in the process
of responsibly carrying out their own professional goals they were
also contributing to mine, my children's, and society's, too.

I have made a strong plea for broader perspectives on the
problem of educational accountability. I have pointed out what
seems to me to be an unfortunate and dangerous distortion of
our educational effort brought about by the current preoccupation
with behavioristic and industrial approaches to educational problems. In doing so I have called for greater attention to the humanistic aspects of education. Whenever humanists make such pleas
they are often accused of being anti-intellectual, or of approaching
difficult problems with nicey-nice unwillingness to confront hard
issues.

The humanist does not ask the substitution of humanistic concerns for intellectual ones. As I have pointed out, learning always
consists of two aspects: the gaining of new information on the
one hand and the discovery of its personal meaning on the other.
The humanist's complaint is that this balance is now badly out
of kilter and education is in serious trouble, not so much for lack
of providing information, but from failure to deal effectively with
the meaning half of the learning equation.

What the humanist asks is redress of a balance overloaded
on one half of the problem. Donald Snygg, a former colleague
of mine, used to tell the story of an aboriginal tribe which believed
that the worst thing that could happen to a man was that his
spirit should escape from his body. Accordingly, when a man
got sick people began to worry that his spirit might escape and,
if local medicines and the witch doctor's charms did not prove
enough, the family would gather about the patient's cot and stuff
all of his body openings with a mixture of grass, leaves, and
mud to keep his spirit from escaping from his body. Under this
treatment, of course, the patient always died — but everyone
felt better for having done something about it! Many a wrong
in human history has been carried out by men of good intentions
without proper perspective. The plea of the humanist for education
is not that we give up behavioral approaches, but that we realistically recognize their assets and liabilities, and thereafter use them
in proper balance with the humanistic aspects of the problem.

I am not opposed to accountability or even to behavioral objectives. I am opposed to oversimplification of the problem. Unfortunately, the behavioral objectives approach sounds infallible to
the lay public, to industrialists, businessmen, and legislators. To
them, the behavioral objectives, performance-based criteria

approach seems like the perfect solution to education's problems. Professional educators should know better. If they permit this distorted view to prevail unchallenged as the primary approach to educational accountability, they will have failed everyone: themselves, the schools, society, but most of all a generation of students who will have to live out the consequences of such unquestioning capitulation to a partly right idea. At least four steps seem necessary to prevent such a tragedy from occurring:

1. Since people do only what seems important to them, *humanistic goals* for education must be rescued from oblivion and raised to front rank. There seems little hope of counteracting the iron grip of behavioristic approaches in which we currently find ourselves without much deeper understanding and appreciation of viable alternatives to accountability. These alternatives must be clearly stated, and stoutly debated in every possible arena.

2. Humanistic aspects of education and the kind of alternatives advocated here clearly must be valued. Humanistic thinking and objectives expressed in practice must be systematically recognized and rewarded wherever they are found throughout the system.

3. A moratorium on the current press for behavioral objectives should be called in order to give time for careful study of the consequences of this approach on students and teachers. Whatever is done in the name of accountability must, itself, be carefully assessed to assure that its ultimate outcomes do not interfere with the larger objectives of education. Special attention should therefore be given to the distorting effect behavioral approaches impose by almost exclusive preoccupation upon skills and the simplest, most primitive aspects of education. Whatever is done in the name of accountability must be used appropriately, and the accounters themselves must be held accountable for the effect of the practices they impose on the system.

4. A major effort designed to explore the nature of humanist thought and its implications for educational practice is called for. The effort might begin with the issues outlined here but, almost certainly, would soon find itself moving far beyond these questions to new and exciting possibilities as yet undreamed of. A place to begin might be with the deflection to more humanistic concerns of a lion's share of the funds and human energies currently devoted to championing behavioral objectives. Such a diversion would provide the means and the manpower. It would also contribute to the moratorium called for. It might even result in saving the taxpayers a great deal of money.

REFERENCES

[1]A. W. Combs, editor. **Perceiving, Behaving, Becoming: A New Focus for Education.** ASCD 1962 Yearbook. Washington, D.C.: Association for Supervision and Curriculum Development, 1962.

[2]A. W. Combs, D. L. Avila, and W. W. Purkey. **Helping Relationships: Basic Concepts for the Helping Professions.** Boston: Allyn and Bacon, Inc., 1971.

[3]Some sample titles are: C. R. Rogers. **Freedom to Learn.** Columbus, Ohio: Charles E. Merrill Publishing Company, 1969; A. H. Maslow. **Motivation and Personality.** New York: Harper & Row, Publishers, 1954; A. W. Combs and D. Snygg. **Individual Behavior: A Perceptual Approach to Behavior.** New York: Harper & Row, Publishers, 1959; E. C. Kelley. **Education for What is Real.** New York: Harper & Row, Publishers, 1947; G. W. Allport. **Personality and Social Encounter.** Boston: Beacon Press, 1964; W. W. Purkey. **Self Concept and School Achievement.** Englewood Cliffs, New Jersey: Prentice-Hall, Inc., 1970.

[4]Combs, **Florida Studies in the Helping Professions,** University of Florida Social Science Monograph No. 37, University of Florida, Gainesville, Florida, 1969.

[5]G. W. Allport, **The Use of Personal Documents in Psychological Science,** Bulletin No. 49, New York: Social Science Research Council, 1942.

[6]A. W. Comb. **The Professional Education of Teachers: A Perceptual View of Teacher Preparation.** Boston: Allyn and Bacon, Inc., 1965.

The Effective Helper: A Model of Personal Accountability

ANNE COHEN RICHARDS

FRED RICHARDS

I. DAVID WELCH

Accountability must be understood to mean that each of us is now accountable for promoting the success and growth of each and every member of the school community and, consequently, society.

It has been said, perhaps facetiously, that the educator who both innovates for constructive change and survives professionally is rare. A more rare specimen of the educator may be one who doesn't experience, as a consequence of dutifully performing his professional role, periods of feeling profoundly isolated and alone. Indeed, the recent decade of assaults upon educational institutions and educators, whether made by an angry public, protesting students, or enraged legislators, have often left educators with the uncomfortable feeling that they are ill-fated targets of the society they seek to serve. In addition, their immediate school environment may be a hierarchy of suspicion and mistrust; from the school board on down to the students, persons may view one another as potential threats rather than helping members of a community. Often educators have only a few fellow professionals to whom they feel free to disclose their deepest, real selves. Too often they feel isolated and alone, objects of external criticism rather than participants in a situation that promotes their maximum growth and well-being.

Both educuators and educational institutions are on trial. Critics continue to describe the school climate as joyless, sterile, dull and impersonal. Purkey comments that the "school communicates a sense of personal failure" and cites studies which found a tragic decrease in the students' sense of self-worth and self-esteem from grade school into high school.[1] Others were disturbed and alarmed that the classroom climate endured by students is to a large degree a repressive and crippling one.[2] The professional educator, *himself* working, learning and growing in such an environment, *himself* expected to perform adequately and effectively in such an environment, is now being charged with "murder in the classroom."

Without question, we educators need to recognize and accept responsibility for our decisions and actions — or the lack of them — which have helped make the schools what they are. Indeed, failure to recognize both the crisis in education and our responsibility for it is one of the charges filed against us. But for years before the issue of teacher accountability received such national attention we have been feeling and shouldering (but too often not sharing) the burden of working and living in schools that have failed to meet the needs of both ourselves and the students. Perhaps it is true that in accepting passively our assignment of being the giver of the grade and the keeper of the book of student accountability, we have helped to fashion the school environment that is now attacked as stifling, crippling, and inhumane. However, to accept passively again the decree of those who demand that the *teacher* is now fully accountable for how the students perform is to become the willing target or victim of that very inadequate system we so dutifully imposed upon our students. We must insist, along with Robert E. Campbell, that *"everyone who is party to the process must be accountable. Just as school people must be asked some very pointed questions, so must society and the student."*[3] A concept of accountability which only concerns itself with educational outcomes — with the cognitive and affective experience and performance of the student in the classroom — may eventually compound the crisis. While focusing our concern on the child or student we must not lose sight of ourselves who, seeking adequate human nourishment and adequacy in schools too often humanly inadequate, are equally in need of understanding, trust, respect, free expression, and material and personal resources which promote our maximum growth and well-being. That is, maturely recognizing our responsibility to the students in our classrooms, we must never lose sight of our responsibility to our fellow educators and ourselves.

Accountability must be understood to mean that each of us is now accountable for promoting the success and growth of each and every member of the school community and, consequently, society. We need more than a growing — and also fashionable — national debate over the degree to which *teachers* can be held responsible for what children learn in the classroom. We need a growing national acceptance of accountability, a growing awareness that the healthy, humane society is the helping society in which each of us becomes the responsible caretaker of ourselves, others, and the total natural and human environment. The need for such an approach to accountability is an urgent one, for "the crisis in the classroom is but one aspect of the larger crisis of American society as a whole, a crisis whose resolution is problematical at best."[4] At present, the debate over the issue of accountability clearly reflects a society and a school system in which the search for a scapegoat rather than a realistic sharing of responsibility is embraced mindlessly as a breakthrough rather than part of the breakdown.

We propose a concept of accountability which concerns itself not merely with the performance of measurable, designated, and limited educational goals, but with the goal of facilitating the increased adequacy and well-being of every person in the school environment. Our proposal is a basic one. It does not assume to define specific procedures for *imposing* accountability on anyone. It focuses on an understanding of accountability without which no attempt to make others accountable will succeed in making the school environment more healthy and humane.

Essentially we suggest that each of us become increasingly more responsible helpers, individual sources of health who, insisting on meeting our own needs for trust, respect, and free expression, are freed to transform the schools into humane places to learn and grow. We suggest that being accountable means choosing or striving to become what Combs calls the effective helper.[5]

The effective helper or adequate person is openly and spontaneously himself. In interpersonal relationships he is genuinely *present*. He is authentic. He establishes his presence. Respecting himself and his needs for health and well-being, he is not a passive victim of the demands of others or of an environment which stifles and sickens him. Trusting in his own experiencing of himself and others, he is free to move through the world without a mask, a front, or a facade. He sees himself and others as persons and not merely as professional roles. However, he comfortably views his "role" in school as a coat he is free to put on or take off when it is helpful and responsible to do so. Thus when "performing his professional duties" he is first and always himself, a person. Though a chairman or a principal, a teacher or a student, he is honestly and openly himself. Others say of him, "He's real," "He's trustworthy," "He's not a fake," and "I feel like I can be myself and talk openly and honestly when I'm around him."

The effective helper or healthy personality sees himself and others as able rather than unable, as persons of worth and dignity. Seeing himself in essentially positive ways, he can free himself and others to be themselves and learn and grow in terms of their own personal meanings. He has no need to play the role of the school policeman or watchdog, no need to control and dominate others traditionally viewed as his subordinates. Trusting others, he can share responsibility rather than impose it. Others say of him "I feel I'm an important and significant person when I'm with him," or "After I've talked with him I feel, I know, I can do well things that are important to me!"

The effective helper attempts to solve problems by seeing them from the other person's point of view. He is empathic and capable of wide identification with others. Feeling adequate as a person, he has no need to act as if the paired terms - student/teacher, principal/teacher, citizen/public servant - are mutually exclusive opposites. He needs no scapegoat. Not rigid and restricted but adequate and growing, he can "put on the shoes" of the other person and walk around in his world. Thus, he has no need to hide or lose himself in a professional role; he feels secure and adequate enough to stop playing the "outsider" and become a responsible, decision making member of the community. Others say of him, "He helps me understand things about myself I was only dimly aware of before," "He helps me accept my responsibility for community problems because he's willing to share it," or "I really enjoy talking with him because he knows how I feel inside."

Such an approach to accountability includes and goes beyond a concern with teacher and student achievement because it calls for creating a community which promotes, not imposes (which is impossible), the personal adequacy needed to accept responsibility and become agents of constructive change. It searches for a concept of accountability which, rather than insisting we do more efficiently what we have done mindlessly in the past, seeks to free all of us to function more fully and to create the humane climate so urgently needed in our schools and society. It proposes that simply making educators accountable or "responsible" for meeting goals and standards, usually imposed upon them from an external frame of reference, is grossly inadequate.

A humanistic approach to accountability calls on each of us to transform our schools into healthy communities where both the educators and the students know and believe they are freed to be spontaneously, responsibly, and deeply themselves. It calls on us to become effective helpers adequate enough to hold ourselves accountable for the kind of humaneness we embody and for the consequences of our own decisions and actions. It suggests that the issue of accountability, if detached from a realistic concern and desire for increased community, will compound rather than correct the inefficiency and inhumaneness in our schools.

REFERENCES

[1]William W. Purkey, **The Self and Academic Achievement,** Research Bulletin, Florida Educational Research and Development Council, Vol. 3, no. 1, Spring, 1967.

[2]John Holt, **How Children Fail,** New York: Pitman Publishing Corporation, 1964, 1968; Neil Postman and Charles Weingartner, **Teaching as a Subversive Activity,** New York: Delacorte Press, 1969; Jonathan Kozol, **Death at an Early Age,** Boston: Houghton Mifflin Company, 1967.

[3]Robert E. Campbell, "Accountability and Stone Soup," **Phi Delta Kappan,** Vol. 53, no. 3, November, 1971, p. 177.

[4]Charles E. Silberman, **Crisis in the Classroom,** New York: Random House, 1970, p. 524.

[5]Arthur W. Combs, "The Human Aspect of Administration," **Educational Leadership,** Vol. 28, no. 2, November, 1970, pp. 197-205. See also Arthur W. Combs, Ed., **Florida Studies in the Helping Professions,** University of Florida Monographs in the Social Sciences, No. 37, Gainesville, Florida, University of Florida Press, 1969; Arthur W. Combs, **The Professional Education of Teachers,** Boston: Allyn and Bacon, 1965; Arthur W. Combs, Donald L. Avila and William W. Purkey, **Helping Relationships,** Boston: Allyn and Bacon, Inc., 1971.

Accountability for the Humanists

ROBERT PRIMACK

Humanists must devise new, experimentally and experientially validated standards which would insure humanistic outcomes more effectively than do the current ones.

When someone states — and this the literature does with broken-record repetitiveness — "We must humanize education," my automatic response, silent fortunately, because I do not have the courage of bad manners, is, "Of course, my friend. Do you know anyone outside a psycho ward who advocates the brutalization, the animalization, the barbarization of education?"

"But that ain't the problem, Bob, at all," I continue in my imaginary dialogue. The real problem, or problems, are: What is humanized education in the real world? What theoretical framework does humanization require? How will I be different and how will others be different once they are humanized? Is one man's notion of what constitutes humanization likely to be the next man's notion of what constitutes savagery? Is humanization a never-ending process or does it have a terminal point? How do I know if I'm making progress in the direction of humanization?

But even if we can come to some kind of agreement on the meaning of the term "humanization of education," and even if we can make some operational judgments on whether we are moving in the direction of our goals, we are still left with some very serious dilemmas. What are the best means of achieving our goals in the most efficient manner possible? Are there activities which are intrinsically dehumanizing, or must all such activities be judged in some situational context? What must be abandoned

Robert Primack, "Accountability for the Humanists," **Phi Delta Kappan,** 620-621, June, 1971. Reprinted by permission.

and what must we add to current practices in education to make it more human, keeping in mind that both politics and education are arts of the possible? How much are we willing to sacrifice in terms of work, money, time, comfort, privileges, and perquisites in order to bring about a more humanized education? There are hundreds of questions of like nature which have to asked about humanizing education. It is my contention that too many who rushed to associate themselves with the notion of humanized education have not bothered to ask themselves some of these most difficult questions and, where they have, have not cared to examine the issues reflectively and thoughtfully enough.

There is an additional consideration. Terminology converts itself into jargon, and it begins to develop a momentum and a prestige and a life of its own, if the conditions are favorable. Concepts become sloganized and emasculated from all significant content. Terms such as "democratic," "child-centered," and "progressive" begin to attract a following who want to adopt the terms for purposes antithetical or not relevant to some, or all, of the implications originally associated with the concept.

In programmatic form, let me over-simplify and make the following suggestions for humanists to consider, not necessarily in their order of importance:

1. Humanists must develop their techniques to the point where those who accept and profess humanism will feel and function better. This has not always been true of humanists, and one acid test of whether you are practicing the humanism you profess is whether in fact this is taking place.

2. Humanists must develop a more clearly defined philosophy with which to undergird some of the humanist assumptions and then examine some of the implications of their philosophical position in terms of therapy, social action, and education. This does not mean that the philosophy should be characterized by some kind of absolutist temper or series of dogmatic fundamentals, but rather that the full implications of the humanist position, as a guide to both past and future actions, should be explored with some thoroughness and sophistication and some tentative deductions and guidelines set up on the basis of this investigation.

3. Humanists should be able to specify, fairly clear-cut patterns or types of behavior which must accompany a humanist orientation. Without necessarily accepting the full implications of the behaviorist orientation, one can accept their criticism that in terms of measurable outcomes the humanist position has been weak. This need not be so. Behavior and meaning need not be antithetical. And whereas humanists have stressed the meaning behind behavior, it may now be time to stress behavioral outcomes and their measurable characteristics with equal vigor.

4. Humanists must make clearer and act on the principle that one cannot effectively segment one's life and still be a humanist. That is, one cannot be a humanist in the classroom and then exploit one's family. One cannot be a humanist in a therapy session and then turn one's back on the problems of poverty, race, and war which distort the society. Humanism must have its social and political counterparts as well as its philosophical, educational, and psychological ones.

5. One cannot be effectively humanistic without the use of intelligence, scholarship, and research. In the recent past there may well have been an overemphasis on intellectuality, or at least the wrong kind of intellectuality, and a denigration of the affective-emotional aspects of the human situation. But I would contend that the "cult of gut response" has now gone too far. There is now widespread distrust of intelligence and scholarship per se among those who claim to be humanistically oriented. It is my contention that without the method of reflective intelligence the goals of the humanists are beyond attainment. The either-or posture of some humanists — either cognition or emotion — must be replaced with a both-and orientation. Furthermore, where there seems direct and unavoidable conflict between the two, intelligence must be the court of last resort. This is especially necessary where communal and social goals are concerned. Within oneself, or within the bosom of an intimate family, one can allow freer reign to emotionality, since in this environment emotions have the ability to communicate almost as directly and precisely as intelligence to members of an empathic group. But when we attempt to extend this form of communication to the political sphere, for instance, distortion and demagoguery become real dangers. If we resolve conflict in this arena by nonevidential and nonreflective processes, then the only method of meaningful communication is abandoned.

This is not to eschew all emotion. First, it is impossible; but where conjoint action for precise goals is required — for example, in designing a humanistic school curriculum — emotion by itself is not precise or effective enough, even in its most exquisite form. To speak about the "child-centered curriculum" may make you feel warm all over, but it just won't do, unless it is also accompanied by the necessary research, the necessary techniques, and the necessary systems of precise evaluation which would make such sweet feelings relevant in a hard, dynamic world. There is a need for more peak experiences in school life, but on the other hand there is also a need for some slogging, straight-forward research, when the Holts, the Leonards, Goodmans, and others of the romantic cult grab us by our bowels.

6. Humanism must be very cautious that it does not transform itself from its present claim of being a movement of fresh new insights with respect to psychology and education into a movement with its own rigid ideology, excommunicating tendencies, and ultramontanism for the humane pope. It seems that humanists must face up to this danger, and there is enough evidence in the tone of some of the writings being produced by humanists, as well as in some of the conventions and meetings where humanists gather, to lend credence to this warning. Historians well know that the past is replete with instances where today's heterodoxy is tomorrow's orthodoxy. Humanism should not allow itself to develop into a cult or dogma. Fallibilism is a much more sensible philosophical posture than is absolutism, and humanists would do well to end each day by murmuring their devotions on their knees about how "God don't make me inhuman by making me believe I'm absolutely right."

7. In education and in psychology, the areas where humanists have had the greatest impact thus far, they must be careful not to so worship the spontaneous and the notion of equality that they abandon all reasonable levels of assured competence. Humanists, perhaps infected with a kind of dogmatic Jacksonianism, seem frequently to be arguing that it is undemocratic as well as antihumanistic to be selective and demanding when filling the roles in society which require professional competence. One may legitimately object that many professional standards and goals are now obsolete, that they do not encourage the kinds of competencies now needed, that they are unwisely exclusionary; but this is not the same as asserting that any empathic person can successfully engage in group therapy, or all that's required to be a good teacher is to be a good human being. We probably should radically change our standards of how to induct a medical doctor, a psychologist, or a teacher into the profession, but, if anything, we may have to make the minimum standards more demanding, though different, rather than less so. . . . Humanists must devise new, experimentally and experientially validated standards which would insure humanistic outcomes more effectively than do the current ones.

8. It seems to me that the humanist orientation requires a much more significant and wider sense of community to be engendered by those who have undergone humanist education or therapy. For the modern era requires that the new sense of community which must be developed include all of mankind and all of his major problems. It will have to deal with the local community as well as the international community; it will have to establish a system of appropriate concerns and priorities for individual conflicts

of interest, as well as for conflicts among families, regions, and nations. At the same time the humanist must be careful that in developing these techniques of overarching "communitizations" he does not alienate the individual from his true self or from significant personal experiences.

9. Humanists must learn better how to open the channels of expression for the great emotions. Humanists talk a good game of freeing the self for courage, joy, and love, but their record for creating these emotions in themselves and in others is not particularly outstanding. Humanists are to be highly commended for refocusing attention on the centrality of these emotions for meaningful existence — they have made a real beginning in making Dionysius respectable again — but they must do better in developing healthy means by which the great emotions can be more freely expressed.

10. Humanists must be sensitive to, and willing to tackle, the great issues of the day. In a sense they must be working social philosophers, economists, and political scientists. They must be willing to extend the humanist orientation into any of the major problems confronting the society. There may be many such problems where humanism has but little to give, but the willingness to examine and inquire must be there, if humanism is to remain vital and accept its challenges.

Humanists must develop a more precise scenario for the future. If humanists begin to produce carefully conceived programs along the lines herein indicated and the outcome is a significant number of human beings who are effective and healthy functioners, as individuals and as groups, we can then in good conscience say that all those interested in the well-being of themselves and of all mankind had better travel the humanist route. And the humanist school will then indeed build the door to a non-Orwellian 1984.